WHAT FISH?

A BUYER'S GUIDE TO MARINE FISH

Tristan Lougher

D1302198

BARRON'S

First edition for the United States
and Canada published in 2006 by
Barron's Educational Series, Inc.

First published in 2006 by
Interpet Publishing.
© Copyright 2006 by
Interpet Publishing.

*All inquiries should be
addressed to:*
Barron's Educational Series, Inc.
250 Wireless Boulevard
Hauppauge, NY 11788
www.barronseduc.com

ISBN-13: 978-0-7641-3256-8
ISBN-10: 0-7641-3256-3

Library of Congress Control
Number 2004118231

Printed in China
9 8 7 6 5 4 3 2 1

The star rating ★★★★★

We include a guide to the prices that aquarium owners might
expect to pay for individuals of each species. The range of
prices for each group of fish is given on the opening page
of the section. Sometimes, the star rating will cover more
than one price category. This might be because specimens
are offered for sale as small juveniles and large adults with
varying degrees of availability. The larger the fish, the greater
the cost of importing it. The final price of a fish may also
reflect where the dealer has purchased it. Directly imported
fish may command a lower price than those sourced through
wholesalers. Similarly, captive-bred species may have a
premium attached because of the difficulties involved in their
production. As a rule, price should only be considered after
establishing the health, suitability, and vitality of the
fish concerned.

Author

Tristan Lougher has been keeping
aquariums for over 25 years, and
his interest in all things animal led to
a degree in zoology in 1992. Since
then he has worked as a professional
aquarist, mainly with Cheshire WaterLife
Ltd., where he specializes in marine fish
and invertebrates. He has written for several
publications, including *Practical Fishkeeping*,
Today's Fishkeeper, *Tropical World*, and *Tropical Fish*. He
currently contributes to *Marine World*, where his articles include
a "Fish Focus" on different fish genera and a feature called
"Top Marques," in which he describes rare or expensive species
and their husbandry. Tristan is interested in all aspects of
aquarism and ichthyology, including fish paleontology. He is also
an enthusiastic scuba
diver and tries to get
away to the Red
Sea at least
once a year.

Introduction

There is nothing worse than buying a
marine fish and stocking it in your
aquarium only to have it bully or eat its
tankmates, or fall victim to the existing
residents' territorial dispositions. This book aims to
provide concise information concerning the compatibility of a
wide variety of tropical saltwater fish species with each other, with other species,
and with corals and other commonly kept invertebrates. Territoriality may depend
on which species is stocked first, and this topic is also discussed where relevant.

The increase in popularity of live rock as the biological filter medium of
choice means that I distinguish between three main types of aquarium. A
reef aquarium is usually live rock-based and stocked with plenty of
corals and other sessile invertebrates. A live rock-based fish-only
aquarium usually houses species that may nip at corals but do not
thrive in a more artificial aquarium, namely the third category, the
fish-only aquarium. In such a system, the only living things
will be the filtration bacteria and the fish stocked by the
aquarist; all the decor is inert.

The ability to provide the correct long-term diet
for tropical marine fish is another subject covered in this
book. I also attempt to highlight species that should be observed
feeding before you acquire them. Other information includes the areas of
origin of each species, their breeding potential, and their maximum size, so
that you can avoid introducing small juveniles into an aquarium that they will
outgrow with ease.

Finally, please remember that this book is meant as a guide and is based on my
own experiences with all the species listed here. Rogue individuals of any species
can and do occur, and contradict the best researched information at your disposal.

Tristan Lougher

Contents

In this listing, the common name of each fish is followed by its scientific name. In sections featuring more than one group of fish, the species are presented in A–Z order of scientific name within each group.

▲ The tomato anemonefish grows rapidly in aquariums.

▼ *The emperor snapper needs a very large aquarium to thrive.*

180–185

Cowfishes, Boxfishes, and Filefishes

186–207

Miscellaneous

208

Picture credits and acknowledgments

Small wonders

Anemonefishes and damselfishes are closely related, but cardinalfishes are included in this section because they, too, usually achieve a modest maximum size and tolerate other individuals of the same species. However, cardinals are much less active than damsels or anemonefishes, and may even be nocturnal. All three groups are likely to breed in an aquarium, given good care. Another shared characteristic is their use of invertebrates for protection. Anemonefishes are known to inhabit any one of nine different species of host anemone, and some juvenile damsels share this behavior. Juvenile cardinals of many species have been observed close to, or in, anemones but also use other invertebrates such as sea urchins for protection. Most fish from this section are easy to care for in the home aquarium, but with some of them there are territorial issues to consider before buying.

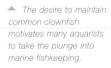

▲ The desire to maintain common clownfish motivates many aquarists to take the plunge into marine fishkeeping.

▼ Damselfish are perennial favorites due to their bold colors and hardy disposition.

Price guide

★	Up to $20
★★	$20–$30
★★★	$30–$40
★★★★	$40–$50
★★★★★	$50–$75

Amphiprion akindynos

Australian anemonefish

FISH PROFILE

The Australian anemonefish is an attractive species available only infrequently from the Coral Sea. It is similar in appearance to many other anemonefishes, particularly those belonging to the "Clarkii" complex, but can be distinguished by its overall ginger-brown coloration, white tail and caudal peduncle, and black-edged vertical bars.

WHAT size?
Males are unlikely to be more than $2^3/8$ in (6 cm); females achieve $3^1/2$ in (9 cm).

WHAT does it eat?
In the wild, zooplankton and occasionally seaweeds. Captive individuals should readily accept most foods offered, including brineshrimp, mysis, flake, pellet, and similar foods.

WHERE is it from?
Western Pacific, Great Barrier Reef, Coral Sea eastwards to Tonga.

WHAT does it cost?
★★★★★
Wild-collected specimens available as pairs are expensive. Single individuals are more reasonably priced.

HOW do I sex it?
Females are the largest individuals in wild-collected pairs.

WHAT kind of tank?
Fish-only, reef, or live rock-based fish-only system with plenty of swimming space.

WHAT minimum size tank?
48 gal (180 l).

HOW do other fish react?
In the presence of a suitable anemone this fish is not threatened by even the most territorial species. Without a host, it could be bullied by large damsels or dwarf angels. Do not stock it if other anemonefishes are already present.

WHAT to watch out for?
Avoid non-feeding specimens or those with any signs of turbidity on their skin. Fins should be intact and the fish should have a steady breathing rate.

▼ *This specimen has made its home among the tentacles of a carpet anemone (Stichodactyla sp).*

HOW compatible with inverts and corals?
May cover sessile invertebrates with the sand it moves away from its host anemone using vigorous sweeps of its tail. Should largely ignore ornamental shrimp.

WHAT area of the tank?
Spends much of its time in or around its host anemone, where present. Otherwise, it occasionally roams around in midwater, often adopting another invertebrate as a surrogate anemone.

HOW many in one tank?
Keep singly or in pairs.

HOW does it behave?
When guarding eggs or protecting its anemone, it can prove a threat to almost any fish, regardless of size. However, unprovoked aggression is unlikely and it is largely peaceful.

WILL it breed in an aquarium?
Yes. It has been successfully spawned and reared in captivity.

Amphiprion bicinctus

Red Sea anemonefish

Amphiprion bicinctus, part of the "Clarkii" complex, is a pretty, quite hardy fish that takes up residence in most host anemone species. It is not the commonest species available; if you want one or two, perhaps for a Red Sea biotope aquarium, you should be able to obtain them with a little patience and perseverance.

▲ *This species only has two prominent vertical white bands. Pictured here with a bubble anemone (Entacmaea quadricolor).*

WHAT size?
Males no more than 4 in (10 cm), large females up to 5½ in (14 cm).

WHAT does it eat?
In the wild, algae and zooplankton. Readily accepts suitable substitutes in the aquarium. Offer brineshrimp and mysis to smaller individuals (less than 2 in/5 cm), together with dried algae in a lettuce clip. Once fully acclimatized to aquarium life, larger fish will take most meaty foods, including flake and pellets.

WHERE is it from?
Red Sea and the Chagos archipelago in the Western Indian Ocean.

WHAT does it cost?
★★★★☆ ★★★★★
More costly than other more commonly available anemonefish.

HOW do I sex it?
Females of pairs are larger.

WHAT kind of tank?
Fish-only; live rock-based fish-only system; or reef aquarium.

WHAT minimum size tank?
13 gal (50 l), assuming excellent water quality.

HOW do other fish react?
Most fish will ignore anemonefish, but possible exceptions include territorial damselfishes, small, pugnacious wrasses, and resident dottybacks, particularly if no host anemone species is present.

WHAT to watch out for?
Make sure fish are feeding before purchase. As with any species of anemonefish, check for signs of cloudy eyes or turbidity of the skin, as these symptoms can indicate a protozoan infection, which is difficult to treat.

HOW compatible with inverts and corals?
Will not harm sessile invertebrates unless it uses them as a surrogate anemone, in which case some corals become irritated by the fish's presence. Should not harm ornamental shrimp.

WHAT area of the tank?
Thrives with or without an anemone, but behaves more naturally when a suitable host is present. Small individuals stay close to the host, but larger ones roam all over the aquarium, returning frequently to the anemone.

HOW many in one tank?
Keep singly or in male/female pairs.

HOW does it behave?
Anemonefish vigorously defend their anemone and the immediate area, but are content for other fish to leave the area, rather than chase them relentlessly.

WILL it breed in an aquarium?
Yes. The larvae have been successfully raised in captivity.

Amphiprion clarkii

Clarke's anemonefish

FISH PROFILE

A hardy anemonefish and the only species to occupy all nine of the anemone species known to act as hosts. Its body color can vary quite significantly, ranging from jet-black to pale brown. This can depend on the country of origin, with many of the best individuals coming from the Coral Sea and Maldives.

WHAT size?
Males maximum 4 in (10 cm), females maximum 5⁷/₈ in (15 cm).

WHAT does it eat?
Accepts most aquarium foods. Offer a varied diet, including enriched brineshrimp, mysis, chopped shellfish, and flake.

WHERE is it from?
Widespread in the tropical Indo-Pacific, including Indonesia and the Philippines. Collected for the aquarium trade in the Indian Ocean and exported through Sri Lanka.

WHAT does it cost?
★☆☆☆☆　★★☆☆☆
Relatively inexpensive. Price range is for tank-raised fish; wild fish up to twice as much.

HOW do I sex it?
In the context of a pair, females are larger than males. Large specimens of 4 in (10 cm) or more are notoriously difficult to determine.

WHAT kind of tank?
Live rock-based fish-only system or a reef aquarium. Best kept with an anemone, although many individuals will do without.

WHAT minimum size tank?
66 gal (250 l), assuming excellent water quality.

HOW do other fish react?
Small specimens of *A. clarkii* are the most vulnerable, but seem quick and clever enough to avoid more aggressive fish. Mature individuals can hold their own among significantly larger fish.

WHAT to watch out for?
Avoid specimens with white blemishes on the skin, as these may be a sign of protozoan parasite infections and are common in newly-imported fish. Specimens should feed readily in the dealer's tanks.

HOW compatible with inverts and corals?
When stocked with a suitable anemone, *A. clarkii* can move rocks away from the immediate area if it deems them to be in the way, whether they are home to corals or not. Should not harm most ornamental invertebrates, although there are reports of some large individuals "feeding" their anemones by repeatedly butting herbivorous snails until they fall into their host.

WHAT area of the tank?
In the absence of an anemone, the fish remains close to rockwork. Otherwise, it stays with its host, wherever it is located.

HOW many in one tank?
Keep singly or in true pairs.

HOW does it behave?
Clarke's anemonefish is a belligerent species when large, attacking anything that threatens its anemone, including the aquarist's fingers. It is quite capable of drawing blood. Choose robust tankmates.

WILL it breed in an aquarium?
Yes. It has been raised in captivity and is sometimes available commercially.

◀ *The body color of Clarke's anemonefish ranges from light brown to jet black.*

Amphiprion frenatus

Tomato anemonefish

FISH PROFILE

The commonly-encountered tomato anemonefish is one of a large number of similar species available in the marine aquarium hobby. Its correct identification centers on the two black stripes present on the front edge of the pelvic fins. Consider its rapid growth and large final size before you commit to buying it. Although not essential for the successful maintenance of *A. frenatus*, the bubble anemone *(Entacmaea quadricolor)* is ideal. In its natural environment, the tomato anemonefish also occupies *Heteractis crispa*.

◁ *The tomato anemonefish can be distinguished from closely-related species by the black leading edge of the pelvic fins.*

WHAT size?
Females 5½ in (14 cm); males smaller.

WHAT does it eat?
Omnivorous; consumes zooplankton and algae in the wild. Settled individuals accept dried algae, mysis, brineshrimp, and any small particulate foods.

WHERE is it from?
Tropical Western Pacific.

WHAT does it cost?
★☆☆☆☆   ★★☆☆☆
Inexpensive. Small captive-bred fish (price range given here) are particularly cheap.

HOW do I sex it?
In a true pair the larger fish is always female.

WHAT kind of tank?
Live rock-based fish-only or reef aquarium. A fish-only system is acceptable.

WHAT minimum size tank?
80 gal (300 l) for a fully-grown pair.

HOW do other fish react?
Other clownfishes and damsels may behave with some aggression towards this species, but it is more than capable of looking after itself, particularly when stocked with a suitable host anemone.

WHAT to watch out for?
The stunning fiery coloration of small individuals becomes more subdued with time. Avoid specimens with torn fins or body damage – typical of individuals kept in groups, where the largest often bullies smaller individuals.

HOW compatible with inverts and corals?
May harm corals it adopts as "surrogate anemones," which usually occurs where anemones are not present. It should not harm ornamental shrimp.

WHAT area of the tank?
Will dominate an entire aquarium when mature, but usually spends most of its time in a host anemone or surrogate where present, venturing forth for food or to defend its home. Small juveniles can spend extended periods close to rockwork or beneath corals.

HOW many in one tank?
Keep singly or in pairs.

HOW does it behave?
A powerful species, prepared to attack any fish that threatens either it or its host anemone. The bites it inflicts in the defense of its territory can be painful for aquarists, although usually not serious.

WILL it breed in an aquarium?
Yes. It has been successfully raised in captivity, even though it is not as commercially viable as the two clownfish species.

Amphiprion melanopus

Pacific fire anemonefish

FISH PROFILE

Recently imported, wild-collected pairs are among the most stunning and vibrant anemonefish, and highly prized by aquarists lucky enough to source them. They are easy to confuse with other, similar anemonefish, but can be identified by their completely black pelvic fins.

WHAT size?
Females 4³/₄ in (12 cm), males smaller.

WHAT does it eat?
In the wild, mainly zooplankton. In the aquarium, accepts mysis, chopped shellfish, brineshrimp, and formula foods almost immediately, and flake or granular foods after a short while.

WHERE is it from?
Tropical Pacific: Bali and the Philippines eastwards to Vanuatu and Marshall Islands.

WHAT does it cost?
★★☆☆☆   ★★★☆☆
Single individuals are relatively inexpensive. True, wild-collected pairs can be very costly, but their stunning coloration justifies the expense. Tank-raised price given here.

▶ *All-black pelvic fins distinguish this fish from other "tomato" anemone fishes.*

HOW do I sex it?
Females are larger than males. The point at which males become females depends on circumstances, but seldom occurs at lengths less than 2³/₄ in (7 cm).

WHAT kind of tank?
Live rock-based fish-only or reef aquarium. Anemones are not necessary to maintain this clownfish successfully, so a fish-only system is acceptable.

WHAT minimum size tank?
46 gal (175 l) for a pair, assuming excellent water quality.

HOW do other fish react?
Most fish completely ignore this species, particularly if it is introduced where an anemone is already in situ. Do not stock it with other *Amphiprion* species.

WHAT to watch out for?
When buying two individuals, try to ensure that they are a true pair, as fish of this species do not pair easily. Specimens that appear to tolerate each other in a dealer's tank may not do so in the presence of an anemone. Although this species will adopt other anemones, it is best maintained with the bubble, *Entacmaea quadricolor*.

HOW compatible with inverts and corals?
May move corals or cover them with sand, sweeping them out of the way with vigorous tail movements. Should not harm ornamental shrimp.

WHAT area of the tank?
In, or very close to, their host anemone where present. Ventures into the water column for food or to defend territory.

HOW many in one tank?
Keep singly or in true pairs.

HOW does it behave?
Once established, this species can react extremely aggressively towards new introductions or any species that appears to threaten its territory. This area tends to include an anemone; individuals stocked without one will be far less belligerent.

WILL it breed in an aquarium?
Yes. It has been successfully reared in captivity.

Amphiprion nigripes

Maldive anemonefish

A. nigripes is also known as the black-footed anemonefish due to its jet-black pelvic fins. Captive-bred specimens are perhaps more readily available than wild-collected fish. This is excellent news for aquarists, as tank-raised marine fish are generally hardier and easier to maintain.

▶ *Tank-raised fish may take more time to settle into an anemone than their wild counterparts. This one has chosen* Heteractis crispa.

WHAT size?
Females up to 4.3 in (11 cm); males around 3.2 in (8 cm).

WHAT does it eat?
In the wild, zooplankton and algae. Offer enriched brineshrimp, mysis, and chopped shellfish. Tank-raised individuals usually accept most high-protein flake and granular foods, too.

WHERE is it from?
Sri Lanka and the Maldives.

WHAT does it cost?
★★☆☆☆   ★★★★☆
Wild-collected fish can be expensive due to their overall poor survival rate. Tank-raised individuals (rated here) are much more reasonably priced.

HOW do I sex it?
When observing a pair or group, the largest individual will be a female, or at least in the process of becoming one.

WHAT kind of tank?
Fish-only; live rock-based fish-only system; or reef aquarium.

WHAT minimum size tank?
40 gal (150 l).

HOW do other fish react?
If this fish is stocked without a host anemone, it may be targeted for aggression by damselfishes or other clownfishes.

WHAT to watch out for?
Cloudiness of the skin and eyes is typical in wild-collected fish. They will also prove very reluctant to feed.

HOW compatible with inverts and corals?
Should be perfectly safe with corals, ornamental shrimp, and various sessile invertebrates.

WHAT area of the tank?
Close to rockwork or in a host anemone, where present. Will swim into open water once settled.

HOW many in one tank?
Keep singly, in pairs, or in groups introduced simultaneously.

HOW does it behave?
Can be aggressive towards other species in defense of its host anemone. Otherwise, largely peaceful.

WILL it breed in an aquarium?
Yes. It has been successfully raised in captivity.

Amphiprion ocellaris
Common clownfish

FISH PROFILE

An instantly recognizable and hugely popular, long-lived marine species. Wild-collected specimens are rare and can be delicate. Given the availability of beautifully-marked, healthy, captive-bred specimens, it is difficult to justify large-scale collection of this species from the wild.

WHAT size?
Males 2.4–2.75 in (6–7 cm), females can reach 4.3 in (11 cm).

WHAT does it eat?
Wild specimens feed on zooplankton and benthic invertebrates, both of which are easily substituted in the home aquarium. To begin with, offer mysis and brineshrimp, gradually increasing the diversity of foods as the fish settle. Most individuals should accept flake and pellet foods with time.

WHERE is it from?
Eastern Indian Ocean and much of the Tropical Pacific, including the popular collection regions of Indonesia and the Philippines.

WHAT does it cost?
★☆☆☆☆ ★★☆☆☆
Wild-collected pairs can be very expensive, but individuals and captive-bred fish are much more affordable (rated here).

HOW do I sex it?
Females are significantly larger.

WHAT kind of tank?
Live rock-based fish-only or reef aquarium. Anemones are not necessary to maintain this clownfish successfully, so a fish-only system is acceptable.

WHAT minimum size tank?
25 gal (100 l) for a pair, assuming excellent water quality.

HOW do other fish react?
Most fish will not react adversely to clownfishes, with the possible exception of territorial damsels. The smallest clownfishes are the most vulnerable.

WHAT to watch out for?
Common clownfishes are prone to problems with a protozoan called *Brooklynella*, which can cause lethargy, skin sloughing, eye cloudiness, and general malaise. Avoid newly-imported fish and ensure that specimens are feeding before you buy them.

HOW compatible with inverts and corals?
Should not harm sessile invertebrates unless a fish chooses a sensitive coral as a surrogate anemone. If this happens, the coral may not expand its tentacles. Ignores most ornamental invertebrates. The natural host anemones of this species are *Heteractis magnifica*, *Stichodactyla gigantea* and *S. mertensii*.

WHAT area of the tank?
Newly-introduced specimens often swim at the water surface, even when a host anemone is present. Many captive-bred juvenile clownfish have no experience of an anemone and can take some time to find their host and move in.

HOW many in one tank?
Keep singly, in pairs, or small groups. If you plan to keep a number of specimens, stock them as small juveniles measuring less than 2 in (5 cm).

HOW does it behave?
Bickers with its own species and defends its anemone from potential aggressors. Otherwise, it is quite peaceful.

WILL it breed in an aquarium?
Yes. May spawn many hundreds or thousands of times in the home aquarium. One of the most popular fish raised in captivity.

▼ *The body color of the common clownfish is variable, ranging from pale yellow to red-orange.*

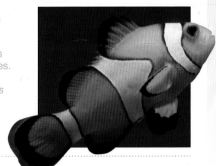

Amphiprion percula

Percula clownfish

FISH PROFILE

Although very similar to
Amphiprion ocellaris, the
percula generally has more
black pigment on the body. It
lives with three host anemone
species: *Heteractis magnifica*,
H. crispa and *Stichodactyla
gigantea*. Although it will
adopt other anemones in time,
introducing a "familiar" species
usually results in host and
clownfish uniting more quickly.

WHAT size?
Males 2.4–2.75 in (6–7 cm);
females up to 4.3 in (11 cm).

WHAT does it eat?
In the aquarium, wild-collected
specimens should accept
finely chopped shellfish, mysis,
and brineshrimp, and dried
foods with time. Tank-raised
specimens often accept
dried flake and pellet foods
immediately.

WHERE is it from?
Australia, New Guinea, and
Melanesia eastwards to the
Solomon Islands.

WHAT does it cost?
★☆☆☆☆ ★★☆☆☆
Wild-caught pairs can be quite
expensive. Individuals from
the same source are
more affordable and
captive-bred fish
are cheap (rated
here).

HOW do I sex it?
Females are larger than males.

WHAT kind of tank?
Live rock-based fish-only; reef
aquarium; fish-only system.

WHAT minimum size tank?
25 gal (100 l) for a pair, assuming
excellent water quality.

HOW do other fish react?
Most fish will not react adversely
to clownfishes, with the possible
exception of territorial damsels.
The smallest clownfishes are the
most vulnerable.

WHAT to watch out for?
Wild-collected specimens should
swim in their characteristic
undulatory fashion and have clear
eyes and no turbidity of the skin.
They should feed readily and have
a steady breathing rate. Scrutinize
captive-bred fish for congenital
deformities, such as misshapen
heads, missing gill covers, etc.

▼ *Some percula clownfish have a
great deal of black on the body.*

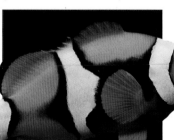

HOW compatible with inverts and corals?
Will not harm ornamental shrimp
or most sessile invertebrates. In
the absence of a host anemone
deemed suitable by the clownfish,
it may adopt a "surrogate."
Favorites include *Sarcophyton*
spp. soft corals and *Goniopora*
spp. hard corals. This can cause
the coral to become irritated, so
that polyp expansion is reduced or
sometimes does not occur.

WHAT area of the tank?
In the absence of a host anemone
or surrogate, this fish may spend
prolonged periods at the water
surface, appearing unsettled.
Given time, it will descend to the
reef or rockwork. Where a suitable
host anemone is present, the fish
lives inside or beneath its tentacles
and follows it wherever it goes.

HOW many in one tank?
Keep singly, in pairs, or in small
groups. In this fish's natural range,
up to six individuals are recorded
sharing host anemones, of which
two are the breeding pair and the
rest are non-breeding juveniles.

HOW does it behave?
Although a clownfish will vigorously
defend its host anemone
against potential aggressors,
it reserves its real temper for
its own species.

WILL it breed in an aquarium?
Yes. This long-lived species may
spawn hundreds of times in the
home aquarium. One of the most
popular fish raised in captivity.

Amphiprion perideraion

Pink skunk anemonefish

FISH PROFILE

A. perideraion has the dorsal band typical of all of the "skunk" complex, but can be distinguished from many of its close relatives by a vertical band across the gill cover. Tank-raised individuals are sometimes available, but not as regularly as the more popular members of the genus.

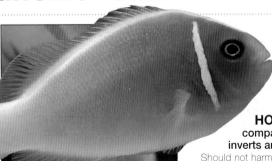

◀ *Less colorful than its relatives, but very rewarding to keep.*

WHAT size?
Females up to 4 in (10 cm) or so, males up to 2.75 in (6–7 cm).

WHAT does it eat?
In the wild, macro-algae and diatoms, tunicates, copepods, benthic worms, and many of the animals associated with zooplankton. In the aquarium, offer enriched brineshrimp, mysis, chopped shellfish, and dried algae.

WHERE is it from?
Eastern Indian Ocean to Western Pacific Ocean, Tonga and the Great Barrier Reef.

WHAT does it cost?
★☆☆☆   ★★☆☆☆
Single specimens are quite reasonably priced. Pairs (rarely collected) are significantly more expensive. Price range shown is for tank-raised fish.

HOW do I sex it?
Like all anemonefish, this species is a protandrous hermaphrodite, meaning that it is a male before it becomes a female. Thus the largest fish will be female.

WHAT kind of tank?
Fish-only; live rock-based fish-only system; or reef aquarium.

WHAT minimum size tank?
13 gal (50 l), assuming excellent water quality.

HOW do other fish react?
Newly-introduced pink skunk anemonefishes or unsettled individuals can fall victim to territorial fish such as damselfishes or wrasses. Those that are settled into a host anemone have little to worry about from other fish.

WHAT to watch out for?
Some specimens arrive in quite poor condition; leave them to settle for some time before buying. Ensure that individuals are feeding and select active, swimming individuals or true pairs with a vigorous disposition.

HOW compatible with inverts and corals?
Should not harm invertebrates unless it adopts a long-tentacled coral species as a surrogate anemone. This may irritate the coral and prevent it from expanding its polyps.

WHAT area of the tank?
Close to a host or surrogate anemone, venturing into open water to feed or defend its territory.

HOW many in one tank?
Keep singly, in small groups added simultaneously as juveniles, or as wild-collected true pairs.

HOW does it behave?
Can be pugnacious towards other fish that it perceives as a threat to its anemone. However, it is more tolerant than most anemonefishes and, although it is safer to maintain a single species from the genus *Amphiprion* per aquarium, the pink skunk is known to share its anemone with *A. akallopisos* in the wild.

WILL it breed in an aquarium?
Yes. It has been successfully raised in the home aquarium.

Amphiprion sandaracinos

Orange skunk anemonefish

FISH PROFILE

An attractive anemonefish species, identifiable by the single broad stripe running along its back from the upper jaw to the base of the tail. Its close relative *A. akallopisos* is very similar in appearance and husbandry requirements, but has a white, not orange, tail. *A. sandaracinos* is a hardy fish and rewarding to keep, yet often overshadowed by more commonly available members of this genus.

WHAT size?
Females up to 4.3 in (11 cm); males 0.75 to 2.5 in (3–6.5 cm).

WHAT does it eat?
Most individuals readily accept enriched brineshrimp, chopped mysis, and chopped shellfish. Settled individuals should accept dried, granular, or flaked foods. This species may also nip at dried algae.

WHERE is it from?
Specimens will either be tank-raised or obtained from the Western Pacific, in particular the Philippines and Christmas Island.

WHAT does it cost?
★☆☆☆☆ ★★☆☆☆
True wild-caught pairs are expensive, but tank-raised individuals are quite cheap (rated here).

HOW do I sex it?
Females are larger than males. Specimens below about 2 in (5 cm) are either males or juveniles.

WHAT kind of tank?
Fish-only, live rock-based fish-only system; or reef aquarium.

WHAT minimum size tank?
40 gal (150 l).

HOW do other fish react?
Anemonefishes are seldom victimized for long, other than by members of the same genus and sometimes damsels. Any problems are usually worse in the absence of a host anemone, but this is not essential for the successful maintenance of this species.

WHAT to watch out for?
Fish should have a clean appearance and feed readily. Avoid specimens with cloudy eyes or turbidity of the skin. These problems generally only manifest themselves in wild-collected fish.

▼ *The orange skunk anemonefish is a beautiful and hardy species, yet not commonly kept by hobbyists.*

HOW compatible with inverts and corals?
Should not harm any invertebrates, but can sometimes adopt a surrogate host, which becomes irritated by its presence.

WHAT area of the tank?
Remains close to its host anemone where present. Otherwise it is associated with rockwork, venturing into open water to feed.

HOW many in one tank?
Keep in pairs or small groups introduced simultaneously as juveniles.

HOW does it behave?
Any resident anemonefish can be aggressive in the defense of its anemone or territory. It is quite capable of driving off any potential aggressors, even those much larger than themselves. Although this can be a nuisance for the aquarist, it seldom results in any major problems to fish health.

WILL it breed in an aquarium?
Yes. It has been successfully raised in captivity.

Premnas biaculeatus

Maroon anemonefish

Many species of anemonefish can possess incomplete vertical bands.

FISH PROFILE

The maroon anemonefish is the only species belonging to the genus *Premnas*. In the wild, it exclusively inhabits bubbletip anemones *(Entacmaea quadricolor)*. In the aquarium it can often fend for itself in the absence of an anemone.

WHAT size?
Specimens around 3–4 in (8–10 cm) could be large males or small females. Large females can attain 6.7 in (17 cm).

WHAT does it eat?
Many aquarists with experience of keeping this species might be surprised to know that it includes algae in its natural diet. However, zooplankton forms the bulk of its normal daily intake. It accepts most foods offered.

WHERE is it from?
A widespread species found in a large percentage of the tropical Indo-Pacific. Specimens from Sumatra have bright yellow, thick, vertical bands, rather than the usual white; this color morph has been extensively bred in captivity.

WHAT does it cost?
★★☆☆☆   ★★★★★
Relatively inexpensive. Wild specimens are at the upper end of the price range.

HOW do I sex it?
Females are usually much larger.

WHAT kind of tank?
Fish-only; live rock-based fish-only system; or reef aquarium.

WHAT minimum size tank?
Due to its large maximum size, house it long-term in a system of 24 gal (90 l) or more.

HOW do other fish react?
Do not keep this species with other anemonefish.

WHAT to watch out for?
A maroon anemonefish will dominate an aquarium, particularly when living with a host anemone. It will scatter sand from the aquarium floor, move rocks, and attack any fish that strays too close. Will aggressively defend its anemone against any threat, including an aquarist's hand if it gets too close. Large individuals are capable of drawing blood.

HOW compatible with inverts and corals?
May move corals or cover them with sand.

WHAT area of the tank?
Will follow host anemone where present.

HOW many in one tank?
Keep singly or in male/female pairs.

HOW does it behave?
Of all species of fish with a symbiotic relationship with anemones, this one usually takes up residence the quickest. Some individuals have been observed swimming into the open bag of an acclimating anemone!

WILL it breed in an aquarium?
Yes. The larvae have been raised successfully.

Chromis cyanea

Blue reef chromis

A lively and active species that is highly prized by aquarists. Grows larger than its close relative, the blue-green chromis (*Chromis viridis*), and should only be purchased by aquarists who can provide the open swimming space that this species needs.

WHAT size?
Males 6 in (15 cm), females are smaller.

WHAT does it eat?
Wild specimens feed on zooplankton and therefore adapt well to frozen foodstuffs. Settled individuals often readily accept flake and dried foods.

WHERE is it from?
The Caribbean and Western Atlantic, including Southern Florida and Bermuda.

WHAT does it cost?
★★☆☆☆   ★★★☆☆
Generally more expensive than most other species of *Chromis* or damselfish, but this can vary considerably depending on where they are offered for sale. Understandably, it is more expensive in Europe than in North America due to freight costs.

▶ *Don't be fooled by the small retail size of this species. Adult males can attain a length of 6 in (15 cm).*

HOW do I sex it?
Male specimens will often be the larger and more dominant individuals within a group.

WHAT kind of tank?
Live rock-based fish-only system or large reef aquarium.

WHAT minimum size tank?
120 gal (450 l).

HOW do other fish react?
Do not keep with predatory fish species, especially when stocking with small individuals.

WHAT to watch out for?
Specimens showing signs of stress or bullying often do not survive for long. It is best to acquire individuals measuring at least an inch (2–3 cm), despite the availability of smaller specimens.

HOW compatible with inverts and corals?
Can be housed with corals and invertebrates with few problems.

WHAT area of the tank?
An open-water-swimming species that quickly retreats into the rockwork when it feels threatened.

HOW many in one tank?
Best kept in groups as large as the aquarium will safely accommodate.

HOW does it behave?
A busy species that often bickers incessantly with members of its own species. It can be found swimming in aggregations with other species.

WILL it breed in an aquarium?
Yes, in larger aquariums.

Chromis viridis

Blue-green chromis

FISH PROFILE

A small, schooling species that is very popular among marine aquarists due to its undemanding disposition, hardiness, and wonderful colors that seem to change as the fish moves. A small shoal will encourage timid fish of other species out into the open water of the aquarium.

▲ *The appearance of this chromis depends on how the light catches it.*

WHAT size?
Males maximum 3.1 in (8 cm), females are smaller.

WHAT does it eat?
Phytoplankton and zooplankton on tropical reefs. Will accept almost any meaty, flake, or particulate foods offered. Feed several small amounts regularly.

WHERE is it from?
Wide-ranging throughout the tropical Indo-Pacific.

WHAT does it cost?
★☆☆☆☆
Inexpensive. The reasonable price and amiability of this species guarantees its inclusion in many aquariums.

HOW do I sex it?
Males are often larger, with a black dorsal fin.

WHAT kind of tank?
Almost any aquarium will house this species adequately, but it will undoubtedly do best in a reef aquarium that closely simulates its natural environment.

WHAT minimum size tank?
13 gal (50 l) will comfortably house a trio.

HOW do other fish react?
Do not keep with predatory fish species.

WHAT to watch out for?
Since blue-green chromis are such active, mobile swimmers, they often consume all the food offered before slower, more timid species have the opportunity to feed. Take care that such species do not starve when chromis are stocked.

HOW compatible with inverts and corals?
Should not directly harm any sessile invertebrates. If it enters a spawning cycle it could damage invertebrates that it chooses to act as the nest site, but this phenomenon is rare.

WHAT area of the tank?
An open-water-swimming species that retreats into rockwork when disturbed.

HOW many in one tank?
Do not keep singly. Groups of three or more are best.

HOW does it behave?
An easy species to maintain in the home aquarium. It will behave completely naturally and reward the aquarist with hours of entertainment. Be aware that territorial males can bully weaker males, so that they stop feeding and eventually die.

WILL it breed in an aquarium?
Yes. This is a substrate-spawning species in which males dominate harems of females. Males guard the nest site vigorously.

Chrysiptera cyanea

Blue damselfish

The blue damselfish still has a place in the modern marine aquarium, despite its reputation for aggressive territoriality. At one time, it was recommended for early introduction into a new marine aquarium because it is better able to withstand the poor water quality associated with immature filters. However, these days, the advice is to make it one of the final introductions, thus reducing its territoriality.

▲ *Males from certain regions have striking orange markings on the tail and body.*

WHAT size?
Males reach almost 3.5 in (9 cm), females seldom more than 2.5 in (6.5 cm).

WHAT does it eat?
In the wild, zooplankton and benthic invertebrates, particularly copepods. Also grazes on certain forms of algae. In an aquarium, mysis, brineshrimp, chopped shellfish, flake, and freeze-dried offerings.

WHERE is it from?
Wide-ranging, found from the Eastern Indian Ocean and throughout the tropical Pacific.

WHAT does it cost?
★☆☆☆☆   ★★★☆☆
Large males from Micronesian and Australian waters are moderately expensive compared to most other damselfishes. Juveniles and females are inexpensive.

HOW do I sex it?
Females and juveniles have a black spot at the base of the dorsal fin. Males from certain areas have a bright red or orange edge to the tail fin.

WHAT kind of tank?
Fish-only; live rock-based fish-only system; or reef aquarium.

WHAT minimum size tank?
13 gal (50 l).

HOW do other fish react?
May be threatened by other damselfishes, some wrasses, and other small robust species, but is usually able to withstand any initial victimization soon after being introduced to the aquarium.

WHAT to watch out for?
Ignore individuals with damage to the fins or body received as a result of bullying by other members of the same species.

HOW compatible with inverts and corals?
Should not harm corals or sessile invertebrates, with the possible exception of tunicates or ornamental shrimp.

WHAT area of the tank?
Found all over the aquarium, in rockwork and in open water.

HOW many in one tank?
Keep singly, in male/female pairs or in a male-dominated harem of three or four individuals.

HOW does it behave?
This fish is very territorial, so make it one of the last introductions. Males are more aggressive than females, but neither can be trusted completely. Introduce more delicate species before this one.

WILL it breed in an aquarium?
Yes.

Chrysiptera parasema

Yellow-tailed blue damselfish

FISH PROFILE

A commonly available species of damselfish, generally regarded as one of the more peaceful from this family of small reef fish. However, in order to avoid any problems with territorial aggression, it is best to introduce it when all delicate species are already in residence.

WHAT size?
Males 2.75 in (7 cm); females slightly smaller.

WHAT does it eat?
This naturally planktivorous species will readily accept most foods. Offer dried flakes and granules in addition to frozen marine fish preparations.

WHERE is it from?
Tropical Pacific, including the Solomon Islands and the Philippines.

WHAT does it cost?
★☆☆☆☆
Inexpensive.

▶ *This species of damselfish is an aquarium favorite, having a more peaceful disposition than some of its larger relatives.*

HOW do I sex it?
Males may be slightly larger and usually more aggressive.

WHAT kind of tank?
Fish-only; live rock-based fish-only system; or reef aquarium.

WHAT minimum size tank?
13 gal (50 l).

HOW do other fish react?
Most fish will ignore this species.

WHAT to watch out for?
Because these fish are often kept in large groups in the dealer's tanks, try to avoid any that show evidence of bullying by more dominant fish. The body color should be solid blue and the fins intact.

HOW compatible with inverts and corals?
Should not harm any sessile invertebrates or ornamental shrimp.

WHAT area of the tank?
Close to and among the rockwork. It will venture into the open to feed or drive away intruders, but quickly returns to the patch it regards as its territory. This reflects the natural situation, as this species is found in and around densely, branching hard corals.

HOW many in one tank?
Best kept singly, in pairs, or in small groups in a large aquarium.

HOW does it behave?
Moderately aggressive towards similar-sized and smaller fish. This behavior can be worse when the fish is introduced as one of the first species in a new aquarium.

WILL it breed in an aquarium?
Yes.

Chrysiptera taupou

Fijian blue-and-gold damselfish

A beautifully-colored damselfish that has been given the somewhat misleading alternative common name of Southseas Devil or Blue Devil by some authorities. In fact, from an aquarist's point of view it is one of the more suitable damselfish for the home aquarium. It is often possible to house a group together, providing individuals are stocked simultaneously and at a small size.

WHAT size?
Males up to 3.1 in (8 cm); females slightly smaller.

WHAT does it eat?
The natural diet includes algae and an assortment of benthic invertebrates, such as copepods and mysids. In an aquarium, it accepts almost any food, including flake and granules, and will pick at dried algae. A varied diet will ensure that it retains its vibrant coloration.

WHERE is it from?
Tropical Eastern Australia and scattered island groups to Fiji.

WHAT does it cost?
★☆☆☆☆   ★★☆☆☆
Slightly more expensive than the more commonly available species of damselfish.

▶ *This male fish shows the black-edged dorsal fin typical of its sex.*

HOW do I sex it?
Males larger and more aggressive. They have a black edge to the front part of the dorsal fin. This region is yellow in females.

WHAT kind of tank?
Fish-only; live rock-based fish-only system; or reef aquarium.

WHAT minimum size tank?
13 gal (50 l) for a single specimen.

HOW do other fish react?
Most species ignore damselfish if they themselves are left alone. Exceptions can include other damselfishes, anemonefishes, and dottybacks.

WHAT to watch out for?
Individuals that show signs of being bullied, such as discoloration of the body or torn fins, may be more susceptible to infections than undamaged specimens.

HOW compatible with inverts and corals?
Should be safe with all invertebrates.

WHAT area of the tank?
Open water-swimmer; seeks refuge in rocks when threatened.

HOW many in one tank?
The upper limits will be dictated by the size of the aquarium. Four is not unreasonable in a 100-gallon (400 l) aquarium, but allow space for the fish to grow.

HOW does it behave?
Fijian blue and gold damsels typically occupy small territories that are often home to small amounts of the algae that they graze on. It does not appear to be necessary to simulate these areas in an aquarium environment. Take care with small fish species that have a similar lifestyle to this damselfish. *C. taupou* may react aggressively towards other damselfishes and dottybacks (*Pseudochromis* spp.), but can coexist with species such as green chromis and anthias.

WILL it breed in an aquarium?
Yes.

Dascyllus aruanus

Humbug aruanus

FISH PROFILE

A popular and attractive species, one of the hardiest available, and offered for sale when very small. It resembles *D. melanurus*, the four-stripe, or blacktail, humbug, but the latter has a black tail margin and only grows to 3.1 in (8 cm). Both species require virtually the same care.

▲ *Four-stripe humbug* D. melanurus.

WHAT size?
Males up to 4 in (10 cm; females 3.1 in (8 cm) or less.

WHAT does it eat?
In the wild, zooplankton and algae. Offer meaty foods, including mysis (chopped if necessary), brineshrimp, and chopped shellfish. Settled specimens accept many dried foods, including flake.

WHERE is it from?
Much of the tropical Indo-Pacific, from the Red Sea to Southern Australia.

WHAT does it cost?
★☆☆☆☆
Inexpensive.

HOW do I sex it?
Males are larger and more belligerent than females.

WHAT kind of tank?
Fish-only; live rock-based fish-only system; or reef aquarium, providing you can tolerate its behavior.

WHAT minimum size tank?
66 gal (250 l).

HOW do other fish react?
Small specimens may be singled out for aggression by wrasses or other damsels, but due to their hardiness and low price, they are often stocked before species that can cause them problems.

WHAT to watch out for?
Avoid individuals that have been picked on by other members of the same species. Very small juveniles are sometimes available, but do not buy them in "shoals," as they will reduce

◀ *Although often available at a small size, this fish grows moderately large and becomes highly territorial.*

their number through interspecific aggression to a single male and group of females.

HOW compatible with inverts and corals?
This species does not consume any desirable invertebrates, but mature groups can prove problematic because the male will strip coral tissue from its stony or fibrous skeleton in order to provide a space for the female to deposit her eggs.

WHAT area of the tank?
Juveniles seldom stray too far from refuge, but adults swim confidently into open water.

HOW many in one tank?
Keep singly or in male-dominated harems. One male and three females is acceptable.

HOW does it behave?
Although small juveniles are quite peaceful, their aggression increases as they grow. Fairly robust species introduced before the damselfish should not be threatened, but sensitive species or those added after the humbugs may be harassed at least and killed at worst.

WILL it breed in an aquarium?
Yes. Males clear a nesting site and entice the female to deposit her eggs, which he then guards.

Dascyllus trimaculatus

Domino damselfish

An attractive species that many aquarists are tempted to buy, particularly when it is at the very small size commonly offered for sale. However, despite its hardiness and the fact that it thrives in captivity, it is not an ideal species for the marine aquarium. Its presence can preclude the introduction of almost any other fish and its growth rate is prodigious.

▶ *Small juveniles become increasingly confident and aggressive as they grow.*

WHAT size?
Males up to 5.5 in (14 cm); females up to 4 in (10 cm) at best.

WHAT does it eat?
In the wild, algae and planktonic organisms. In the aquarium, settled individuals will accept almost anything, including flaked, granular, and other dried foods, but mix these with frozen meaty foods for the best long-term results.

WHERE is it from?
Much of the tropical Indo-Pacific, from the Red Sea to Southern Australia.

WHAT does it cost?
★☆☆☆☆
Inexpensive.

HOW do I sex it?
Males are larger and more belligerent than females.

WHAT kind of tank?
Fish-only; live rock-based fish-only system; or very large reef aquarium (160 gal/600 l or more).

WHAT minimum size tank?
80 gal (300 l).

HOW do other fish react?
Most fish will ignore the spritely, highly alert juvenile specimens. Adults are large and sturdy enough to hold their own against some of the most aggressive marine fish.

WHAT to watch out for?
Groups of juveniles shoal well and use hard corals and anemones for refuge. However, they grow rapidly and you will soon have cause to regret a rash purchase.

HOW compatible with inverts and corals?
Damage to invertebrates is seldom deliberate. Large specimens may rearrange rockwork or attack ornamental shrimp. Their sand-moving behavior can also smother sessile invertebrates.

WHAT area of the tank?
Keep singly or in male/female pairs.

HOW many in one tank?
Juveniles seldom stray too far from refuge, but adults will swim confidently into open water.

HOW does it behave?
Juveniles are shy and although they bicker among themselves, small fish (1–1.5 in/3–4 cm) are seldom a problem. However, as they grow, their territorial aggression increases exponentially and they will attack, and sometimes kill, any new introductions or residents that are not strong enough to look after themselves. If you must own this fish, be sure to keep it with very hardy species.

WILL it breed in an aquarium?
Yes. Males clear a nesting site and entice the female to deposit her eggs, which he then guards.

Pomacentrus alleni

Andaman damselfish

FISH PROFILE

Many aquarists are tempted to buy this stunning species of damselfish, only to discover that it can turn its incredible color and patterning on and off at will. This appears to be the result of a pecking order, whereby dominant individuals earn the right to display their full beauty.

WHAT size?
The largest males grow to 2.4 in (6 cm); females slightly smaller.

WHAT does it eat?
Almost any meaty particulate food offered, plus the dried algae available for tangs and other more herbivorous fish.

WHERE is it from?
Thailand and Indonesia.

WHAT does it cost?
★☆☆☆☆   ★★☆☆☆
Moderately priced for a damselfish.

HOW do I sex it?
Males are larger than females, but this is only apparent when observing a pair. Otherwise, there are no obvious external differences.

WHAT kind of tank?
Peaceful reef or live rock-based fish-only system.

WHAT minimum size tank?
50 gal (200 l).

HOW do other fish react?
Do not keep *P. alleni* with other damselfishes, with the possible exception of the more peaceful *Chromis* species, such as *C. viridis*. *P. alleni* is not as robust as many other damsels, and constant chasing by dwarf angelfishes or tangs may cause it to become stressed and therefore reluctant to leave the refuge of rockwork.

WHAT to watch out for?
Try to avoid specimens with torn or ragged fins. Although these will heal quickly when the fish is settled, they do indicate individuals that have been subjected to some aggression by their own species. Such fish may not be able to tolerate the initial territoriality of existing fish in their new home.

HOW compatible with inverts and corals?
Perfectly suited to a reef aquarium.

WHAT area of the tank?
Swims close to, but above, rockwork and sand.

HOW many in one tank?
Keep in small groups for the best chance of seeing the true colors of this species.

HOW does it behave?
P. alleni does not generally bother other fish species, but sometimes bickers incessantly with its own.

WILL it breed in an aquarium?
Potentially, yes. Other *Pomacentrus* species are known to spawn in captivity, and there is no reason why this should not be the case here.

◀ *A beautiful and relatively peaceful species of damselfish.*

Pterapogon kauderni

Banggai cardinalfish

An untypical cardinalfish species, but one of the easiest marine fish to breed and raise successfully in captivity. It has achieved considerable popularity with marine aquarists over recent years and the increasing availability of captive-bred specimens should ensure its availability to the hobby indefinitely.

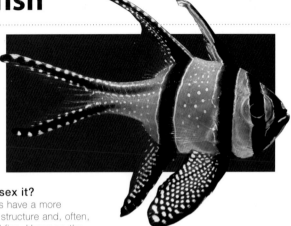

▶ *Tank-raised specimens of this striking cardinalfish are often on sale. Breeds readily.*

WHAT size?
Males and females 3 in (8 cm).

WHAT does it eat?
Wild specimens feed on zooplankton in open water. Captive specimens readily accept most foods, including chopped shellfish, mysis, and brineshrimp. Males do not feed when brooding eggs and therefore require regular feeding between breeding cycles; otherwise, they can consume the egg mass.

WHERE is it from?
Originally restricted to the Banggai Islands in Indonesia, but the loss of specimens from collectors' boats has actually increased the natural range of this species.

WHAT does it cost?
★★★★☆ ★★★★★
Probably the most expensive commonly available cardinalfish species.

HOW do I sex it?
Mature males have a more massive jaw structure and, often, longer dorsal fins. However, the latter feature is unreliable due to fin loss as a result of infighting between individuals.

WHAT kind of tank?
A peaceful aquarium with plenty of sea grass or *Caulerpa* spp. algae is ideal, but fish will settle into most quiet aquariums containing live rock and/or corals.

WHAT minimum size tank?
15 gal (50 l).

HOW do other fish react?
The Banggai cardinalfish does not react well to the presence of busy or aggressively territorial species.

WHAT to watch out for?
Males have a distended mouth when brooding a clutch of eggs and refuse to feed during this time.

HOW compatible with inverts and corals?
Will not harm corals, but may attack small ornamental shrimp such as *Thor amboinensis*.

WHAT area of the tank?
Swims in open water, but often found close to rockwork.

HOW many in one tank?
Can be kept in large shoals in a sufficiently large aquarium.

HOW does it behave?
Try to obtain male/female pairs, otherwise fighting can occur, often resulting in the death of the weaker individual. The Banggai cardinalfish is not the most active fish—usually hanging motionless in the water column—but its good looks and fascinating breeding behavior more than make up for this. If a long-spined sea urchin is provided, it is also possible to observe the unique relationship that the juveniles and adults have with this invertebrate.

WILL it breed in an aquarium?
Yes. Females deposit eggs in the form of a cluster or ball.

Sphaeramia nematoptera

Pajama cardinalfish

FISH PROFILE

Its benign behavior and attractive coloration make this cardinalfish very popular with marine aquarists. It is active at night, often spending large parts of the day hiding in the branches of small-polyp stony corals. It often appears to be more adventurous under blue actinic lighting.

WHAT size?
Males up to 4 in (10 cm); females slightly smaller.

WHAT does it eat?
In the wild, small, free-living benthic invertebrates on the coral reefs. Aquarium individuals readily accept small meaty foods, such as brineshrimp, mysis, and various frozen foods. Most fish will take flaked and granular foods. It is vital to feed mature fish several times each day, especially when breeding.

WHERE is it from?
Western Pacific, including Indonesia and the Great Barrier Reef.

WHAT does it cost?
★☆☆☆☆ ★★☆☆☆
Inexpensive.

▶ *Good looks and an even temperament make this fish a perennial favorite with marine aquarists.*

HOW do I sex it?
Males are generally larger and have a larger mouth.

WHAT kind of tank?
Fish-only; live rock-based fish-only system; or reef aquarium.

WHAT minimum size tank?
45 gal (175 l).

HOW do other fish react?
Being a shy and unassertive species, the pajama cardinalfish can become the victim of more aggressive species. Damsels and dwarf angelfishes can be problematic if resident in a smaller aquarium before the cardinalfish is introduced.

WHAT to watch out for?
Avoid non-feeding specimens or those with signs of fin or body damage. Since this species is usually collected and shipped in large numbers, there will always be weaker individuals in the shoal. These are more easily caught in a net, so inspect fish carefully before buying.

HOW compatible with inverts and corals?
Will not harm sessile invertebrates or most ornamental shrimp.

WHAT area of the tank?
In a brightly lit reef aquarium, it will hide in the rockwork for much of the day. More active at night or under blue actinic lights.

HOW many in one tank?
Keep singly, in pairs or in small groups.

HOW does it behave?
Reserves most aggression for other pajama cardinalfish, but even this is not particularly problematic.

WILL it breed in an aquarium?
Yes. Males brood eggs in their mouths. The fry are much smaller than those of the Banggai cardinalfish and therefore more difficult to rear, but they have been raised successfully in captivity.

Aquarium personalities

▶ True angelfishes (family Pomacanthidae) include the genera *Pomacanthus, Apolemichthys, Chaetodontoplus, Pygoplites* and *Holacanthus*, all medium to large fish—often with personalities to match. They are often available as small juveniles, some with a markedly different appearance to the adult. Given sufficiently good water quality, most settle well into the aquarium, but do not be tempted by beautiful juveniles if you cannot house a large specimen long-term. Most dwarf angelfishes (genus *Centropyge*) remain fairly small (less than 6 in/15 cm). They are a favorite of aquarists, particularly those with reef aquariums, even though they can never be fully trusted not to nip at invertebrates. The swallowtail angelfishes are small to medium-sized fish. Males are not only larger, as in other angelfishes, but also have a different color or pattern. These fish are ideal for the larger reef aquarium.

Price guide

★	$25–$35
★★	$35–$60
★★★	$60–$105
★★★★	$105–$175
★★★★★	$175–$525

FISH PROFILE

A small species of dwarf angelfish that is available at less than 2 in (5 cm), yet proves extremely hardy in an aquarium situation. The obvious colored band along its back varies from intense orange to golden yellow. It resembles the western Atlantic flameback angelfish *(Centropyge aurantonotus)*, which has similar aquarium attributes, but the latter fish has deep blue pigment in the tail fin that is absent in the fireball.

WHAT size?
Males 3.1 in (8 cm); females 2.4 in (6 cm).

WHAT does it eat?
In its natural environment, its diet is quite cosmopolitan and it should not prove difficult to feed in the home aquarium. Offer a variety of meaty foods, including chopped shellfish, enriched brineshrimp, chopped mysis, and dried algae. Fish should accept flaked and granular foods, although it may take some time to wean them onto these.

WHERE is it from?
Western Indian Ocean.

WHAT does it cost?
★★☆☆☆
Size for size, it is more expensive than many other dwarf angelfishes. Small individuals (less than 2 in/5 cm) are commonly available.

Fireball dwarf angelfish

HOW do I sex it?
Males are significantly larger than females. The very largest specimens are likely to be males.

WHAT kind of tank?
Fish-only; live rock-based fish-only system; or reef aquarium.

WHAT minimum size tank?
33 gal (125 l) is ample for a single individual, assuming excellent water quality.

HOW do other fish react?
The fireball angelfish is quite robust even when small, and usually able to avoid any major aggression from resident fish such as wrasses, tangs, surgeonfish, and larger species of dottyback.

▼ *A small but beautiful dwarf angelfish.*

WHAT to watch out for?
Ensure that specimens are feeding before you buy them. The vast majority will feed readily within a day or so after importation. Check for pale discoloration of the body, which is particularly obvious on the deep purple flanks of the fish.

HOW compatible with inverts and corals?
Sometimes nips at large-polyp stony corals, but is generally safe with most corals. The mantle of tridacnid clams is also under threat from this fish, but seems to be nipped out of inquisitiveness, rather than a desire to consume the mollusc.

WHAT area of the tank?
Although predisposed to spend extended periods in the rockwork from where it can avoid predators, an individual in a peaceful aquarium will have much more confidence and swims boldly into open water in the anticipation of being fed.

HOW many in one tank?
Keep singly, in pairs or in small groups where space allows.

HOW does it behave?
The fireball has a personality that exceeds its diminutive size. If stocked early in the lifespan of the aquarium, this can prove a problem for the aquarist, because the fish bullies new introductions incessantly.

WILL it breed in an aquarium?
Yes. A good candidate for captive breeding attempts.

Centropyge argi
Cherub (pygmy) angelfish

FISH PROFILE

The smallest member of the genus *Centropyge* is also the most popular and reasonably priced of those species found in the Western Atlantic and Caribbean.

WHAT size?
Males 3.1 in (8 cm); females 2.4 in (6 cm).

WHAT does it eat?
In the wild, mainly various forms of algae. Offer dried algae in the aquarium, together with small-sized particulate food, such as chopped mysis, brineshrimp, and chopped shellfish.

WHERE is it from?
Caribbean and subtropical and tropical Western Atlantic.

WHAT does it cost?
★★☆☆☆
Moderately priced; generally available when very small (less than 2.5 in/5 cm).

HOW do I sex it?
Males are significantly larger than females. The very largest specimens are likely to be males.

WHAT kind of tank?
Fish-only; live rock-based fish-only system; or reef aquarium.

WHAT minimum size tank?
26 gal (100 l) is ample for a single individual, assuming excellent water quality.

HOW do other fish react?
C. argi can fall victim to resident fish that would not otherwise attack dwarf angelfish. These can include small wrasses, e.g. the sixline (*Pseudocheilinus hexataenia*) and even dotty-backs such as the bluestreak (*Pseudochromis springeri*), both of which are protective around the rockwork retreat. For this reason, it is a good idea to stock *C. argi* earlier rather than later.

▼ *Good specimens appear bright-eyed and have a uniform blue body color.*

WHAT to watch out for?
Individual fish should be feeding well before you buy. Check the body for discoloration or lack of good condition. All angelfish can be prone to *Brooklynella* infestations, so avoid specimens with turbidity of the skin or cloudy eyes.

HOW compatible with inverts and corals?
Can be problematic with some hard corals, particularly those with large polyps such as *Trachyphyllia, Platygyra, Favia, Favites* and *Lobophyllia*. Should not harm ornamental shrimp.

WHAT area of the tank?
Spends much of its time in and among rockwork towards the bottom of the aquarium. Ventures out over the substrate, particularly where rubble is present, as this mirrors its natural behavior.

HOW many in one tank?
Keep singly, in pairs, or in small groups where space allows.

HOW does it behave?
Despite its small size, it can be at least as belligerent as other members of this genus when the mood takes it. Will vigorously defend its territory, even against much larger fish such as tangs and surgeonfish.

WILL it breed in an aquarium?
Yes. It has been successfully reared in captivity.

Centropyge aurantia

Golden angelfish

FISH PROFILE

This enigmatic little fish is highly prized by many marine aquarists, not least for its beauty. The overall copper base color can sometimes lead to some confusion with the rusty angelfish *(Centropyge ferrugatus)*. The lack of blue on the dorsal and ventral fins in the golden angelfish and its high price are distinguishing features.

▲ *A shy angelfish species that needs a peaceful aquarium if it is to thrive.*

WHAT size?
Males 4 in (10 cm); females 3.1 in (8 cm).

WHAT does it eat?
In the wild, algae, benthic crustaceans, and some tunicates. Can be difficult to feed in captivity, but offer brineshrimp (enriched with spirulina and Omega 3) and plenty of dried algae.

WHERE is it from?
Samoa, Indonesia, and Great Barrier Reef.

WHAT does it cost?
★★★★☆
An expensive fish.

HOW do I sex it?
Males are larger than females because the latter change sex as they reach the maximum size for the species.

WHAT kind of tank?
A mature (ideally established for 12 months or more) live rock-based fish-only or reef aquarium.

WHAT minimum size tank?
60 gal (240 l).

HOW do other fish react?
Forget about adding *C. aurantia* to any aquarium housing boisterous fish. If aggressive species are present, you will not see this fish at all, and will have no idea whether it is ailing or in need of attention.

WHAT to watch out for?
Strictly speaking, you should not buy any fish without first observing it feeding. However, *C. aurantia* can be so shy in the dealer's tank that it will not feed while you are watching it closely. A specimen that is feeding well in this situation is highly prized.

HOW compatible with inverts and corals?
Should not harm corals or ornamental invertebrates, with the possible exception of sponges and tunicates.

WHAT area of the tank?
Close to the rockwork if it ventures into open water at all.

HOW many in one tank?
Can be kept singly or in pairs.

HOW does it behave?
Very peaceful. May bicker with other members of the same species.

WILL it breed in an aquarium?
Potentially, yes.

Centropyge bicolor

Bicolor dwarf angelfish

The stunning contrasting coloration of the bicolor, or oriole, dwarf angelfish guarantees its continued popularity as a marine aquarium fish. However, it has a reputation among reef aquarists as a polyp-nipper that can cause sessile invertebrates major problems.

WHAT size?
Males maximum 6 in (15 cm); females 4 in (10 cm) or less.

WHAT does it eat?
The natural diet consists of sponges, tunicates, algae, small worms, and crustaceans. It is vital to reproduce this variety in the aquarium and to offer dried algae on which the fish can browse. Add vitamin supplements to frozen formula foods, brineshrimp, and mysis. In time, fish should take flake or granular food.

WHERE is it from?
Found throughout many of the tropical reef zones in the Indo-Pacific as far east as Samoa.

WHAT does it cost?
★★☆☆☆
A relatively inexpensive dwarf angelfish.

▶ *Check that this fish will feed before buying it. Provide a varied diet in captivity.*

HOW do I sex it?
As with all angelfishes, this species is a protogynous hermaphrodite (meaning females become males), so the very largest specimens will be males.

WHAT kind of tank?
Fish-only; live rock-based fish-only system; or reef aquarium.

WHAT minimum size tank?
60 gal (240 l).

HOW do other fish react?
Avoid keeping *C. bicolor* with closely related species, such as the lemonpeel or Herald's dwarf angelfish.

WHAT to watch out for?
Avoid emaciated fish or those with slightly faded colors, which may signify a weak or ailing fish. Specimens must be feeding well and have a relaxed breathing rate.

HOW compatible with inverts and corals?
Most dwarf angelfish target large-polyp stony corals for particular attention, but the bicolor's tastes can stretch to other corals and sessile invertebrates. It should not harm ornamental shrimp.

WHAT area of the tank?
Bicolor angelfish can be quite shy when first introduced, hiding in the rockwork. They become bolder with time and should behave like most dwarf angelfishes, regularly examining the rockwork for food.

HOW many in one tank?
Can be kept singly or in pairs where space allows (200 gal/750 l or more). Introduce two individuals simultaneously wherever possible.

HOW does it behave?
Can be aggressive towards similar species, particularly dwarf angelfishes, but this is likely to be shortlived. Where territoriality might be an issue, introduce fish that are significantly larger or smaller than the specimen of this species. The bicolor dwarf angelfish is only moderately aggressive towards new aquarium introductions.

WILL it breed in an aquarium?
Has the potential to spawn in the aquarium, but would prove a great challenge to rear successfully.

Centropyge bispinosa
Coral beauty

FISH PROFILE

One of the most commonly kept marine fish, this species embodies the beauty and aquarium hardiness for which the genus *Centropyge* is famed. Specimens have varying patterns depending on where they were collected.

▲ *The amount of purple pigment varies significantly in this species of dwarf angelfish.*

WHAT size?
Males 4 in (10 cm); females slightly smaller.

WHAT does it eat?
In the wild, algae, sponges and tunicates from rocks. Settled captive fish enjoy almost anything offered to them, including chopped seafood, flake, and pellets. Dried algae is vital for long-term success.

WHERE is it from?
Tropical Indo-Pacific. Most specimens are imported through Indonesia and the Philippines.

WHAT does it cost?
★★☆☆☆
Among the least expensive dwarf angelfishes.

HOW do I sex it?
Males are larger than females.

WHAT kind of tank?
Fish-only; live rock-based, fish-only system; reef aquarium.

WHAT minimum size tank?
40 gal (150 l).

HOW do other fish react?
The coral beauty may fall victim to larger or more aggressive species, particularly if introduced after these fish. It is best to make the coral beauty one of the first introductions into the aquarium.

WHAT to watch out for?
Observe fish closely before buying to ensure that they are moving naturally, with a slow breathing rate. Although most individuals usually feed well, reluctance to do so can indicate a recently imported or relocated specimen. Avoid such fish until they have had time to settle.

HOW compatible with inverts and corals?
The coral beauty is very unlikely to cause any problems.

WHAT area of the tank?
Close to rockwork, which it scours for food.

HOW many in one tank?
Keep singly unless the aquarium is large enough (100–130 gal/ 400–500 l minimum) to house a pair.

HOW does it behave?
Any aggression is generally very shortlived, even towards members of the same genus.

WILL it breed in an aquarium?
Yes. Males court the females and induce them to spawn. In their natural environment, individual males defend a territory containing a number of females.

Centropyge eibli

Red stripe dwarf angelfish

A commonly imported fish, not as colorful as some members of the genus, but very attractive nonetheless and can prove a hardy addition to most aquariums. It is mimicked by juvenile specimens of the Indian Ocean mimic surgeonfish, *Acanthurus tristis*.

◀ *This is a young adult specimen. These fish do not change significantly through life.*

WHAT size?
Males 6 in (15 cm) maximum; females around 4 in (10 cm) or less.

WHAT does it eat?
The natural diet has been recorded as consisting of stony coral polyps and algae. Although the latter is important for the long-term maintenance of this species, the former is not and *C. eibli* can often be kept with corals without any problems. Supplement dried algae in a lettuce clip with formula foods developed for angelfishes, enriched brineshrimp, and mysis. Feed the fish at least three times per day to prevent any weight loss.

WHERE is it from?
Sri Lanka to Indonesia and Malaysia in the Tropical Indo-Pacific.

WHAT does it cost?
★★☆☆☆
A medium-priced fish.

HOW do I sex it?
As with all angelfish, this species is a protogynous hermaphrodite, so the very largest specimens will be males.

WHAT kind of tank?
Fish-only; live rock-based fish-only system; or reef aquarium.

WHAT minimum size tank?
63 gal (240 l).

HOW do other fish react?
C. eibli shares the typically streetwise nature of dwarf angelfish and can be housed with most other marine fish species. Even other members of the genus *Centropyge* are unlikely to pester this fish to any major extent.

WHAT to watch out for?
Avoid skinny specimens or those that refuse to feed in the dealer's tank. Once acquired, keep an eye on the fish's bodyweight, as it appears prone to weight loss if it does not receive a sufficiently varied diet.

HOW compatible with inverts and corals?
May nip at the occasional polyp, paying particular attention to large-polyp stony corals, which it can reduce to a skeleton very quickly.

WHAT area of the tank?
Investigates the aquarium decor looking for tasty morsels to eat. Quickly retreats to the safety of the rockwork should danger threaten.

HOW many in one tank?
Can be kept singly or in pairs where space allows (200 gal/750 l or more). Introduce two individuals simultaneously wherever possible.

HOW does it behave?
Generally peaceful; may bicker with other dwarf angelfishes, surgeonfish, and tangs, but seldom to any great degree.

WILL it breed in an aquarium?
Has the potential to spawn in the aquarium, but would prove a great challenge to raise successfully.

Centropyge flavissimus

Lemonpeel dwarf angelfish

FISH PROFILE

The lemonpeel is a tempting aquarium favourite. Its colors may vary from brilliant yellow to bright orange, depending on the area from which individual fish have been collected. In common with many dwarf angelfishes it is hardy and long-lived, with a maximum recorded age of 11 years. Most specimens are imported through Hawaii, despite the fact that it is not found there.

WHAT size?
Males maximum 5.5 in (14 cm); females around 4 in (10 cm) or less.

WHAT does it eat?
In the wild, principally algae; provide this in dried form, supplemented with frozen and formula foods, plus marine flake and granules if possible. Brineshrimp and mysis are also useful, preferably enriched with vitamins.

WHERE is it from?
Found throughout many tropical Pacific island chains.

WHAT does it cost?
★★☆☆☆
A medium-priced fish.

▶ *A beautiful fish that can grow to become highly territorial.*

HOW do I sex it?
The very largest specimens will be males.

WHAT kind of tank?
Fish-only; live rock-based fish-only; some reef aquariums.

WHAT minimum size tank?
80 gal (300 l).

HOW do other fish react?
Most fish ignore the lemonpeel when it is first introduced, as it remains out of harm's way in the rockwork. Tangs and other dwarf angelfishes are likely to present the greatest threat to it.

WHAT to watch out for?
Avoid non-feeding or pale fish, as either condition may be symptomatic of greater problems.

HOW compatible with inverts and corals?
The lemonpeel has a reputation for attacking many corals in the reef aquarium. It should be safe with species that it is unlikely to predate, such as *Sinularia* and *Sarcophyton*. Should not harm ornamental shrimp.

WHAT area of the tank?
Despite its potentially aggressive nature, this fish will never be particularly bold or leave the rockwork for prolonged periods. It often remains hidden as it searches both the underside and upper surface of the rocks for food.

HOW many in one tank?
Keep singly or in pairs where space allows (200 gal/750 l or more). Wherever possible, introduce two individuals simultaneously.

HOW does it behave?
A large, mature lemonpeel angelfish can be fiercely territorial and relentlessly attack newly introduced fish. At this size it can dominate the rest of the aquarium inhabitants. Stock small specimens as one of the final introductions to the aquarium.

WILL it breed in an aquarium?
It has the potential to spawn in the aquarium, but would prove a great challenge to rear successfully.

Centropyge ferrugatus

Rusty dwarf angelfish

FISH PROFILE

Although one of the less popular dwarf angelfish species, the rusty is nonetheless one of the hardiest and best-suited to a marine aquarium that the group has to offer. Unfortunately, its colors are rather drab, but it might rate as a possible alternative to the coral beauty *(Centropyge bispinosa)*, albeit without the brilliant purple coloration of the latter species.

▲ *The rusty angelfish is an inexpensive, hardy member of the genus* Centropyge.

WHAT size?
Males 4 in (10 cm); females 3.1 in (8 cm).

WHAT does it eat?
Includes tunicates and coral polyp tentacles in its natural diet, but algae is the mainstay. This should be available in dried form at all times to satisfy the fish's grazing instincts and reduce any tendencies towards coral nipping. Supplement this diet regularly with flake, pellet, and frozen foods.

WHERE is it from?
Western Pacific, including the Philippines.

WHAT does it cost?
★★☆☆☆
One of the least expensive dwarf angelfish species.

HOW do I sex it?
Individuals are female first, becoming males as they become larger, so determining sex is difficult, except to say that the largest specimens will be males.

WHAT kind of tank?
Fish-only; live rock-based fish-only system; or reef aquarium.

WHAT minimum size tank?
63 gal (240 l).

HOW do other fish react?
Avoid introducing this species into an aquarium containing the similarly marked coral beauty *(Centropyge bispinosa)*, Potter's angelfish *(C. potteri)* or Shepard's angelfish *(C. shepardi)*, as they are likely to attack it with a vengeance. Tangs and surgeonfishes may also take exception to it, at least in the hours after its introduction.

WHAT to watch out for?
Avoid recently imported specimens that have not been quarantined and always ensure specimens are feeding before you buy. Fish should have bright eyes and inquisitive behavior.

HOW compatible with inverts and corals?
May occasionally nip at coral polyps and tentacles. This behavior seems limited to large-polyp stony corals, but as with most other dwarf angelfishes it is difficult to trust them totally. It should not harm most other corals and ornamental shrimp.

WHAT area of the tank?
In and over rocks, corals, or coral rubble patches in their natural environment and in the aquarium.

HOW many in one tank?
Keep singly or in pairs. Small groups need an aquarium larger than 130 gal (500 l).

HOW does it behave?
Rusty angelfishes can be quite belligerent towards other fish when the latter are first introduced. It may chase small wrasses, tangs, surgeonfish, gobies and blennies, but provided the aquarium has plenty of hiding places, this should not present a threat to the long-term tranquillity of the aquarium.

WILL it breed in an aquarium?
Yes. This species has been successfully reared in captivity.

Centropyge loricula

Flame dwarf angelfish

FISH PROFILE

The flame angelfish is an instantly recognizable aquarium icon and seldom confused with any other species. It commands a generally high price, depending on whether it has been imported directly or acquired through a wholesaler.

WHAT size?
Males 6 in (15 cm) maximum; females 4 in (10 cm) or less.

WHAT does it eat?
Algae and the invertebrates associated with it, so be sure to offer plenty of grazing material. Also provide some of the formula foods designed for dwarf angelfishes, plus the usual mysis, brineshrimp, and other meaty foods.

WHERE is it from?
Most aquarium specimens are collected from the Marshall Islands and exported through Hawaii, but the flame angelfish can also be found in many of the scattered island locations in the tropical Pacific. It is reported to be most common in Palau and the Caroline, Marshall and Society Islands.

WHAT does it cost?
★★★☆☆ ★★★★☆
A medium to high-priced marine fish.

HOW do I sex it?
The largest specimens will be males.

WHAT kind of tank?
Fish-only; live rock-based fish-only; some reef aquariums.

WHAT minimum size tank?
80 gal (300 l).

HOW do other fish react?
Flame angelfishes can usually withstand the aggression of resident fish when first introduced to a new aquarium. The initial belligerence of tangs and surgeonfishes is shortlived.

WHAT to watch out for?
Avoid fish with a high breathing rate, that do not feed, or have a labored swimming motion.

HOW compatible with inverts and corals?
Commonly maintained in reef aquariums, despite a tendency to peck at corals. Many aquarists avoid keeping species that the flame angelfish attacks, whereas others will forgive it anything provided it is happy, such is its overall beauty. It should not harm ornamental shrimp.

WHAT area of the tank?
Can be quite secretive in the wild, yet proves one of the boldest species in a marine aquarium. Rarely ventures too far from the caves and crevices and becomes very wily as it ages.

HOW many in one tank?
Can be kept singly or in pairs where space allows (130 gal/500 l or more). Introduce two individuals simultaneously wherever possible or try to find specimens with significant size differences. Aquarists with a very large system (200 gal/750 l or more) could consider keeping small groups called harems, as typically one individual will become a male, the rest females.

HOW does it behave?
Can be quite aggressive towards similarly sized fish, and will attack tangs and surgeonfishes when they are first introduced to the aquarium. This should subside quickly, but occasional altercations can still occur.

WILL it breed in an aquarium?
It has been recorded spawning in the home aquarium and larvae have been reared in captivity.

◀ *Its vivid coloration makes this a desirable, if expensive, addition to the marine aquarium.*

Centropyge multicolor

Multicolor dwarf angelfish

FISH PROFILE

Although an expensive rarity within the hobby, the determined aquarist should still be able to obtain a specimen or two of *C. multicolor*. Its high price is the result of a combination of factors. Firstly, it is found in scattered localities throughout the tropical Western Pacific – an area with inherent transport issues from collector to exporter to importer. Secondly, it is usually found at depths in excess of 82 ft (25 m), making its net capture difficult for divers who are approaching their maximum operating depth on compressed air.

◄ *This shy species justifies its high price tag and proves hardy once settled into a peaceful aquarium.*

WHAT size?
Males grow to 3.5 in (9 cm); females maximum 3.1 in (8 cm).

WHAT does it eat?
In the wild, algae and tunicates. In the aquarium, a variety of foods, including dried algae, brineshrimp, and mysis, all with vitamin supplements. Fish may accept dried foods after some time in the aquarium.

WHERE is it from?
Pacific Ocean: Micronesia, Marshall, to Society Islands and occasionally Hawaii, through which it is exported.

WHAT does it cost?
★★★★★
Expensive.

HOW do I sex it?
In a pair, the male is the larger fish.

WHAT kind of tank?
Fish-only; live rock-based fish-only system; some reef aquariums.

WHAT minimum size tank?
50 gal (200 l).

HOW do other fish react?
The usual territorial suspects can make life difficult for this small species, although it does share the robust nature typical of most dwarf angelfishes. Its high price means that aquarists take few chances with its safety.

WHAT to watch out for?
Avoid skinny or very small specimens unless you can put them into an aquarium where they can be fed several times per day under close observation.

HOW compatible with inverts and corals?
Should not harm ornamental shrimp but may occasionally nip some corals, particularly large-polyp forms of hard corals.

WHAT area of the tank?
Seldom strays far from the rockwork, even when fully settled.

HOW many in one tank?
Keep singly or in male/female pairs.

HOW does it behave?
This is one of the most peaceful dwarf angelfishes and should not be aggressive towards all but the most delicate tankmates.

WILL it breed in an aquarium?
Yes, it has been recorded spawning in the home aquarium.

Centropyge multifasciata

Multibanded dwarf angelfish

FISH PROFILE

A small, peaceful, but timid dwarf angelfish, closely related to *Centropyge venustus*, with which it can form hybrids. As it is typically found in deeper water (65–230 ft/20–70 m), it may become more adventurous under blue actinic lighting.

WHAT size?
Males 4.7 in (12 cm); females slightly smaller.

WHAT does it eat?
Wild specimens have been recorded eating coral polyps, algae, and tunicates, but this is likely to be a small fraction of their varied diet. Make sure that specimens are feeding on frozen foods such as brineshrimp before buying them. Extending the range of foods accepted by the fish is crucial for its long-term vitality.

WHERE is it from?
Mostly collected from Indonesia, the Philippines, and Micronesia, but can be found as far north as southern Japan and the Ryukyu Islands.

WHAT does it cost?
★★★☆☆   ★★★★☆
Moderately expensive.

> ▶ *Specimen selection and a varied diet are the keys to long-term success with this peaceful species.*

HOW do I sex it?
Males are likely to be larger. This species is found singly or in small groups, which are usually male-dominated harems.

WHAT kind of tank?
A well-established system (more than 12 months old) with plenty of live rock is essential.

WHAT minimum size tank?
At least 66 gal (250 l) to accommodate sufficient live rock.

HOW do other fish react?
The philosophy behind stocking this species in a live rock-rich aquarium is to supplement its diet with natural browsing material on the rock surfaces. It is counterproductive to stock this species with other fish that might compete for this resource, e.g., other dwarf angelfishes, unless the aquarium is very large. In the presence of many busy or territorial species, *C. multifasciata* is unlikely to venture out.

WHAT to watch out for?
Make sure the fish is feeding in the dealer's tank before buying it. Sadly, many individuals will not feed on any aquarium foods and are destined to starve.

HOW compatible with inverts and corals?
The multibanded dwarf angelfish includes sponges and tunicates in its natural diet. Aquarists also report that it targets large-polyp stony corals.

WHAT area of the tank?
Remains very close to the substrate, be it rockwork or the aquarium bottom, and often swims upside-down in caves and beneath overhangs.

HOW many in one tank?
Most aquarists will only be able to maintain a single specimen, although it is possible to keep this species in small groups.

HOW does it behave?
A very timid species that can settle well into the aquarium.

WILL it breed in an aquarium?
It has the potential to breed, but the problems associated with the selection, care, and maintenance of two or more fish means that few aquarists will ever witness a spawning event in the aquarium.

Centropyge potteri

Potter's dwarf angelfish

Potter's dwarf angelfish is one of the most beautifully-marked aquarium fish, yet often overlooked in favor of some of its gaudier relatives. Unfortunately, many dealer tanks are not sufficiently brightly lit to show off the amazing variation in its color or patterning. This shallow-water species is accustomed to intense light and best observed under metal-halide illumination.

◄ *This Hawaiian beauty has a wonderful pattern and coloration that are seen at their best under strong lighting.*

WHAT size?
Males 4 in (10 cm); females 3.1 in (8 cm).

WHAT does it eat?
The natural diet of this species includes certain hard-coral polyps, algae, and tunicates. In an aquarium it will readily accept most frozen particulate foods, such as mysis, brineshrimp, etc. Offer dried algae in a lettuce clip on which the fish can browse all day and frozen specialist foods developed for angelfish.

WHERE is it from?
Johnston Islands and Hawaii.

WHAT does it cost?
★★☆☆☆ ★★★☆☆
Moderately expensive, particularly larger specimens.

HOW do I sex it?
Males are larger.

WHAT kind of tank?
Fish-only; live rock-based fish-only system; or reef aquarium.

WHAT minimum size tank?
63 gal (240 l).

HOW do other fish react?
Potter's angelfish provokes a similar response from other aquarium fish as any other dwarf angelfish. Although it is able to look after itself, it is safer to mix individuals of significantly different sizes where territorial aggression is anticipated.

WHAT to watch out for?
Avoid specimens that do not feed or appear to have problems maintaining their position in the water. Poorly-nourished fish will appear thin or even emaciated; do not buy them.

HOW compatible with inverts and corals?
May feed on large-polyp stony corals, although many fish will not even nibble at them. Does not harm any other ornamental invertebrates.

WHAT area of the tank?
Does not venture too far away from the safety of a bolthole and is perhaps a little more timid than many other members of the genus.

HOW many in one tank?
Keep singly or in pairs.

HOW does it behave?
Potter's angelfish is similar in disposition to the coral beauty (*Centropyge bispinosa*), one of the more placid *Centropyge* angelfish. It is likely to react aggressively towards other dwarf angelfish for a few hours in order to assert its dominance over the newcomer. Tangs and surgeonfish invariably receive the same short-term welcome.

WILL it breed in an aquarium?
Potentially, yes.

▲ *The valentini pufferfish will inflate its body to deter the aggression of other fish.*

120–131

Triggerfishes and Pufferfishes

132–155

Groupers, Grammas, and Dottybacks

Contents

▲ *The Red Sea mimic blenny has an endearing personality.*

66–81

Butterflyfishes

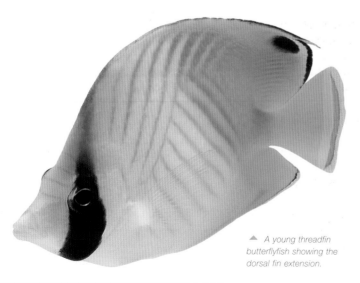

▲ *A young threadfin
butterflyfish showing the
dorsal fin extension.*

Contents

82–97

Wrasses and Hogfishes

▼ *The powder blue surgeonfish is impressive but needs care in the aquarium.*

98–119

Tangs and Surgeonfishes

Apolemichthys arcuatus

Bandit angelfish

FISH PROFILE

Although the black-and-white coloration of this wonderful species may not immediately endear itself to the aquarist with a taste for the more obviously stunning true angelfish, it should be highly prized for its hardiness and ability to settle into the home aquarium. These attributes, coupled with the fact that it is a fairly uncommon import, mean that it does have its fans among hobbyists, but its high price precludes many from obtaining a specimen.

WHAT size?
At 7 in (18 cm) or so, this is one of the smallest members of the genus *Apolemichthys*.

WHAT does it eat?
In the wild, it supplements its natural diet of sponges with whatever else it can find, including algae and fish eggs. In the aquarium, offer a wide variety of foods, including preparations designed for sponge-eating angelfish. Dried algae satisfies the fish's browsing requirements. Feed the fish several times a day.

WHERE is it from?
Endemic to the Hawaiian and Johnston Islands.

WHAT does it cost?
★★★★★
Expensive.

HOW do I sex it?
No known external differences.

WHAT kind of tank?
Fish-only or live rock-based fish-only. It may be possible to keep this species in a reef aquarium housing invertebrate species that it finds unpalatable, including many species of soft coral.

WHAT minimum size tank?
90 gal (350 l).

HOW do other fish react?
Apart from the usual in-built aggression of some surgeonfish, tangs, and wrasses, this species should not elicit any particular adverse reaction from other fish. Given its high price, it would be sensible to stock this species into a fairly peaceful aquarium to avoid any undue stress to the fish—or even the aquarist.

WHAT to watch out for?
Specimens should be feeding and have a good body shape. Otherwise, as with most true angelfishes, they should have clear eyes and an inquisitive disposition.

HOW compatible with inverts and corals?
It may be possible to stock this fish with certain corals that it finds distasteful. It is highly likely to consume large-polyp stony corals, but should not harm ornamental shrimp.

WHAT area of the tank?
All areas.

HOW many in one tank?
Best kept singly unless you can obtain a true pair. It may be possible to raise two small individuals together.

HOW does it behave?
An angelfish with a big personality and one that loses no opportunity to boss other fish around. It is not especially aggressive, but seems to like being involved in everything that is going on in the aquarium.

WILL it breed in an aquarium?
No.

▼ *The exquisite patterning of the bandit angelfish is instantly appealing.*

Apolemichthys trimaculatus

Flagfin (threespot) angelfish

FISH PROFILE

The popular flagfin angelfish is suited to the aquarist making a first foray into keeping species from this fantastic group – but be sure to acquire juveniles and meet their nutritional demands. In common with the rest of the genus *Apolemichthys*, adults are less aggressive than angelfishes from other genera.

WHAT size?
Males 10.2 in (26 cm); females slightly smaller.

WHAT does it eat?
Most *Apolemichthys* species are specialist feeders on sponges and tunicates, but accept a wide variety of foods in the aquarium. Provide meaty foods, such as shellfish, mysis, and brineshrimp, plus dried marine algae and flaked foods. Sponge-based foods for angelfish are also recommended.

WHERE is it from?
A widespread species found along the East African coastline to Sri Lanka and the Maldives, and the Western area of the tropical Pacific, including southern Japan and Australia.

WHAT does it cost?
★★★☆☆ ★★★★☆
Small juveniles (less than 2 in/ 5 cm) are relatively inexpensive when compared with similar-sized specimens of other angelfish.

HOW do I sex it?
Males are larger, but determining this from an individual fish is almost impossible unless it is approaching the maximum recorded size for this species.

WHAT kind of tank?
Fish-only or live rock-based fish-only system. It may be possible to introduce this species into a reef aquarium when small.

WHAT minimum size tank?
120 gal (450 l) for adult specimens.

HOW do other fish react?
As with many other species of angelfish, the flagfin will avoid a certain amount of territorial aggression from its tankmates by acting as a cleaner fish. Dwarf *Centropyge* angelfishes may react adversely when it is first introduced, but this behavior should not continue for long.

WHAT to watch out for?
Avoid skinny or non-feeding specimens. Adults are generally less adaptable than juveniles to aquarium life and should be selected very carefully. The smallest juveniles can lose weight very quickly if not encouraged to feed, so be sure to observe a fish feeding heartily before buying it.

HOW compatible with inverts and corals?
Will not harm most species of larger ornamental shrimp,

▶ *The flagfin angelfish is best acquired as a juvenile specimen.*

such as *Lysmata*. Can be stocked in a reef aquarium containing *Sarcophyton* leather corals with reasonable confidence. Other corals may also remain unharmed.

WHAT area of the tank?
Spends most of its time scouring the rockwork for browsing material. As its confidence grows it becomes more adventurous, especially when anticipating the introduction of food.

HOW many in one tank?
Best kept singly. Hobbyists have maintained pairs acquired as small juveniles and grown on to adult size, but their coexistence could not be described as harmonious.

HOW does it behave?
Juvenile flagfin angelfishes are very peaceful and will not generally bother other fish. Adults can react aggressively to other closely related or similar species.

WILL it breed in an aquarium?
No.

Apolemichthys xanthopunctatus

Goldflake angelfish

FISH PROFILE

Not all expensive fish are difficult to maintain or require a degree of specialization before they can be successfully maintained in a home aquarium. The goldflake angelfish is actually hardier than its close relative the flagfin angelfish *(Apolemichthys trimaculatus)*. Its high price is associated with the difficulties in its collection, since it is only found in some remote island locations in the Pacific Ocean.

WHAT size?
Males 10 in (25 cm); females slightly smaller.

WHAT does it eat?
Wild specimens feed on sponges and tunicates, but most individuals readily accept a variety of foods in an aquarium. Offer dried algae, shellfish (some with the shell still in place, such as whole cockle or mussel) and the readily available shrimp varieties. In time, fish may accept flake and granular food.

WHERE is it from?
Tropical Pacific Ocean. Gilbert Islands to the Line Islands.

WHAT does it cost?
★★★★★
Small, medium, or large, all specimens are expensive.

HOW do I sex it?
No known external differences.

WHAT kind of tank?
Fish-only; live rock-based fish-only; or a reef aquarium containing corals known to be distasteful to this fish, such as *Sarcophyton* soft corals.

WHAT minimum size tank?
90 gal (350 l).

HOW do other fish react?
The goldflake angelfish is quite robust and capable of looking after itself. A small specimen may have a problem with larger individual *Centropyge* dwarf angelfish. Its high price usually means that aquarists do not take risks with compatibility.

WHAT to watch out for?
Many aquatic outlets will not stock this fish unless they know they have a buyer. However, do not feel compelled to buy if it is not feeding or its health appears to be compromised in any way.

HOW compatible with inverts and corals?
Will not harm many corals, but can cause terminal damage to large-polyp stony corals. Should not harm most larger ornamental shrimp species.

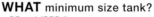

▲ *Expensive, but easy to maintain.*

WHAT area of the tank?
Searches for food among the rocks. Stocking a fish into a system with a healthy growth of encrusting sponge (encouraged by feeding phytoplankton) helps to keep it occupied. It becomes tame after a very short time.

HOW many in one tank?
Best kept singly, although where aquarists have maintained two individuals in the same aquarium there were very few instances of aggression between them.

HOW does it behave?
With the possible exception of aggression towards other, very similar or closely related species, the goldflake is a peaceful fish.

WILL it breed in an aquarium?
No.

Apolemichthys xanthurus

Cream angelfish

FISH PROFILE

The cream angelfish is one of the cheapest angelfish species available. Fortunately, it is also easy to maintain in captivity and, despite not being the most highly decorated fish, it is attractive enough to ensure that it will remain popular for many years to come.

WHAT size?
Males 6 in (15 cm); females slightly smaller.

WHAT does it eat?
Primarily sponges and tunicates and is known to browse on seaweeds. Specialist foods for angelfishes are important, but many aquarists have had success with feeding dried algae, mysis, brineshrimp, and chopped shellfish. Should accept flake and granular foods with time and perseverance on the part of the aquarist.

WHERE is it from?
Eastern Indian Ocean, including Sri Lanka and Mauritius. Replaced by the similar *Apolemichthys xanthotis* in the Red Sea.

WHAT does it cost?
★★☆☆☆
Inexpensive, especially small specimens (less than 2.3 in/ 6 cm).

▶ *Not the most colorful angelfish available, but* A. xanthurus *is hardy and rewarding to keep.*

HOW do I sex it?
No known external differences, except that males are likely to be larger in adult pairs.

WHAT kind of tank?
Fish-only; live rock-based fish-only; or reef aquarium with corals that this species finds distasteful.

WHAT minimum size tank?
90 gal (350 l).

HOW do other fish react?
As a general rule, do not keep species from the same genera together. May fall victim to large angelfishes from different genera, to particularly aggressive dwarf angelfishes, or to tangs. Acts as a cleaner of other fish to try to distract their aggressive urges.

WHAT to watch out for?
Always ensure that a specimen has clear eyes and is feeding well before you buy it. The general hardiness of this species is reflected in the fact that fish generally look very well in the dealer's aquarium.

HOW compatible with inverts and corals?
May nip at large-polyp stony corals, but will leave most soft corals and polyps alone. Does not harm the larger species of ornamental shrimp.

WHAT area of the tank?
Spends much of its time investigating the rockwork for food, only swimming into open water when the aquarist approaches the aquarium at feeding time.

HOW many in one tank?
Keep singly. With care, it may be possible to maintain pairs in a sufficiently large aquarium (120 gal/500 l or more), which would reflect the species' natural behavior.

HOW does it behave?
Not particularly aggressive, although larger specimens will assert their authority over newly-introduced fish.

WILL it breed in an aquarium?
No.

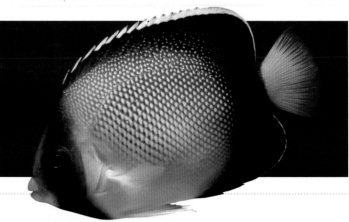

Chaetodontoplus duboulayi

Scribbled angelfish

FISH PROFILE

Most specimens are exported through Australia and therefore shipped quickly and efficiently. The benefit of this is healthy, vibrant imports, but the care taken over their welfare is reflected in their price.

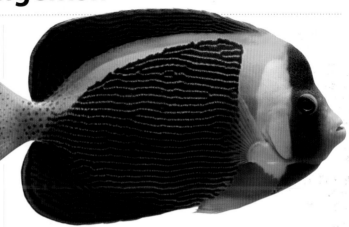

▶ *Given good care and a varied diet, this species will thrive in most marine aquariums.*

WHAT size?
Males 11 in (28 cm); females slightly smaller.

WHAT does it eat?
In the wild, sponges and tunicates. Offering suitable substitutes in the aquarium is not easy, but some suppliers of frozen foods have produced formulations for fish that require plenty of sponge tissue in their diets. Use these where possible and supplement them with mysis, chopped shellfish, enriched brineshrimp, and dried algae. Vitamin supplements are also recommended.

WHERE is it from?
Northern Australia and Indonesia.

WHAT does it cost?
★★★★☆
Moderately expensive.

HOW do I sex it?
Males are larger than females when approaching their maximum size. All individuals are female first, becoming males as they approach their upper growth limits. This phenomenon is known as protogyny.

WHAT kind of tank?
Fish-only or live rock-based fish-only.

WHAT minimum size tank?
120 gal (450 l).

HOW do other fish react?
Juvenile scribbled angelfish can be quite vulnerable, so do not introduce them into an aquarium containing boisterous or aggressive species.

WHAT to watch out for?
The fish's breathing rate should be slow and steady. Avoid specimens that are thin, discolored, or refusing to feed.

HOW compatible with inverts and corals?
Will nibble most sessile invertebrates given the opportunity, but should not harm ornamental shrimp.

WHAT area of the tank?
Juveniles are shy and remain close to rockwork until they settle. Fully acclimatized specimens are bolder and venture all over the aquarium.

HOW many in one tank?
Keep singly.

HOW does it behave?
Not aggressive as such, but its large personality and boisterous temperament could easily be mistaken for less sociable behavior. Do not keep this fish with very nervous species.

WILL it breed in an aquarium?
No.

Chaetodontoplus meredithi

Queensland angelfish

This is one of two species of Australian angelfish commonly sold as "personifer" angelfish (The other is *Chaetodontoplus personifer*, which requires exactly the same aquarium care.) The Queensland angelfish has a completely yellow tail fin, whereas in *C. personifer* there is a black band running through it or it is nearly all black.

WHAT size?
Males 10 in (25 cm); females slightly smaller as they are protogynous hermaphrodites.

WHAT does it eat?
In the wild, sponges and tunicates. In the aquarium, provide specially formulated proprietary foods containing sponge material, supplemented with dried algae, mysis, and chopped shellfish. Juveniles generally feed more readily than adults.

WHERE is it from?
Queensland and New South Wales in Australia. Replaced by the closely related *C. personifer* in northwest Australia.

WHAT does it cost?
★★★★☆
Prices are consistently high for this species in line with equivalent-sized juveniles and adults of angelfish from the genus *Pomacanthus*.

HOW do I sex it?
Males are larger than females, but this is only apparent when they are fully grown.

WHAT kind of tank?
Fish-only aquarium or live rock-based fish-only system.

WHAT minimum size tank?
120 gal (450 l).

HOW do other fish react?
Most fish will not react too aggressively towards this species. Juveniles may be vulnerable to attack from tangs, large wrasses, other angels, and surgeonfishes, so are best stocked before such fish.

WHAT to watch out for?
It is vitally important that specimens are feeding and that their dietary requirements are well known before you buy them. Generally speaking, it will not thrive on a monotonous diet. Given its

point of origin and high price, it is invariably shipped with the utmost care for its wellbeing and settles quickly in the right aquarium.

HOW compatible with inverts and corals?
Cannot be trusted with many corals, particularly large-polyp stony corals, and may nibble any sessile invertebrate. It should not harm ornamental shrimp.

WHAT area of the tank?
A settled individual will dominate the aquarium, swimming in open water as well as searching for food in the rockwork.

HOW many in one tank?
Keep singly.

HOW does it behave?
Adults can become quite boisterous and will dominate the rest of the aquarium inhabitants. It is rarely aggressive to any real extent and exhibits behavior typical of a large angelfish.

WILL it breed in an aquarium?
No.

◀ *This species has not yet achieved the same popularity as some of its gaudier relatives, yet is quite easy to care for in the home aquarium.*

Chaetodontoplus mesoleucos

Vermiculated angelfish

FISH PROFILE

The vermiculated angelfish is sometimes confused with the hardier—and infinitely more suitable—aquarium species, the cream angelfish (*Apolemichthys xanthurus*). Although easy to acquire, check specimens thoroughly before buying them, as *C. mesoleucos* can be difficult to care for in the aquarium. It commonly refuses foods available to the aquarist for species that eat sponges and tunicates in the wild. This is surprising, given that other hardy angelfish species with a similar diet readily accept these foods.

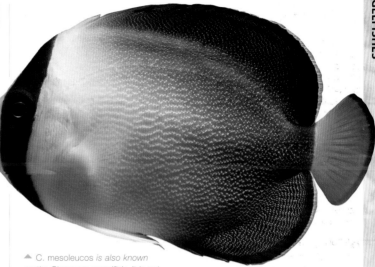

▲ *C. mesoleucos is also known as the Singapore angelfish. It is not the easiest species to maintain.*

WHAT size?
Males 7 in (18 cm); females slightly smaller.

WHAT does it eat?
Live rock often houses animals that this fish can feed on before it has the confidence to compete with other fish for brineshrimp, mysis, and chopped shellfish. Settled individuals accept flake or pellet foods. Offer specific foods designed for fish that feed on sponges in the wild.

WHERE is it from?
Indian Ocean and Western Pacific.

WHAT does it cost?
★☆☆☆☆
Inexpensive for an angelfish.

HOW do I sex it?
No known visual differences, but males are likely to be larger.

WHAT kind of tank?
Fish-only; live rock-based fish-only system; or reef aquarium.

WHAT minimum size tank?
106 gal (400 l).

HOW do other fish react?
Often shy and may be bullied by larger or more aggressive species, such as dwarf angelfishes, wrasses, or tangs.

WHAT to watch out for?
Try to find specimens that feed readily in the dealer's tank.

HOW compatible with inverts and corals?
May pick at sessile invertebrates, including many species of coral. Should not harm ornamental shrimp.

WHAT area of the tank?
In and among the rockwork.

HOW many in one tank?
Keep singly or in pairs.

HOW does it behave?
Generally non-aggressive.

WILL it breed in an aquarium?
No.

Holacanthus ciliaris

Queen angelfish

FISH PROFILE

The story of the queen angelfish is one of beauty and temptation. Its wonderful coloration makes it instantly endearing, but many aquarists who acquire it as a small and tempting juvenile do not realize that it has a prodigious growth rate and large personality. Try to avoid possible confusion with the similar and less expensive *H. bermudensis*.

WHAT size?
Males and females 18 in (45 cm).

WHAT does it eat?
Adult fish feed almost exclusively on sponges, but their stomachs have been shown to contain traces of many other sessile invertebrates and algae. It is likely that it feeds opportunistically on most foods on the reefs. In the aquarium it accepts a wide variety of meaty foods and dried algae, plus flake and granules, given time.

WHERE is it from?
Western Atlantic and the Caribbean.

WHAT does it cost?
★★☆☆☆
Moderately expensive. Juveniles tend to represent better value for money. Star rating here is for juvenile fish.

▶ *This subadult still bears the vestiges of the juvenile's white bands.*

HOW do I sex it?
Juveniles cannot be sexed. Male fish are likely to be larger than females, but this is only helpful when a mated pair can be observed at length.

WHAT kind of tank?
Fish-only; live rock-based fish only system; or reef aquarium.

WHAT minimum size tank?
200 gal (750 l).

HOW do other fish react?
Apart from conflicts with other angelfish species, the queen will use its juvenile cleaning role to avoid unwanted attention from its tankmates.

WHAT to watch out for?
Be sure that individuals are feeding well before you buy them, particularly adults since as they do not ship as well as juveniles. Remember that the fish grows at an almost unbelievable rate. You have a duty to provide the long-term care requirements of any fish you buy, so if your system is not large enough for a queen angelfish, then leave it in the dealer's aquarium.

HOW compatible with inverts and corals?
Should not harm ornamental shrimp, but will nip at sessile invertebrates.

WHAT area of the tank?
Cruises in and among rockwork, occasionally venturing into open water if it suspects that food may be offered.

HOW many in one tank?
Keep singly. True pairs could be housed in a very large aquarium (2,600 gal/10,000 l or more).

HOW does it behave?
A large adult specimen is bold and dominant when settled. Given its eventual size, choose tankmates with care. Juvenile specimens are unlikely to cause any problems, but adults need robust tankmates, such as hawkfishes, squirrelfishes, puffers, triggers, and large tangs.

WILL it breed in an aquarium?
No.

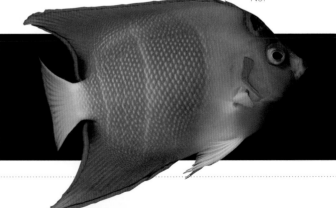

Holacanthus passer

Passer (king) angelfish

FISH PROFILE

◄ *The passer angelfish is almost exclusively available in its juvenile coloration.*

A large, impressive angelfish species, but rarely encountered for sale in full adult coloration. The juvenile is beautifully marked, and, in common with most true angelfish, quite bold, even when very small. Adults and juveniles act as cleaners of other fish and can escape unwanted attention by fulfilling a useful role. Adults have been filmed cleaning parasites from hammerhead sharks!

WHAT size?
Males and females 14 in (35 cm).

WHAT does it eat?
In the wild, adults feed on sessile invertebrates, including tunicates and sponges. They accept a varied selection of offerings in an aquarium situation. Try flaked and granular foods, together with dried algae and a variety of meaty shrimp and shellfish. Vitamin supplements are beneficial.

WHERE is it from?
Eastern Pacific Ocean, including the Gulf of California south to tropical waters off the northern coast of South America.

WHAT does it cost?
★★★☆☆
Juveniles are expensive even when very small.

HOW do I sex it?
Sexing this fish while it is still in juvenile coloration is impossible. Mature adult males have yellow pelvic fins, whereas those of the females are white.

WHAT kind of tank?
Fish-only or live rock-based fish-only aquarium.

WHAT minimum size tank?
145 gal (550 l) is the absolute minimum.

HOW do other fish react?
Most marine fish will not react aggressively to the king angelfish, particularly since it is likely to be stocked as a juvenile.

WHAT to watch out for?
Fish should be feeding well in the dealer's tank and have full, rounded bodies, clear eyes, and be their normal inquisitive selves.

HOW compatible with inverts and corals?
May be housed with certain sessile invertebrates but on the whole not to be trusted with corals. It should not harm ornamental shrimp.

WHAT area of the tank?
Once settled, this species investigates rockwork and sand or swims in open water. As the aquarist approaches it will nose the front glass of the aquarium in anticipation of food.

HOW many in one tank?
Keep singly. Pairs could be maintained in a very large aquarium (2,600 gal/10,000 l or more).

HOW does it behave?
Even when quite small, the king will assert itself over significantly larger fish. Likely to nip or bite newly-introduced fish. Introduce this species last or as a small juvenile. Choose hardy and robust tankmates.

WILL it breed in an aquarium?
No.

Holacanthus tricolor
Rock beauty

FISH PROFILE

The rock beauty is one of the least expensive *Holacanthus* species, but can present the most problems. Specimen selection is of the utmost importance; be prepared to discount many individuals before making a purchase.

◀ *This is a juvenile specimen. The extent of the blue-black coloration increases as the fish matures.*

WHAT size?
Males from around 9.5 in (24 cm) upwards to the maximum wild size of 14 in (35 cm). Females smaller.

WHAT does it eat?
Feeds on a variety of sponges, tunicates, and other benthic invertebrates. Formulations for such fish are available, some gel-bound, which makes them suitable for fish that naturally browse on the rockwork. May accept dried algae, plus mysis and brineshrimp. Offering a variety of different food items is vital. Juvenile specimens have been reported feeding from the mucus of other fish, a characteristic that does not endear them to their tankmates.

WHERE is it from?
Tropical Western Atlantic.

WHAT does it cost?
★☆☆☆☆
Relatively inexpensive for a large species of angelfish.

HOW do I sex it?
Males are the largest individuals, but it may be impossible to sex a largish aquarium specimen.

WHAT kind of tank?
Fish-only or live rock-based fish-only system.

WHAT minimum size tank?
120 gal (450 l).

HOW do other fish react?
Juveniles resemble certain small and extremely "streetwise" damsels, and are often ignored by larger boisterous fish species.

WHAT to watch out for?
There are contradictory reports concerning the survivability of this species in captivity. The consensus is that it is not easy. If you believe you have the skills and resources to keep it successfully, avoid buying very large or very small individuals and try to observe them feeding.

HOW compatible with inverts and corals?
Should not harm larger ornamental shrimp species, but will damage most sessile invertebrates, including hard and soft corals.

WHAT area of the tank?
Juveniles remain close to a suitable bolthole. Adults are more confident and readily venture into open water, especially for food.

HOW many in one tank?
Keep singly.

HOW does it behave?
As domineering and aggressive as any other species of large angelfish and will readily assert itself over other fish. Choose sturdy tankmates. Juveniles are generally better behaved, apart from their mucus-eating tendencies. The rock beauty should integrate well into most aquariums, but introduce smaller individuals before any other particularly aggressive species.

WILL it breed in an aquarium?
No.

Pomacanthus asfur

Asfur (Arabian) angelfish

FISH PROFILE

Do not confuse this species with *Pomacanthus maculosus*, a large species with similar markings found in the same area as the Asfur and also referred to as the Arabian angelfish. The Asfur is a beautiful deep purple, with a vivid yellow vertical band or crescent bisecting the body. Juveniles are seldom available but can settle better than adults. For the best results, try to select small adult specimens measuring 4 in (10 cm) or so.

WHAT size?
Large males up to 18 in (40 cm) or so; females 12 in (30 cm) or slightly more.

WHAT does it eat?
In the wild, sponges, tunicates, and algae. In the aquarium, offer mysis, brineshrimp, chopped shellfish, and frozen formulas that include sponge material. Provide food several times a day.

WHERE is it from?
Red Sea and East Africa.

WHAT does it cost?
★★★☆☆
Reasonably expensive. A typical price for a colorful species of angelfish.

▲ *The dark body color of this fish will reveal the slightest blemish or mark.*

HOW do I sex it?
Don't bother. This species is fiercely aggressive towards conspecifics, and attempting to make pairs from individuals will inevitably lead to disaster. If you do see a pair, the male will be the largest fish.

WHAT kind of tank?
Fish-only or live rock-based fish-only systems.

WHAT minimum size tank?
132 gal (500 l).

HOW do other fish react?
Juveniles can act as cleaners of other fish, so are often ignored by other species. Adults are quite timid when first introduced, remaining hidden in rockwork for prolonged periods to avoid the attention of more aggressive fish.

WHAT to watch out for?
The best fish will always feed readily in the dealer's tank, despite their apparent lack of courage. Avoid specimens that appear faded or have cloudy eyes, since these may be recent imports that have not recovered from the stress of shipping.

HOW compatible with inverts and corals?
Small individuals could be stocked to some coral-rich aquariums, including those containing *Sinularia* or *Sarcophyton* spp. soft corals or species of small-polyp stony corals, but *P. asfur* is not totally trustworthy in such a system.

WHAT area of the tank?
Juveniles and newly-introduced specimens spend long periods in the rockwork. Once settled and confident, they will swim actively all over the aquarium.

HOW many in one tank?
Keep singly unless the aquarium is large enough to accommodate a true pair.

HOW does it behave?
A mature, well acclimatized specimen will boss similar-sized species and chase any fish that upsets it all over the aquarium.

WILL it breed in an aquarium?
No.

Pomacanthus imperator

Emperor angelfish

FISH PROFILE

A favorite marine fish in which the stunning beauty of the juvenile is only surpassed by the incredible looks of the adult. Small individuals (less than 2 in/ 5 cm) can prove extremely hardy; many soon outgrow the aquarium. Adult specimens with brilliant orange tail fins are highly prized; these are imported from the Red Sea and Hawaii.

WHAT size?
Males 16 in (40 cm); females up to about 14 in (35 cm).

WHAT does it eat?
In the wild, sponges and tunicates and, occasionally, marine algae. In the aquarium provide specially formulated foods to help maintain color and vitality. Supplement these with shellfish, mysis, and brineshrimp, plus whole molluscs in shell (e.g., clams and cockles) to keep the fish stimulated. Provide regular vitamin supplements.

WHERE is it from?
Widespread in the Tropical Indo-Pacific, including the Red Sea. As far east as the Hawaiian Islands.

WHAT does it cost?
★★★☆☆
Expensive; even the smallest juvenile commands a fairly high price.

HOW do I sex it?
Males are the largest fish, but it is difficult to establish the sex unless you can observe a pair.

WHAT kind of tank?
Fish-only; live rock-based fish-only system; or a well thought-out reef aquarium.

WHAT minimum size tank?
145 gal (550 l).

HOW do other fish react?
Juveniles are recognized as cleaner fish and therefore not harmed by much larger species. Take care when introducing small specimens to an aquarium housing pugnacious dwarf angelfishes. Adults can look after themselves.

WHAT to watch out for?
Fish undergoing the transition from juvenile to adult are not particularly attractive. The markings of adults undergoing the color change in an aquarium are unlikely to be as vivid as in wild-caught adults. Avoid non-feeding individuals.

HOW compatible with inverts and corals?
Many aquarists have kept juveniles in a reef aquarium with few, if any, problems. However, determining which corals/invertebrates are likely to be nipped at is difficult and may depend on the individual fish. Generally, emperor angelfish ignore *Sarcophyton* and *Sinularia* spp. soft corals, and mushroom anemones, and can be trusted with most small-polyp stony corals.

WHAT area of the tank?
Can be quite secretive when first introduced, but as it settles, its bold character comes to the fore and it can be found almost everywhere in the aquarium. It will charge at the aquarium glass if it thinks it is going to be fed.

HOW many in one tank?
Keep singly.

HOW does it behave?
Although they seldom harass any single fish to death, both large juvenile and adult emperors often assert themselves over their tankmates. This tendency is exacerbated in a smaller aquarium.

WILL it breed in an aquarium?
No.

◀ *Some adult specimens, such as those from the Red Sea, have orange tails.*

Pomacanthus navarchus

Majestic angelfish

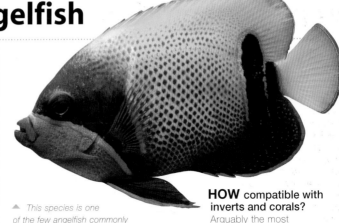

▲ *This species is one of the few angelfish commonly kept in the reef aquarium.*

FISH PROFILE

Due to its generally trustworthy behavior and relatively small maximum size, this is the most popular *Pomacanthus* species to be maintained in reef aquariums. Both it and *P. xanthometapon* (the blue-face angelfish) can undergo metamorphosis to the adult coloration when very small. Fully transformed adults measuring 2.3 in (6 cm) or so are not uncommon and often settle better than larger individuals.

WHAT size?
Males 11 in (28 cm); females smaller.

WHAT does it eat?
In the wild it browses on a variety of sponges and tunicates. Offer aquarium specimens dried algae, mysis, brineshrimp, and a wide variety of shellfish and specialist formula foods for angelfish. Observe newly-introduced specimens closely and target-feed them if necessary.

WHERE is it from?
Indonesia, Papua New Guinea, Philippines, Great Barrier Reef, and Micronesia.

WHAT does it cost?
★★★☆☆
Moderately expensive, but actually one of the cheaper adult angelfishes, due to its ability to change to the mature coloration when very small.

HOW do I sex it?
Males are the largest fish, but it is difficult to establish the sex unless you can observe a pair.

WHAT kind of tank?
Fish-only; live rock-based fish-only; or a well thought-out reef aquarium.

WHAT minimum size tank?
106 gal (400 l).

HOW do other fish react?
The majestic is capable of looking after itself, even when quite small. It is prepared to hide for long periods to avoid the attentions of territorial fish such as tangs or surgeonfishes, and seldom ventures far from a suitable refuge.

WHAT to watch out for?
It is vital to determine whether the fish is feeding before you buy it, since this can be impossible to establish once it is ensconced in the rockwork of its new home.

HOW compatible with inverts and corals?
Arguably the most trustworthy of the genus, but the majestic has been observed biting at some polyps, particularly those of large-polyp stony corals. Some individuals may target bivalve molluscs, but should leave ornamental shrimp alone.

WHAT area of the tank?
Close to or in the rockwork. Settled individuals become more confident over time and will stray into open water to collect food.

HOW many in one tank?
Keep singly.

HOW does it behave?
Fully acclimatized majestic angelfishes will assert themselves over other fish, such as some species of tang, small wrasses, anthias, and any other fish they may take objection to. However, this does not usually escalate into a serious situation requiring outside intervention.

WILL it breed in an aquarium?
No.

Pomacanthus paru

French angelfish

FISH PROFILE

Many aquarists have fallen for the beauty of the juvenile French angelfish and been tempted into making a rash purchase. However, its growth rate is prodigious, and the charming juvenile fish becomes a drab adult with a belligerent attitude towards its tankmates. It is a hardy fish that thrives in the aquarium, but is quite capable of moving or undermining rockwork in its search for food.

WHAT size?
Males 16 in (41 cm); females smaller.

WHAT does it eat?
In the wild, zooplankton, benthic crustaceans, algae, and gorgonian polyps, in addition to sponges and tunicates. Juveniles remove parasites from larger fish. Aquarium fish accept mysis, brineshrimp, chopped shellfish, dried algae, flake, and granular foods. Hiding food inside empty shells or offering whole bivalve shellfish can occupy this species and prevent stereotyped behavior.

WHERE is it from?
Western Atlantic from Florida south to Brazil. Also found in the Caribbean.

WHAT does it cost?
★★★☆☆
Juveniles are fairly expensive for their size. Less costly adults are sometimes offered for sale.

HOW do I sex it?
Males are the largest fish, but it is difficult to establish the sex unless you can observe a pair.

WHAT kind of tank?
Fish-only or live rock-based fish-only system.

WHAT minimum size tank?
160 gal (600 l).

HOW do other fish react?
Because the juvenile acts as a cleaner of other fish, including morays, snappers, wrasses, and surgeonfishes, it can be added to an aquarium containing fairly large species with some confidence that it will not be singled out for aggression.

▼ *This subadult has adult coloration with vestiges of the juvenile's vertical bands.*

WHAT to watch out for?
Aquarium specimens should be feeding and inquisitive. The black ground color clearly shows up any marks or blemishes, and cloudy eyes should also be noticeable when present.

HOW compatible with inverts and corals?
Should not harm larger ornamental shrimp, but likely to nip corals or other sessile invertebrates.

WHAT area of the tank?
Juveniles and adults roam over most of the aquarium, confident and boisterous and permanently on the lookout for food.

HOW many in one tank?
Keep singly.

HOW does it behave?
Adults and large juveniles (13 in/ 8 cm or more) are dominant fish and will force their personalities on every other aquarium inhabitant. They can be highly aggressive if they take a dislike to an individual, so choose very hardy tankmates.

WILL it breed in an aquarium?
No.

▼ *Small juveniles are attractive but grow rapidly.*

Pomacanthus semicirculatus
Semicircle angelfish

FISH PROFILE

The popularity of the semicircle angelfish has waned over recent years, but it remains a suitable fish for the larger marine aquarium. Juveniles are available from very small sizes and many aquarists consider them more attractive than full adult specimens. However, this hardy, long-lived species shares the domineering character traits of other angelfishes.

WHAT size?
Males 15.7 in (40 cm); females smaller.

WHAT does it eat?
In the wild, sponges, tunicates, and algae, plus zooplankton and benthic invertebrates. Most individuals are easy to feed in the aquarium, readily accepting chopped shellfish, mysis, brineshrimp, formula recipes for angelfish, dried algae, flake, and pellet. Aquarists also report its likings for cyanobacteria, the so-called "slime algae" found in many aquariums.

WHERE is it from?
Red Sea, East Africa, and much of the tropical Indo-Pacific.

WHAT does it cost?
★☆☆☆☆
One of the least expensive members of the genus *Pomacanthus*.

HOW do I sex it?
Males are the largest fish, but it is difficult to establish the sex unless you can observe a pair.

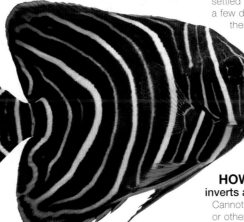

WHAT kind of tank?
Fish-only or live rock-based fish-only system.

WHAT minimum size tank?
120 gal (450 l).

HOW do other fish react?
Due to the fairly large size at which this species undergoes the transformation from juvenile to adult coloration (4.7–7 in/ 12–18 cm), most specimens introduced to a new aquarium will be youngsters, with the typical blue-black-white banded pattern. Most other fish therefore recognize them as potential cleaner fish and otherwise aggressive species often ignore them.

WHAT to watch out for?
Avoid very small specimens in favor of individuals with decent body weight. They should be settled in the dealer's tank for a few days before you buy them, particularly if imported directly, rather than through a wholesaler.

◀ *This striking species is almost exclusively sold when in juvenile coloration, as shown here.*

HOW compatible with inverts and corals?
Cannot be trusted with corals or other sessile invertebrates; should not harm ornamental shrimp.

WHAT area of the tank?
A bold fish that dominates the whole aquarium, constantly roaming in search of food.

HOW many in one tank?
Keep singly.

HOW does it behave?
Large juveniles are bossy and ensure that new fish are left in no doubt regarding who is at the top of the aquarium's pecking order.

WILL it breed in an aquarium?
No.

Pomacanthus xanthometapon

Blueface angelfish

FISH PROFILE

The blueface angelfish can be found in full adult coloration when very small (2.3 in/6 cm or so) and therefore tempts many aquarists without the aquarium capacity to care for it in the long term. Although it requires the best water quality, this species should be fairly easy to maintain in a mature, stable aquarium.

WHAT size?
Males 15 in (38 cm); females smaller.

WHAT does it eat?
In the wild, marine algae, sponges and tunicates. In the aquarium, you can offer it dried algae, but you must also supply sponge diets in the form of specialized frozen recipes available from good marine dealers. Supplement this diet with a variety of other meaty or dried foods.

WHERE is it from?
Found from the Maldives in the Western Indian Ocean to Vanuatu in the tropical Pacific.

WHAT does it cost?
★★★☆☆
Juveniles are quite economical, but small, fully-colored adults represent the best value. They are still expensive, but can adapt better to the aquarium than larger specimens.

HOW do I sex it?
Males will be the largest individuals, but perhaps not noticeably so.

WHAT kind of tank?
Fish-only or live rock-based fish-only.

WHAT minimum size tank?
160 gal (600 l).

HOW do other fish react?
Most fish will not react adversely to the introduction of a juvenile blueface angelfish, as its coloration tells larger species that it is a potential cleaner and therefore useful. Small fish may sometimes bully juveniles, but, in common with most small angelfishes, it is canny and streetwise. Small adults may attract the unwanted attention of tangs and surgeonfishes, but are usually more than capable of looking after themselves.

WHAT to watch out for?
Be sure that adults and juveniles are feeding before you buy them. Small individuals can be extremely shy when first introduced to the aquarium and food is one tool that you can use to encourage them out into the open.

HOW compatible with inverts and corals?
Should not harm larger ornamental shrimp, but likely to nip corals or other sessile invertebrates.

WHAT area of the tank?
Juveniles and adults roam over most of the aquarium, confident and boisterous and permanently on the lookout for food.

HOW many in one tank?
Keep singly.

HOW does it behave?
Large juveniles (3 in/8 cm or more) and adults are dominant fish that force their personalities on every other aquarium inhabitant. They can be highly aggressive if they take a dislike to an individual, so choose very hardy tankmates.

WILL it breed in an aquarium?
No.

◀ *The adult blueface is a stunning fish and relatively easy to care for in a suitably-sized aquarium.*

Pygoplites diacanthus

Regal angelfish

FISH PROFILE

A relatively peaceful angelfish species that was once considered nearly impossible to maintain in captivity. However, many more-experienced aquarists are achieving long-term success with it.

WHAT size?
Males and females 10 in (25 cm).

WHAT does it eat?
Good specimens feed on most frozen foods. With time and patience, they will also take dried and flake foods. Use vitamin supplements and preparations designed for species that feed on sponges in their natural environment. Provide dried seaweed such as Nori for this species to graze.

WHERE is it from?
Red Sea and Tropical Indo-Pacific. Red Sea and Indian Ocean specimens have a yellow pelvic region and these should be the only individuals attempted by marine aquarists.

WHAT does it cost?
★★★☆☆
Less expensive than adult specimens of the desirable angelfish species within the genus *Pomacanthus*.

HOW do I sex it?
No external visual differences.

WHAT kind of tank?
Fish-only; live rock-based fish-only; a reef system with care.

WHAT minimum size tank?
120 gal (450 l).

HOW do other fish react?
Often the victim of bullying by larger tangs and other angels. Best kept as the largest fish in a peaceful aquarium.

WHAT to watch out for?
Leave non-feeding specimens in the dealer's tanks, together with specimens obtained from Pacific-based exporters.

HOW compatible with inverts and corals?
Will completely ignore most hard and soft corals, but in common

▲ *The yellow pelvic region suggests that this fish originates from the Indian Ocean or Red Sea.*

with most angelfishes, it cannot be completely trusted. It includes sponges and tunicates in its natural diet and often nips the tube feet of starfish.

WHAT area of the tank?
A shy species that remains close to rockwork, but settles in time.

HOW many in one tank?
Keep singly.

HOW does it behave?
Peaceful, although established specimens can dominate an aquarium of less assertive species.

WILL it breed in an aquarium?
No.

Genicanthus bellus

Ornate swallowtail angelfish

FISH PROFILE

The remarkable differences between male and female specimens from the genus *Genicanthus* are nowhere more defined than in *G. bellus*. Males are rarely offered in the aquarium trade and should be highly prized, but lack of familiarity with this species can mean that the link between male and female specimens is not always recognized.

◀ *The female ornate swallowtail angelfish is more brightly coloured than the yellow and white male fish.*

WHAT size?
Males up to 7 in (18 cm); females rarely more than about 14.7 in (2 cm).

WHAT does it eat?
Feeds almost exclusively on zooplankton. Offer suitable alternatives in the aquarium. Accepts flake and other dried foods, but appreciates chopped shellfish, mysis, and brineshrimp. Dried algae in a lettuce clip is also a good idea.

WHERE is it from?
Limited in the Indian Ocean to Cocos-Keeling Atoll. More widespread in the Pacific, being found throughout the Philippines and island chains as far east as Tonga. This deepwater fish is found as far down as 300 ft (100 m).

WHAT does it cost?
★★★☆☆
Medium-priced; equates fairly well with similar-sized dwarf angelfish.

HOW do I sex it?
Males have no blue pigment on the body, but very obvious longitudinal yellow bands on an off-white base. Females have an exquisite combination of blue stripes with black on the body.

WHAT kind of tank?
Fish only; live rock-based fish-only system; or reef aquarium.

WHAT minimum size tank?
70 gal (270 l) for a single female. 106 gal (400 l) or so for a single male. Pairs require 120 gal (450 l) or more.

HOW do other fish react?
Dwarf angelfishes may take exception to its presence.

WHAT to watch out for?
As with any fish collected at depths, *G. bellus* can display swimming problems if brought up too quickly. The motion is likely to appear labored and the fish might adopt a head-up or head-down position in the aquarium.

HOW compatible with inverts and corals?
Should not harm sessile or ornamental invertebrates.

WHAT area of the tank?
Swims in the open water when settled. Being a deepwater fish, it may take some time to adjust to a brightly-lit reef aquarium.

HOW many in one tank?
Can be kept singly or in pairs. Harems of up to seven individuals dominated by a single male would require a large (200 gal/750 l) aquarium.

HOW does it behave?
Major conflicts only occur with fish that have a similar lifestyle. Not an inherently aggressive species, although males can harass fish such as fairy wrasses almost without compunction.

WILL it breed in an aquarium?
Potentially, yes.

Genicanthus lamarck

Lamarck angelfish

FISH PROFILE

Another elongate fish with elaborate V-shaped tail fins. The group as a whole shows marked definitions between male and female individuals, opening up the possibility of housing pairs or harems in the aquarium. The lamarck is perhaps the least likely to be confused with any other commonly available *Genicanthus* species, due to the bold black horizontal bands on the body, but it also has the most subtle differences between males and females.

WHAT size?
Males reach 10 in (25 cm). Females from just 2 in (5 cm) or so upwards. They are unlikely to achieve 7.8 in (20 cm) before they begin to change into male individuals.

WHAT does it eat?
In the wild, feeds primarily on zooplankton. Offer a variety of meaty foods in the aquarium, including chopped shellfish, mysis, and brineshrimp. Should accept flake and granular food with time.

WHERE is it from?
Indonesia, Malaysia, Philippines eastwards to Vanuatu and the Great Barrier Reef in the South.

WHAT does it cost?
★★☆☆☆
Relatively inexpensive.

HOW do I sex it?
Females are smaller, with an arc-shaped black stripe close to the lateral line. The pelvic fins are white in females, black in males.

WHAT kind of tank?
Fish-only; live rock-based fish-only system; or reef aquarium.

WHAT minimum size tank?
Single female: 70 gal (270 l). Single male: at least 132 gal (500 l). Pairs: 145 gal (550 l) or more.

HOW do other fish react?
Most fish will have no problem with the lamarck angelfish, particularly as it does not closely resemble other species. It may fall afoul of territorial surgeonfishes or tangs, because they attack anything that enters their space.

WHAT to watch out for?
Individuals should feed well, have bright eyes and undamaged fins.

HOW compatible with inverts and corals?
Should not harm sessile invertebrates nor threaten any but the smallest ornamental shrimp.

WHAT area of the tank?
Smaller individuals may spend time in the rockwork but gain confidence as they grow. Settled specimens swim actively in open water seeking food.

HOW many in one tank?
Keep singly or in male/female pairs. Can be kept in groups of up to five females and one male. Introduce a number of small females into the aquarium and allow them to sort out their genders as they grow.

HOW does it behave?
Rarely aggressive. Never introduce more than one angelfish species to the aquarium. Given the color and pattern difference between male and female specimens, having a pair can mean introducing two contrasting, though equally spectacular, individuals.

WILL it breed in an aquarium?
Potentially, yes.

▼ *This female has a bold curved line that is absent in the larger male.*

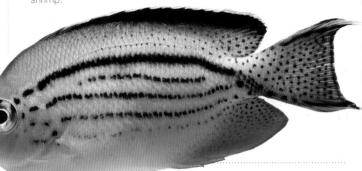

Genicanthus melanospilus

Yellow swallowtail angelfish

FISH PROFILE

A medium-sized angelfish with a truly pelagic (open water) existence. Although it may not be one of the most extravagantly colored, even for a *Genicanthus* species, it is inexpensive and very rewarding to keep.

WHAT size?
Males up to 7 in (18 cm). Females are smaller but there can be some overlap between large females at around 4.7 in (12 cm) and small males of the same size.

WHAT does it eat?
Zooplankton substitutes in captivity, including flake and granular food with time. Also known to browse on dried algae, offered in a lettuce clip where possible.

WHERE is it from?
Widespread from the extreme east of the Indian Ocean and from the Western Pacific to Fiji and Tonga.

WHAT does it cost?
★★☆☆☆
Perhaps the least expensive of the swallowtailed angelfishes. Compares well with some of the less costly dwarf angelfishes and can be less problematic than some of these species in the reef aquarium.

HOW do I sex it?
Males have obvious vertical banding; the female is yellow and white.

WHAT kind of tank?
Fish only; live rock-based fish-only system; or reef aquarium.

WHAT minimum size tank?
Female: 93 gal (350 l) tank or so, especially if bought at 2–3 in (6–8 cm) and allowed to grow. Male: 120-gallon (450-l) system. Pair: at least 132 gal (500 l) to provide plenty of swimming space.

HOW do other fish react?
Most fish will not react adversely to the yellow swallowtail. Possible exceptions include other open-water-swimming species, such as wrasses or some triggerfishes.

WHAT to watch out for?
All specimens should be bright-eyed and have undamaged fins. Reject non-feeding individuals. Pairs can command a premium, but if you come across a male it should not be a problem to introduce a female at a later date.

HOW compatible with inverts and corals?
May nip at sessile invertebrates, but generally more trustworthy than most other angelfishes, including many *Centropyge* species. Will not harm most *Lysmata* species of ornamental shrimp.

WHAT area of the tank?
Regularly swims in open water, but also investigates caves and overhangs in rockwork.

HOW many in one tank?
Keep singly, in pairs, or in male-dominated harems of one male to two or three females.

HOW does it behave?
Large males sometimes chase females, but this is usually only temporary. May chase rivals for its swimming space and food resources, such as anthias, wrasses, and even chromis, but will not harass them to death.

WILL it breed in an aquarium?
Spawning is possible in a large aquarium stocked with pairs.

▲ *This female differs markedly from the zebra-striped male.*

Genicanthus watanabei

Blackedged swallowtail

FISH PROFILE

The blackedged swallowtail is gaining popularity with aquarists as they become familiar with its excellent temperament and beauty. The powder blue of the female is exquisite in its own right, but in the male, the combination of this base color, plus stripes and a more vivid blue dorsal area is simply stunning.

▼ *Male blackedged angelfish like this have a more elaborate pattern than the powder blue female.*

WHAT size?
Males up to 6 in (15 cm). Females seen in the trade rarely measure more than 4.7 in (12 cm).

WHAT does it eat?
In the wild, zooplankton. In an aquarium it should accept mysis, brineshrimp, and any meaty particulate foods. Dried algae and vitamin supplements are also recommended.

WHERE is it from?
Found throughout much of the Western tropical Pacific, including the east coast of Australia and many of the island chains eastwards to Tuamotu. Most aquarium specimens arrive through Philippine exporters.

WHAT does it cost?
★★★☆☆
Fairly expensive.

HOW do I sex it?
Males are larger, with different patterning from the females.

WHAT kind of tank?
Fish-only; live rock-based fish-only system; or reef aquarium.

WHAT minimum size tank?
Females: 70 gal (270 l) or so. Males: 106 gal (400 l). Pairs: 120 gal (450 l) plus.

HOW do other fish react?
Take care when introducing this species to a brightly-lit aquarium that is home to several boisterous species. Individuals collected from deeper waters can become stressed, particularly when harassed by resident tangs or surgeonfishes.

WHAT to watch out for?
Newly imported specimens may prove reluctant to venture out, let alone feed. Leave them to adjust to their new environment. Closely observe their swimming behavior, which may be affected by problems associated with gas expansion as they were raised from the depths.

HOW compatible with inverts and corals?
Should not harm sessile invertebrates or ornamental shrimp.

WHAT area of the tank?
An active open-water-swimmer once settled; may sometimes investigate the rockwork for food.

HOW many in one tank?
Keep singly, in pairs, or in small groups with only one male.

HOW does it behave?
Unlikely to react negatively towards any other marine fish, with the possible exception of other zooplankton-feeders, such as fairy wrasses or anthias.

WILL it breed in an aquarium?
Potentially, yes. Its close relative *G. personatus* has been successfully raised in captivity.

Worth the effort

▶ The majority of butterflyfishes available in the aquarium hobby are members of a single genus, *Chaetodon*, and have a very similar body pattern. Notable exceptions are the genera *Heniochus, Forcipiger,* and *Chelmon,* but all require similar care in the home aquarium. The most commonly encountered problems concern the provision of a suitable diet, as many species are obligate coral polyp feeders and will refuse any substitutes. Even those individuals that will accept alternative offerings will usually die through malnutrition in the short term. It is vital to research any potential purchases to determine the long-term requirements of the species. Those that include zooplankon as part of their natural diet are some of the easiest to maintain. When they are chosen with care—and if their individual demands are met—butterflyfish species can prove to be extremely hardy and long-lived.

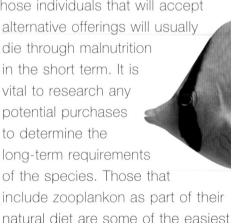

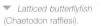
▲ Pyramid butterflyfish (Hemitaurichthys polylepis).

▼ Latticed butterflyfish (Chaetodon rafflesi).

Price guide

★	Up to $35
★★	$35–$70
★★★	$70–$115
★★★★	$115–$130
★★★★★	$130+

▲ Many species of butterflyfish can be maintained in the home aquarium. These are two not covered in detail elsewhere.

Chaetodon argentatus

Black pearlscale butterflyfish

FISH PROFILE

An infrequent import, but one of the hardier butterflyfish species for the aquarium. Although it does not have the stunning pattern or coloration of other butterflyfish, it is still very attractive. The fact that it can be bought with confidence in its long-term survival should ensure its increased popularity in years to come.

WHAT size?
Males and females 7.9 in (20 cm).

WHAT does it eat?
In the wild, benthic invertebrates and zooplankton. (At the northern part of its distribution in the Japanese Islands it is found where corals are absent.) In the aquarium, readily accepts a variety of substitutes, including mysis and brineshrimp.

WHERE is it from?
Western Pacific rim, including Japan and the Philippines.

WHAT does it cost?
★☆☆☆☆   ★★☆☆☆
Relatively inexpensive.

HOW do I sex it?
No external sexual differences. Can be acquired as pairs.

WHAT kind of tank?
Fish-only; live rock-based fish-only; reef aquarium with great care.

WHAT minimum size tank?
120 gal (450 l).

HOW do other fish react?
Tangs and surgeonfishes may be temporarily aggressive to newly introduced specimens of *C. argentatus*.

WHAT to watch out for?
Obtain specimens that feed readily and, if possible, are a pair.

HOW compatible with inverts and corals?
Should not harm shrimp, with the possible exception of the smallest ornamental species,

e.g., *Urocaridella* spp. or *Thor amboinensis*. Will ignore most coral species.

WHAT area of the tank?
Open water, scouring rockwork and sand or gravel substrates for morsels of food.

HOW many in one tank?
A single individual or pair. A large aquarium will accommo-date small groups.

HOW does it behave?
Can be aggressive towards other butterflyfish. This busy, active fish demonstrates the remarkable swimming gymnastics of many species of butterflyfish as it forages for food in the aquarium.

WILL it breed in an aquarium?
No.

▼ *Not as striking as some species, but attractive and quite easy to keep.*

Chaetodon auriga

Threadfin butterflyfish

FISH PROFILE

One of the many butterflyfish species with a vertical black band running through the eye and yellow and black body coloration. The threadfin can be identified by the pattern of bands on the body and the single black spot (ocellus) on the rear margin of the dorsal fin. This fin can have a long filament, which gives the species its common name.

WHAT size?
Males and females 7.9 in (20 cm).

WHAT does it eat?
In the wild, benthic algae, polychaete worms, nudibranchs, and an assortment of small crustaceans. In the aquarium, offer foods formulated for butterflyfishes and the usual mysis, brineshrimp, and chopped shellfish at least three times per day. Juveniles may require more regular feeding than this because they are prone to losing weight.

WHERE is it from?
Widespread throughout the Indo-Pacific from the Red Sea and East African coast to the Hawaiian Islands.

WHAT does it cost?
★☆☆☆☆
Inexpensive.

HOW do I sex it?
No external sexual characteristics.

WHAT kind of tank?
Fish-only or live rock-based fish-only.

WHAT minimum size tank?
93 gal (350 l).

HOW do other fish react?
Juvenile threadfins have been reported cleaning other fish in captivity, and such behavior can enable fish with little or no means of protecting themselves against aggressive species to settle into aquarium life without any major incidents.

WHAT to watch out for?
Avoid excessively skinny or small specimens, as they will require a great deal of work on your part if they are to recover sufficiently. All individuals should be feeding before you buy them.

HOW compatible with inverts and corals?
Do not keep with any sessile invertebrates, anemones, bivalve molluscs, or small ornamental shrimp. Should not harm larger species of *Lysmata* spp. ornamental shrimp.

WHAT area of the tank?
This active fish thoroughly investigates every square inch of the aquarium in its perpetual search for food.

HOW many in one tank?
Keep singly or in pairs.

HOW does it behave?
A bossy species that will try to assert itself over other fish. This is generally not a problem with small juveniles, but larger specimens can make a nuisance of themselves, dominating smaller fish.

WILL it breed in an aquarium?
No.

▼ *Despite the fish's common name, the dorsal filament of this species is not always obvious. The dark spot at the top edge of the dorsal fin may be absent in some specimens.*

Chaetodon burgessi

Burgess butterflyfish

FISH PROFILE

A deepwater butterflyfish that inhabits exposed reef fronts may not initially sound like the best species for a home aquarium. However, it is one of the hardiest and most affordable butterflyfishes and one of the few species that does not consume the majority of sessile invertebrates highly prized by marine aquarists.

◀ *A very hardy and robust species that is set to become increasingly popular in the marine hobby.*

WHAT size?
Males and females 4.7 in (12 cm).

WHAT does it eat?
In the wild, small benthic invertebrates and zooplankton. Will accept most aquarium foods, including dried algae.

WHERE is it from?
Indonesia, Philippines, and Palau.

WHAT does it cost?
★★☆☆☆   ★★★☆☆
A mid-priced species, considerably less expensive than the closely-related *Chaetodon mitratus* and *C. tinkeri.*

HOW do I sex it?
No external sexual differences, yet pairs are quite easy to find.

WHAT kind of tank?
A reef aquarium with care, or a fish-only system with live rock present is best for the long-term husbandry of this species.

WHAT minimum size tank?
80 gal (300 l) for a single individual.

HOW do other fish react?
Surgeonfishes and tangs may react aggressively to the introduction of this butterflyfish. Watch also where dwarf angelfishes are already stocked.

WHAT to watch out for?
Burgess' butterflyfish is one of the best potential consumers of *Aiptasia* spp. anemones in the aquarium, and a better choice than the copperband butterfly *(Chelmon rostratus)* for this purpose.

HOW compatible with inverts and corals?
Large-polyp stony corals and tubeworms are likely to be nipped at best, and completely devastated at worst.

WHAT area of the tank?
An open-water-swimmer that does not venture too far from the rockwork that it investigates thoroughly for food items.

HOW many in one tank?
A single individual is acceptable, while a pair will enable you to observe natural behavior.

HOW does it behave?
This peaceful species settles well into most aquariums, which is perhaps surprising, given that many individuals are found at depths below 120 ft (40 m) or in caves. Found in association with black corals and gorgonians.

WILL it breed in an aquarium?
Unlikely, although not impossible in a large aquarium.

Chaetodon collare

Collared butterflyfish

FISH PROFILE

It is difficult to generalize about the collared butterflyfish, because good-quality individuals often prove hardy and long-lived. However, poor specimens will confound the aquarist's best attempts to keep them, often succumbing to starvation or parasitic infections.

WHAT size?
Males and females 7 in (18 cm).

WHAT does it eat?
One of the few species to feed almost exclusively on hard coral polyps, yet can be acclimatized to accept more readily available items. Offer a wide variety of foodstuffs, including dried algae, brineshrimp, mysis, chopped and whole shellfish, plus regular vitamin supplements. Feed at least three times per day.

WHERE is it from?
Found throughout the Indian Ocean, from the Persian Gulf to Indonesia.

WHAT does it cost?
★★☆☆☆
Not particularly expensive.

HOW do I sex it?
No external sexual differences.

WHAT kind of tank?
Fish-only or live rock-based fish-only system.

WHAT minimum size tank?
66 gal (250 l).

HOW do other fish react?
Most fish will tolerate the collared butterflyfish and it is quite capable of looking after itself in most situations. Tangs and surgeonfishes are likely to present the most immediate threat as the fish settles in a new aquarium.

WHAT to watch out for?
Avoid non-feeding individuals in the dealer's aquarium. Try to select specimens measuring 2.3–4.7 in (6–12 cm) long (not the largest or smallest specimens imported) and check them for signs of disease such as turbidity of the skin or cloudy eyes.

HOW compatible with inverts and corals?
Should not harm most larger ornamental shrimp, but not safe with sessile invertebrates.

WHAT area of the tank?
An active species that remains close to rockwork, scouring it perpetually for food. Ventures into open water at feeding time and eventually becomes very tame.

HOW many in one tank?
Best kept singly or in pairs. Pairs require a large system and you must be prepared to endure bickering between specimens.

HOW does it behave?
Fairly peaceful towards other species, although it may chase smaller butterflyfish every now and then.

WILL it breed in an aquarium?
No.

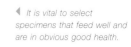

◀ *It is vital to select specimens that feed well and are in obvious good health.*

Chaetodon kleini

Sunburst butterflyfish

FISH PROFILE

Although it is one of the less colorful butterflyfish, the sunburst is nonetheless a popular marine aquarium subject. It is commonly available and proves very hardy. If well cared for, it should thrive for many years.

WHAT size?
Males and females 6 in (15 cm).

WHAT does it eat?
Offer dried green algae to simulate a readily available food item that can be visited at will, and feed with mysis, brineshrimp, chopped shellfish, plus whole bivalves such as cockle or clam. Vitamin supplements can help this fish maintain its coloration.

WHERE is it from?
Widespread in the tropical Indo-Pacific, from the Red Sea to the Hawaiian Islands.

WHAT does it cost?
★☆☆☆☆
Inexpensive for a butterflyfish.

▲ *Both juveniles (here) and subadults can show vertical barring on the body.*

▲ *This species may control nuisance anemones, but also nips at other inverts.*

HOW do I sex it?
May be possible by observing pairs, but even then it is very difficult without actually observing the fish spawning.

WHAT kind of tank?
Fish-only or live rock-based fish-only system. It may be possible to house this species in a hard coral-rich aquarium.

WHAT minimum size tank?
53 gal (200 l).

HOW do other fish react?
May be bullied by tangs, surgeons, or other butterflyfish when first introduced, but will usually endure this onslaught without any major consequence.

WHAT to watch out for?
Ensure specimens are feeding before introduction.

HOW compatible with inverts and corals?
Some aquarists maintain that this species' reputation for controlling *Aiptasia* spp. anemones is unfounded, but most agree that the fish will eat this nuisance invertebrate. However, it will also have a go at many other forms of polyp, much to the consternation of the aquarist. It should not harm larger species of ornamental shrimp. Clams are likely to be nipped.

WHAT area of the tank?
An active swimmer that will investigate every nook and cranny of the aquarium and become hand-tame very quickly.

HOW many in one tank?
Keep singly, in pairs, or small groups.

HOW does it behave?
Generally very laidback and peaceful. Its hardy constitution means it can be safely stocked quite early on in the life of an aquarium, with the confidence that its presence will not preclude the addition of any other species at a later stage.

WILL it breed in an aquarium?
No. A spawning event is possible but not likely.

Chaetodon lunula

Raccoon butterflyfish

FISH PROFILE

An aquarium favorite that proves hardy and long-lived when supplied with a suitably varied diet and excellent water quality. It is one of the best "first" butterflyfish species, provided specimens are selected carefully. The Red Sea raccoon *(Chaetodon fasciatus)* requires similar care, but is more expensive due to its collection area.

WHAT size?
Males and females 7.9 in (20 cm).

WHAT does it eat?
On the reef, this omnivorous fish browses on sessile invertebrates, anemones, benthic crustaceans, polychaete worms, and algae. It is particularly useful for the control of *Aiptasia* spp. anemones in live rock-based fish-only systems. For long-term nutrition in the aquarium, offer a wide variety of foods, including algae, mysis, chopped shellfish, enriched brineshrimp, and formula diets.

WHERE is it from?
Widespread in the tropical and sub-tropical Indo-Pacific from east Africa to the Hawaiian Islands.

WHAT does it cost?
★☆☆☆☆
Relatively inexpensive. One of the cheaper butterflyfish.

▲ C. lunula *has a black spot on the caudal peduncle absent in* C. fasciatus.

HOW do I sex it?
No external sexual differences.

WHAT kind of tank?
Fish-only or live rock-based fish-only systems. Do not be tempted to keep it with corals or other sessile invertebrates.

WHAT minimum size tank?
66 gal (250 l) for a pair, assuming excellent water quality.

HOW do other fish react?
Small specimens of *C. lunula* often act as cleaners of larger fish species and are therefore not chased or bullied unduly. However, it is safer to stock this species before larger or more aggressive species.

WHAT to watch out for?
Avoid non-feeding specimens, skinny individuals, and those with cloudy eyes or torn fins.

HOW compatible with inverts and corals?
Although certain individuals might ignore some corals, such fish are the exception rather than the rule. Even smaller ornamental shrimp may be killed and eaten.

WHAT area of the tank?
An active, open-water swimmer that pauses frequently to investigate the rockwork for any tasty morsels.

HOW many in one tank?
Best kept singly for the most peaceful aquarium, but pairs can be maintained.

HOW does it behave?
Can be bossy towards other butterflyfish species, if not actually aggressive, but generally quite peaceful.

WILL it breed in an aquarium?
No.

Chaetodon miliaris

Milletseed butterflyfish

FISH PROFILE

A commonly imported Hawaiian species, often overlooked in favour of more brightly coloured and often less hardy butterflyfish species. This is a shame, because many aquarists are missing out on a hardy and peaceful aquarium fish that will reward its keeper with a long, trouble-free existence, given adequate water quality. An ideal first butterflyfish for novice marine aquarists.

WHAT size?
Males and females 4.7 in (12 cm).

WHAT does it eat?
A plankton-feeding species in its natural environment, but readily accepts a wide variety of small particulate foods, including chopped shellfish, mysis, brineshrimp, and fish eggs. Settled specimens may even take particulate flaked or dried foods.

WHERE is it from?
Hawaii and Johnston Atoll in the Pacific Ocean.

WHAT does it cost?
★☆☆☆☆   ★★☆☆☆
Relatively inexpensive.

▶ *The black spot on the caudal peduncle distinguishes this fish from the similar C. guentheri.*

HOW do I sex it?
No external sexual differences.

WHAT kind of tank?
Fish-only; live rock-based fish-only; reef aquarium with care.

WHAT minimum size tank?
80 gal (300 l).

HOW do other fish react?
Resident tangs and surgeons may behave aggressively towards this species when it is first introduced. Take care when introducing it to an aquarium housing large planktonivores, such as *Genicanthus* angelfish.

WHAT to watch out for?
Avoid non-feeding specimens or those that appear emaciated. Settled specimens present few problems to the aquarist.

HOW compatible with inverts and corals?
Can be trusted with most corals, with the possible exception of large-polyp stony corals.

WHAT area of the tank?
Open-water-swimming species.

HOW many in one tank?
Keep singly, in pairs or small groups where aquarium capacity allows.

HOW does it behave?
A peaceful species with a relaxed attitude towards other fish. Spends much of its time swimming actively in the water column. Feeding very small amounts of food at regular intervals encourages it to behave as naturally as possible.

WILL it breed in an aquarium?
Possible but unlikely.

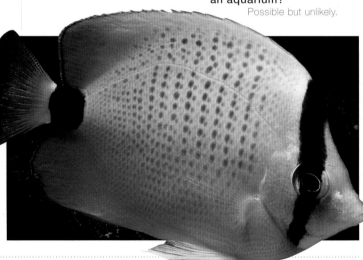

73

Chaetodon punctatofasciatus

Spotband butterflyfish

Chaetodon punctatofasciatus is one of three species (the others being *C. guttatissimus* and *C. pelewensis*) that are very similar in appearance and require the same aquarium care. All have a white-yellow base color and a series of dark spots of varying sizes and shapes over the body. For the most part, the information given here for the spotband butterflyfish applies also to the other species, with the obvious exception of the natural range.

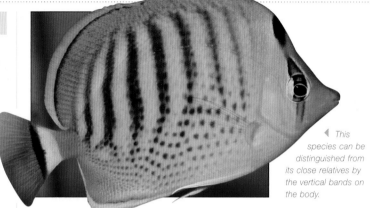

◀ *This species can be distinguished from its close relatives by the vertical bands on the body.*

WHAT size?
Males and females 4.7 in (12 cm).

WHAT does it eat?
In the wild, coral polyps, polychaete worms, algae, and small crustaceans. Aquarium specimens will accept most small particulate foods, including chopped shellfish, formula foods designed for butterflyfishes, chopped mysis, and enriched brineshrimp. It is also worth offering dried algae on a lettuce clip.

WHERE is it from?
Eastern Indian Ocean to Micronesia. (*C. guttatissimus* replaces it in the Indian Ocean.)

WHAT does it cost?
★☆☆☆☆ ★★☆☆☆
Relatively inexpensive.

HOW do I sex it?
No external sexual differences.

WHAT kind of tank?
Fish-only or live rock-based fish-only system.

WHAT minimum size tank?
66 gal (250 l).

HOW do other fish react?
In most cases, the introduction of this species will pass without major incident. Surgeonfishes and tangs are the most likely to react adversely to it. The spotband's peaceful nature means that problems can be avoided if it is added before any aggressive species.

WHAT to watch out for?
Avoid skinny specimens or ones that will not feed in dealer's tank.

HOW compatible with inverts and corals?
Safe in a live rock-based aquarium with a few carefully chosen invertebrates, such as anemones or mushroom polyps. However, it can never really be considered for the reef aquarium. Should not harm ornamental shrimp.

WHAT area of the tank?
Roams all over the aquarium, but not quite as adventurous as some other members of this genus.

HOW many in one tank?
Keep singly or in pairs. Small juveniles are reported to be solitary in their natural environment.

HOW does it behave?
The smallest individuals are not very well suited to a boisterous aquarium, as they can prove difficult to feed and may not compete well with larger or more powerful species. Tolerant of other closely-related species and will not bother smaller, more sensitive, ones.

WILL it breed in an aquarium?
No.

Chaetodon semilarvatus
Masked (addis) butterflyfish

FISH PROFILE

A beautiful butterflyfish, highly prized by marine aquarists. Although by no means the most expensive butterflyfish available to the hobby, any aquarist wanting to obtain an individual of this species will need deep pockets!

WHAT size?
Males and females 9–10 in (23–25 cm).

WHAT does it eat?
In the wild, browses on hard corals and benthic invertebrates. In the aquarium, accepts most foods, including frozen and dried foods, the latter only after some perseverance by the aquarist. Feed this species at least three times per day.

WHERE is it from?
The Red Sea and Gulf of Aden only.

WHAT does it cost?
★★★★☆
Expensive.

▶ *An exquisite and popular species that proves hardy once settled in the marine aquarium.*

HOW do I sex it?
No external sexual differences.

WHAT kind of tank?
Fish only; live rock-based fish-only; a system home to plenty of *Sinularia* spp. soft corals.

WHAT minimum size tank?
130 gal (500 l).

HOW do other fish react?
Try to avoid stocking this species with similarly-colored butterflyfishes. It may suffer if kept with too many active swimmers, such as wrasses.

WHAT to watch out for?
Avoid specimens that do not feed or that appear skinny. Good individuals will readily accept a variety of foods and approach the front of the aquarium when a potential buyer walks past because they expect to be food.

HOW compatible with inverts and corals?
Unlikely to bother small crustaceans, including ornamental shrimp. However, it will nip at sessile invertebrates with the exception of many species of soft coral. Few people maintain this species with corals, but more will do so when they understand that it is possible.

WHAT area of the tank?
Open water or scouring the rockwork for morsels of food.

HOW many in one tank?
Keep singly or in pairs.

HOW does it behave?
Peaceful. Quite tolerant of other fish.

WILL it breed in an aquarium?
Not recorded, even though pairs are commonly kept.

Chaetodon striatus

Banded butterflyfish

FISH PROFILE

At first glance, the banded butterflyfish may not be to everyone's taste. By the standards set by more colorful species, it has a fairly bland appearance and is not a regular import. However, aquarists who have tried it state that it is a hardy species with a useful role in the control of pest anemone species such as *Aiptasia* spp.

▶ *This juvenile specimen will lose the dorsal 'eye spot' (ocellus) as it grows.*

WHAT size?
Males and females 6.3 in (16 cm).

WHAT does it eat?
The tropical Caribbean reefs that this species calls home must appear to it like a colorful smorgasbord. It will eat marine worms, benthic crustaceans, polyps, zooplankton, and fish eggs. Offer aquarium specimens a variety of frozen foods, including mysis, brineshrimp, and chopped shellfish.

WHERE is it from?
Western Atlantic and the Caribbean, straying into subtropical waters.

WHAT does it cost?
★★☆☆☆
Slightly more expensive than other, similarly-sized butterflyfishes available in the hobby.

HOW do I sex it?
No external sexual differences.

WHAT kind of tank?
Fish-only or live rock-based fish-only. It is possible to keep this fish with corals, but they should be selected around the fish, rather than stocking the butterflyfish into an existing aquarium with a great diversity of corals. It should ignore many corals altogether.

WHAT minimum size tank?
100 gal (375 l).

HOW do other fish react?
Juveniles will remove parasites from larger fish, so they are forgiven the intrusion into a territorial fish's area for this useful purpose. Tangs and surgeonfishes may take exception to larger specimens, but any aggression is usually short-lived.

WHAT to watch out for?
Individuals should be feeding on frozen food before you buy them and should not be too thin. Ignore specimens below 1.5 in (4 cm).

HOW compatible with inverts and corals?
Identifying the corals that this species attacks is a case of trial and error. It has been maintained in a diverse reef aquarium with no obvious coral predation, but this may depend on the individual fish concerned. Offering "picking" material, such as dried algae or gel-encased foods, may help to avoid coral damage.

WHAT area of the tank?
Remains close to rockwork, only venturing into open water to feed.

HOW many in one tank?
Keep singly or in pairs.

HOW does it behave?
May take exception to other, similar species of butterflyfish, but is generally peaceful.

WILL it breed in an aquarium?
No.

Chaetodon xanthurus

Pacific pearlscale butterflyfish

FISH PROFILE

One of a group of butterflyfish in which a sector of the rear portion of the dorsal fin and body is colored orange. A closely related species from the Red Sea has a red sector *(C. paucifasciatus)*. Some of the differences between the species are quite subtle and their common names tend to reflect their point of origin, rather than any clue that will help to identify them in a dealer's aquarium. Fortunately, they require almost identical care.

WHAT size?
Males and females 5.5 in (14 cm).

WHAT does it eat?
This species does not include coral tissue in its natural diet, instead preferring benthic invertebrates such as worms and small crustaceans in addition to algae. In the aquarium, offer most meaty foods including chopped shellfish, mysis, brineshrimp, and specific butterflyfish diets, together with dried algae. Vitamin supplements are recommended.

WHERE is it from?
Indonesia and the Philippines.

WHAT does it cost?
★☆☆☆☆ ★★☆☆☆
Inexpensive.

▶ *The beautiful Pacific pearlscale butterfly is a popular aquarium fish.*

HOW do I sex it?
No external sexual differences.

WHAT kind of tank?
Fish-only or live rock-based fish-only.

WHAT minimum size tank?
66 gal (250 l).

HOW do other fish react?
Most species will ignore the pearlscale butterflyfish if it is introduced when small (less than 7cm). Tangs, surgeonfishes, boisterous wrasses, and dwarf angelfishes may react adversely to the arrival of larger individuals, so introduce the pearlscale before these or similar fish.

WHAT to watch out for?
Avoid skinny specimens or fish that refuse to feed in the dealer's aquarium. The best individuals will be at the glass waiting to be fed as you approach and then feed greedily.

HOW compatible with inverts and corals?
Species from the "pearlscale complex" have been cited as "reef-safe" by some aquarists, but they cannot be fully trusted. They will reduce the overall diversity of species present in a reef aquarium and predate useful detritivores. They may also peck at corals, but should not harm larger ornamental shrimp.

WHAT area of the tank?
Small juveniles stay close to the rockwork, only approaching open water when food is introduced. Larger specimens are more confident and will roam all over the aquarium searching for food.

HOW many in one tank?
Keep singly or in pairs. The latter are best introduced as small juveniles and allowed to grow, although they will still bicker between themselves at first.

HOW does it behave?
May bully similar species by chasing them around the aquarium and nipping at their fins, but they do not present a major threat to other fish.

WILL it breed in an aquarium?
No.

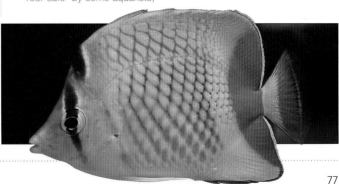

Chelmon marginalis

Margined coralfish

FISH PROFILE

This wonderful species can be thought of as an Australian version of the copperband butterflyfish (*Chelmon rostratus*). The similarities are obvious, but their range overlaps on the Northern Coastline of Australia and both species can be encountered there.

WHAT size?
Males and females 7 in (18 cm).

WHAT does it eat?
In the wild, locates benthic invertebrates in holes and crevices with the aid of its long snout. Accepts a variety of foods in the aquarium, such as chopped and whole shellfish, mysis and brineshrimp. Feed enriched forms of brineshrimp and supplement any offerings regularly with vitamins. It is vital to feed this species several times a day.

WHERE is it from?
The North West Coast of Australia eastwards to Cape York Peninsula.

WHAT does it cost?
★★★★★
An expensive rarity.

▶ *This subadult margined coralfish is in the process of losing the central vertical band.*

HOW do I sex it?
No known external sexual differences.

WHAT kind of tank?
Fish-only; live rock-based fish-only system; a reef aquarium with care.

WHAT minimum size tank?
132 gal (500 l).

HOW do other fish react?
Other butterflyfish species and/or large tangs, surgeonfishes or angelfishes, may all bully this species. Ideally, introduce smaller individuals of potential aggressors after the butterflyfish has been introduced.

WHAT to watch out for?
Avoid skinny or non-feeding specimens. As with most species of butterflyfish, by the time you notice that an individual is looking a little emaciated, it can be too late to do anything about it.

HOW compatible with inverts and corals?
Will nip at tubeworms and, occasionally, corals, but should ignore ornamental shrimp.

WHAT area of the tank?
Open water close to rockwork.

HOW many in one tank?
Keep singly.

HOW does it behave?
Spends hours in the methodical investigation of every nook and cranny that the aquarium offers.

WILL it breed in an aquarium?
No.

Chelmon rostratus
Copperband butterflyfish

FISH PROFILE

A firm favorite among aquarists, despite an undeserved reputation as being almost impossible to maintain in captivity. Selecting a good specimen and offering it a varied diet are the keys to success. The copperband can prove to be a long-lived and hardy species, provided you follow a few simple rules.

WHAT size?
Males and females 7.9 in (20 cm).

WHAT does it eat?
In the wild, tubeworms, free-living polychaetes, and other benthic invertebrates. Make sure specimens in dealers' tanks are feeding energetically before you buy one. Good specimens will approach the aquarium glass as people pass by. Offer a wide variety of frozen foods, including shellfish and particularly mysis shrimp, rather than brineshrimp. Feed several times per day and supplement regularly with vitamins.

WHERE is it from?
Eastern Indo-Pacific.

WHAT does it cost?
★★☆☆☆
Fairly inexpensive.

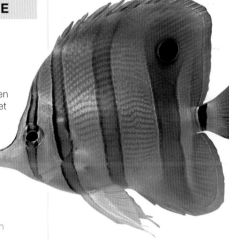

HOW do I sex it?
No external sexual differences. Specimens are usually available singly, yet are commonly (though not always) found in pairs in their natural environment.

WHAT kind of tank?
Fish-only system with plenty of live rock; reef system with care.

WHAT minimum size tank?
120 gal (450 l).

HOW do other fish react?
Likely to be harassed by tangs, dwarf angels, and surgeonfishes if these are introduced before the copperband. It is best to stock this species before any fish that are likely to challenge it. A well-settled, healthy specimen can fend for itself, often "head-standing" to fend off potential aggressors with its erect dorsal fin spines.

◀ *Copperbands need plenty of attention if they are to thrive.*

WHAT to watch out for?
It is vital to monitor the physical shape of this species. At the first sign of emaciation, raise the feeding rate and substitute food items such as brineshrimp for mysis shrimp, which have a much higher fat content.

HOW compatible with inverts and corals?
Will nip at tubeworms but largely ignores most species of sessile invertebrate, with the notable exception of *Aiptasia* spp. anemones. Many aquarists introduce the copperband butterflyfish to control this pest invertebrate without giving due consideration to the fish's long-term requirements.

WHAT area of the tank?
Investigates rockwork for food items. May spend prolonged periods behind rockwork searching for tubeworms.

HOW many in one tank?
Best kept singly unless a compatible and healthy pair can be sourced.

HOW does it behave?
A peaceful species that becomes increasingly confident as it settles into the aquarium.

WILL it breed in an aquarium?
No.

Forcipiger flavissimus

Longnosed butterflyfish

The genus *Forcipiger* is instantly recognizable by the solid body coloration and very long, slender snout. Only two species exist; *F. flavissimus* is the most commonly seen in the trade. Distinguishing between it and *F. longirostris* is difficult unless you have two specimens side by side. One clue is that on the thorax of *F. longirostris* there are scales with a dark pigment in their centers.

◀ *The physical adaptations that enable a fish to remove invertebrates from deep crevices and holes are clear to see in this species.*

WHAT size?
Males and females 8.7 in (22 cm).

WHAT does it eat?
In the wild, browses on a wide range of naturally occurring foods—an important consideration if you are thinking of introducing it to a reef set-up (see also "Invertebrate/coral compatibility"). In the aquarium it accepts most foods—mysis and brineshrimp are favorites. Feed the fish regularly to minimize their impact on sessile invertebrates.

WHERE is it from?
Wide-ranging species found in large parts of the Tropical Indo-Pacific, including the Red Sea and Hawaiian Islands.

WHAT does it cost?
★★☆☆☆
A mid-priced species, depending on the country of origin.

HOW do I sex it?
No obvious external differences.

WHAT kind of tank?
Fish-only; fish-only with live rock; a reef aquarium only with care.

WHAT minimum size tank?
106 gal (400 l).

HOW do other fish react?
Occasionally threatened by large surgeonfishes and tangs. Its response is to "headstand," exposing erect dorsal spines and facing the direction of the threat with these defensive weapons.

WHAT to watch out for?
Without sufficient food and given its active lifestyle, this species is prone to lose weight in an aquarium situation.

HOW compatible with inverts and corals?
Take into account the dietary information supplied for this species, and bear in mind that

it will also feed on the trailing tentacles of Zoanthid polyps and may also nip at large-polyp stony corals. It does not include small-polyp stony corals in its diet and therefore should not present a threat where these are present.

WHAT area of the tank?
Scours every part of the aquarium in its never-ending search for food.

HOW many in one tank?
Best kept singly, although in its natural environment it is found in pairs and small groups.

HOW does it behave?
A lively and peaceful fish that will behave naturally in the aquarium, once settled. The purpose of that seemingly oversized snout soon becomes clear, as it probes every hole and recess for food.

WILL it breed in an aquarium?
No.

Heniochus diphreutes

Wimplefish

FISH PROFILE

The wimplefish, and its close relative the longfin bannerfish (*Heniochus acuminatus*), are often confused by aquarists, but they differ in some subtle physical characteristics and quite markedly in behavior. The wimplefish has a more angular anal fin on which the black and white bands meet at its apex. The longfin bannerfish also has a less-rounded general appearance and more pointed snout. *H. diphreutes* is more gregarious than its close relative and better suited to the reef aquarium.

WHAT size?
Males and females 8.3 in (21 cm).

WHAT does it eat?
In the wild, *H. acuminatus* and *H. diphreutes* feed on zooplankton. In the home aquarium offer particulate foods, such as brineshrimp (enriched with spirulina or Omega 3), mysis, and chopped shellfish. Be sure to provide a variety of such items several times per day.

WHERE is it from?
Red Sea, East Africa, and much of the tropical Indo-Pacific to the Hawaiian Islands.

WHAT does it cost?
★☆☆☆☆ ★★☆☆☆
Relatively inexpensive.

HOW do I sex it?
No known external sexual differences.

WHAT kind of tank?
Fish-only; live rock-based fish-only; or reef system.

WHAT minimum size tank?
66 gal (250 l).

HOW do other fish react?
H. diphreutes is known to act as a cleaner of larger fish, so they are prepared to leave it alone. Tangs

and surgeonfishes may present the most problems, but this can be avoided by stocking the wimplefish before more territorial species.

WHAT to watch out for?
Avoid skinny or non-feeding specimens. It is important to distinguish between the wimplefish and *H. acuminatus* if you intend stocking it in a coral-rich aquarium.

HOW compatible with inverts and corals?
H. diphreutes is largely trustworthy in a reef aquarium, but may find tubeworms too tempting to resist. It will ignore most corals, sessile invertebrates, and ornamental shrimp.

WHAT area of the tank?
Settled specimens are active open-water swimmers.

HOW many in one tank?
Can be kept singly, in pairs or small groups.

HOW does it behave?
This peaceful species reserves its aggression for other members of its species, but this seldom amounts to anything more than bickering.

WILL it breed in an aquarium?
No.

◀ *The wimplefish is not only attractive and hardy, but also reasonably priced.*

From timid to tenacious

▶ There are many species of wrasse available to marine hobbyists; it is not possible to cover them all in detail here, but they vary from the large and belligerent to the very small and reclusive. Many hogfishes and wrasses show widely varying temperaments between individuals of the same species—one aquarist's ideal fish may be another's nightmare. Many wrasses show markedly different coloration as they mature and some are sexually dimorphic. This is another group of marine fish in which a transformation from female to male throughout the course of an individual's life is commonplace. Be aware of any changes in color or form and research the ultimate size potential of attractive juvenile specimens before buying them. The term hogfish is generally applied to some of the larger wrasse species of which only a few do not grow too large for most home aquariums.

Price guide

★	Up to $20
★★	$20–$45
★★★	$45–$60
★★★★	$60–$80
★★★★★	$80–$170

FISH PROFILE

The yellowtailed wrasse is typical in that it shows pronounced sexual dimorphism, meaning that the sexes are very different in appearance. Species from the genus *Anampses* are quite commonly encountered in the marine aquarium trade, but their availability does not reflect their ease of keeping.

WHAT size?
Males 8.7 in (22 cm); females to around 4.7 in (12 cm).

WHAT does it eat?
In the wild, a variety of bottom-dwelling invertebrates such as small worms and crustaceans. In the aquarium offer mysis, brineshrimp, and chopped shellfish several times per day. It may also accept whole clam, mussel, or cockle that it will pull apart. Increase the particle size as the specimen grows.

WHERE is it from?
Indo-Pacific, from the Red Sea to Tuamotu.

WHAT does it cost?
★★☆☆☆
Inexpensive.

Anampses meleagrides

Yellowtailed wrasse

HOW do I sex it?
Females are smaller and have a dark body, white spots, and yellow tail. The male is deep purple with blue flecks and spots.

WHAT kind of tank?
Fish-only; live rock-based fish-only system. Has been maintained in reefs, but larger specimens can be problematic.

WHAT minimum size tank?
120 gal (450 l).

HOW do other fish react?
The yellowtailed wrasse is most vulnerable to attack from other large wrasses. It is canny enough to keep out of trouble for the most part, but will almost certainly be targeted by resident territorial species shortly after introduction.

WHAT to watch out for?
Newly-imported specimens need time to recover. Allow specimens to settle for at least two weeks before buying them. This sensitive species enjoys stable conditions; excellent overall water quality is essential. May jump from an uncovered aquarium.

HOW compatible with inverts and corals?
Can be maintained with corals without any problems. Larger individuals may target smaller species of ornamental crustacean.

WHAT area of the tank?
When small or newly introduced, it spends much of its time close to sand or rockwork. As its confidence grows, it will increasingly swim in open water.

HOW many in one tank?
Keep singly.

HOW does it behave?
A fairly peaceful species that should not prove a nuisance to other fish.

WILL it breed in an aquarium?
No.

▼ *If this wrasse settles after importation, it will often thrive in the home aquarium.*

Cirrhilabrus rubrisquamis

Maldive velvet fairy wrasse

FISH PROFILE

The beautiful Maldive velvet fairy wrasse is becoming increasingly well known as a stunningly colored fish suitable for a peaceful reef aquarium. There are many similar species, but the husbandry and aquarium requirements for each are almost identical.

▲ *This stunning fish is an ideal introduction to the peaceful reef aquarium.*

WHAT size?
Males 3.1 in (8 cm); females 2.5 in (6.5 cm).

WHAT does it eat?
In the wild, zooplankton. Usually accepts enriched brineshrimp, mysis, chopped shellfish, and dried algae in the aquarium. Vitamin supplements help to keep the colors vibrant.

WHERE is it from?
Maldives and the Islands of the Chagos Archipelago.

WHAT does it cost?
★★★★☆
Medium-priced.

HOW do I sex it?
Males are larger and more brightly colored. Typically for the genus, females keep their juvenile coloration, which is not as bright or attractive as that of the males.

WHAT kind of tank?
Live rock-based fish-only system or reef aquarium.

WHAT minimum size tank?
80 gal (300 l).

HOW do other fish react?
Its submissive nature and dietary preferences mean that this fish is often singled out for aggression by other open-water-swimming species. Other fairy wrasses are likely to be problematic, as are larger wrasse species, dottybacks, and swallowtail angelfishes.

WHAT to watch out for?
In common with other species in this group, the Maldive velvet fairy wrasse will sometimes jump out of an uncovered aquarium. Newly acquired specimens may sulk in the corner of the aquarium for short periods, particularly if more boisterous species are present.

HOW compatible with inverts and corals?
Should not harm corals, sessile invertebrates, or ornamental shrimp.

WHAT area of the tank?
Once settled in a peaceful aquarium, this is an open-water-swimming species. It hovers in midwater or swims actively over rockwork and sand.

HOW many in one tank?
Keep males singly. Females can be kept in groups with a single male specimen.

HOW does it behave?
This overwhelmingly peaceful fish does not thrive in the presence of more aggressive species. It reserves its own antagonistic behaviour for very similar fish or same-sex members of its own species.

WILL it breed in an aquarium?
It may spawn. As more people start to keep this fish in home aquariums and observe its behavior, we will learn more about it.

Halichoeres iridis

Iridis wrasse

FISH PROFILE

Such is the beauty of the iridis wrasse that it is often mistaken for fairy wrasses of the genus *Cirrhilabrus*. It is becoming increasingly available and can be considered for most peaceful community aquariums.

WHAT size?
Males and females 4.7 in (12 cm).

WHAT does it eat?
Most *Halichoeres* species feed greedily on a variety of meaty foods. Wild specimens take small molluscs, worms, and crustaceans. Aquarium specimens feed on mysis, brineshrimp and chopped shellfish. Settled individuals may accept dried foods.

WHERE is it from?
Western Indian Ocean, including East Africa, Seychelles, and the Chagos Islands.

WHAT does it cost?
★★☆☆☆ ★★★☆☆
Quite expensive for a species of *Halichoeres*, but not excessively costly.

HOW do I sex it?
Females have a line of reddish pigment along the back, below the dorsal fin.

WHAT kind of tank?
Fish-only or live rock-based fish-only systems.

WHAT minimum size tank?
49 gal (150 l).

HOW do other fish react?
Boisterous or aggressive fish are likely to pick on this wrasse. Being peaceful, it is not well able to defend itself and often falls victim to other midwater swimmers. Best housed with other generally peaceful fish.

WHAT to watch out for?
Poorly acclimatized specimens will have a high breathing rate, and all individuals can be quite timid at first. Avoid fish that do not feed or appear to have difficulty swimming for extended periods. This fish may jump out of an uncovered aquarium.

HOW compatible with inverts and corals?
Should not harm corals, but may target small beneficial snails, such as *Stomatella varia* or even small algae-grazing species. Smaller ornamental shrimp may also become the prey of this fish.

WHAT area of the tank?
Initially shy, hiding in rockwork, but becomes more confident and will swim actively in open water.

HOW many in one tank?
Keep singly. Pairs can be maintained in a sufficiently large system (120 gal/450 l or more).

HOW does it behave?
Not overly aggressive; can be housed with small, peaceful species. It may occasionally chase similar fish, but this is rarely long-lived behavior.

WILL it breed in an aquarium?
It may spawn, but raising the larvae successfully is unlikely.

▲ *Iridis wrasses are very attractive and usually peaceful.*

Labroides dimidiatus

Bluestreak cleaner wrasse

FISH PROFILE

The bluestreak cleaner wrasse is a firm favorite, albeit for the wrong reason. Many see it as useful for removing parasites in the aquarium, but this wrasse does not deal with the types of infestation experienced in a home aquarium, such as white spot or marine velvet. It has also been suggested that the over-collection of cleaner wrasses from the wild leads to a reduction in the health and vitality of the fish that remain on the reef. As a result, the ethics of importing this fish for trade have been questioned.

WHAT size?
Males 4.5 in (11.5 cm); females 3.5 in (9 cm).

WHAT does it eat?
Wild specimens consume mucus and crustacean parasites from other fish. In captivity, they scrutinize other fish, looking for morsels to pick off, but they should also accept small particulate foods, such as chopped mysis or brineshrimp. Enrich these periodically with vitamin supplements.

WHERE is it from?
Red Sea, Indian Ocean, and Western Tropical Pacific.

WHAT does it cost?
★☆☆☆☆   ★★☆☆☆
Inexpensive.

▶ *Only consider specimens that feed greedily in the dealer's tank.*

HOW do I sex it?
Males are larger. Females become males in the absence of the latter, but determining either sex is difficult unless you have a pair.

WHAT kind of tank?
Fish-only; live rock-based fish-only system; or reef aquarium.

WHAT minimum size tank?
26 gal (100 l).

HOW do other fish react?
The vast majority of marine aquarium fish recognize this species as a cleaner and accept its presence in the aquarium. Interestingly, even species that can never before have seen a cleaner wrasse, such as those from the Caribbean region, will still react in the same way as fish that share the wrasse's home range.

WHAT to watch out for?
Ignore skinny or non-feeding specimens. Although the often-repeated idea that this species will not feed in captivity is simply untrue, some individuals will not feed and others require regular offerings to compensate for the energy lost through their active swimming style.

HOW compatible with inverts and corals?
Should not harm corals or ornamental invertebrates.

WHAT area of the tank?
An open-water-swimmer. In larger aquariums, it may form cleaning stations that it rarely leaves and that other fish visit.

HOW many in one tank?
Keep singly or in true male/female pairs.

HOW does it behave?
Never aggressive, but other fish can become irritated if the wrasse takes its cleaning duties too far. A fish visiting a cleaning station shows amazing trust; it opens its gill covers and hovers motionless with its mouth and fins open. Having a piece of dead tissue or a parasite removed can result in a painful nip, which often elicits a chase from the recipient. The wrasse also solicits fish for cleaning, which can irritate them to the point of chasing the cleaner around the aquarium.

WILL it breed in an aquarium?
Potentially, yes.

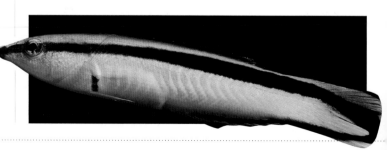

Macropharyngodon meleagris

Leopard wrasse

FISH PROFILE

This sexually dimorphic species has much to offer the modern marine aquarist who understands, and can meet, its demands. It is active during much of the aquarium's daylight period, but burrows into the sand for the night. The presence of live rock improves the chances of keeping this species successfully.

▲ *This female can undergo a significant color change as it becomes a male after some time in the aquarium.*

WHAT size?
Males 5.9 in (15 cm); females seldom more than 4 in (10 cm).

WHAT does it eat?
In the wild, small gastropod molluscs and foraminiferans (small invertebrates associated with live rock). Failure to provide a sufficiently nutritious diet will result in an early demise. Offer a variety of foods, including enriched mysis and brineshrimp, frozen formula products, and dried algae. Feed several times per day.

WHERE is it from?
Eastern Indian Ocean to Western Pacific Ocean.

WHAT does it cost?
★★☆☆☆
Not particularly costly.

HOW do I sex it?
Females have the "leopard" markings, while the larger males have orange and green bands on the head, giving way to a deep rusty red on the body with turquoise spots.

WHAT kind of tank?
This fish does best in a mature aquarium stocked with plenty of live rock. Ideal for a live rock-based fish-only or reef aquarium.

WHAT minimum size tank?
40 gal (150 l).

HOW do other fish react?
Do not stock this species with overly aggressive fish. It is best added before territorial tangs, surgeonfishes, or damselfishes.

WHAT to watch out for?
Specimens that appear to be losing weight require a large number of feeds on enriched particulate foods. Offer small amounts of mysis at regular intervals throughout the day.

HOW compatible with inverts and corals?
Will not harm most invertebrates, but may consume beneficial "hitchhikers" associated with live rock, such as the gastropod mollusc *Stomatella varia*.

WHAT area of the tank?
Close to rockwork or in the substrate at night.

HOW many in one tank?
Keep singly or in pairs. Introducing two females together may result in a pair, as one individual can become a male. Pairs may bicker, but this seldom escalates into real aggression.

HOW does it behave?
A shy species. Can be kept with other *Macropharyngodon* species, but do not overstretch the aquarium's natural resources by keeping too many.

WILL it breed in an aquarium?
Potentially, but no known records.

Novaculichthys taeniourus

Dragon wrasse

FISH PROFILE

The dragon wrasse has a deceptively beautiful juvenile form that encourages many aquarists to acquire it without any research into its maximum size or aquarium behavior. Its alternative name of "rockmover wrasse" is a clue to the problems it can cause in the aquarium. The juvenile body form, and even its swimming motion, have evolved to camouflage the fish among clumps of detached algae such as *Sargassum*.

WHAT size?
Males achieve the maximum size of 11.8 in (30 cm). Females remain a little smaller.

WHAT does it eat?
As this fish turns over rocks, it reveals worms, urchins, molluscs, and various crustaceans. In the aquarium, larger specimens usually accept most meaty foods.

WHERE is it from?
Indo-Pacific from the Red Sea to Central America.

WHAT does it cost?
★★☆☆☆   ★★★☆☆
Almost without exception, only small juveniles measuring no more than 2.3 in (6 cm) are offered for sale. They are not expensive.

▶ *This subadult is beginning to lose its attractive juvenile coloration. Check out those teeth!*

HOW do I sex it?
Differences are only apparent in mature fish. Males are larger, with more elaborate patterning.

WHAT kind of tank?
A fish-only aquarium.

WHAT minimum size tank?
120 gal (450 l).

HOW do other fish react?
Most fish ignore the dragon wrasse. However, without a sufficiently deep substrate (2–4 in/5–10 cm) in which to bury itself, it can become stressed and susceptible to aggression from any fish.

WHAT to watch out for?
As the dragon wrasse grows, its personality changes. From being suitable for the ordinary fish-only aquarium, it becomes a specimen for whom robust tankmates are essential. It has a reputation for jumping out of the aquarium. Ensure that very small specimens are feeding before buying them.

▶ *Do not be tempted by a juvenile of this species unless you can provide for it long, term.*

HOW compatible with inverts and corals?
Not safe with invertebrates.

WHAT area of the tank?
Small fish remain very close to rockwork or sand. Adults are more confident, swimming actively all over the aquarium.

HOW many in one tank?
Keep singly.

HOW does it behave?
This dominant species will target small fish for bullying and may sometimes even eat them if they are not quick enough to escape. Keep it with other sturdy, active species, including puffers and triggers. Try to choose species that will achieve a similar size.

WILL it breed in an aquarium?
No.

Paracheilinus carpenteri

Carpenter's flasher wrasse

FISH PROFILE

The genus *Paracheilinus* contains about 15 stunningly beautiful species that are fairly easy to maintain in a marine aquarium, provided you follow a few rules. Their popularity is not as great as it should be due to a lack of familiarity with the group as a whole and, perhaps, the perception that something so beautiful must be difficult to keep in the aquarium.

WHAT size?
Males 3.1 in (8 cm), females 2.5 in (6.5 cm).

WHAT does it eat?
In the wild, zooplankton and, once settled, readily accepts substitutes in the aquarium. Enriched brineshrimp and chopped mysis offered several times per day should yield enough energy for this active fish. Supplement these items with chopped shellfish. Try to accustom the fish to feeding on flake and granular foods. Some fish will nibble at dried algae.

WHERE is it from?
The Philippines, Indonesia and other localities in the Western Pacific.

WHAT does it cost?
★★☆☆☆
A mid-priced marine fish.

▲ *A gorgeous species that requires a peaceful aquarium to thrive.*

HOW do I sex it?
Males are more brightly colored and larger. They also have a long filament on the dorsal fin that is absent in female specimens.

WHAT kind of tank?
Best kept in a live rock-based fish-only or reef aquarium.

WHAT minimum size tank?
A 46-gallon (175-liter) system should provide enough swimming space.

HOW do other fish react?
Many fish will take exception to Carpenter's flasher wrasse if they are stocked before it. These include any other zooplanktivorous fish with an even remotely territorial bent, dottybacks, other wrasses, damselfishes, and even dwarf angelfishes. Stock this wrasse into a peaceful aquarium only.

WHAT to watch out for?
Make sure that specimens are feeding before you buy them.

In a sparsely decorated dealer's aquarium, they will often sit motionless on the substrate, but good fish will be very alert and become active when food is introduced to the system.

HOW compatible with inverts and corals?
Should not harm any corals or ornamental invertebrates.

WHAT area of the tank?
Settled specimens swim actively in open water.

HOW many in one tank?
Keep one male only per tank. It is possible to maintain small groups or harems with a number of females present.

HOW does it behave?
A very peaceful species that usually ignores other fish, even if they are introduced after it. It will display to females and other males by erecting all its fins to show off its wonderful coloration.

WILL it breed in an aquarium?
Has the potential to spawn in the home aquarium.

Pseudocheilinus hexataenia

Pajama (sixline) wrasse

FISH PROFILE

A "Jekyll and Hyde" fish that elicits strong emotions from aquarists with experience of keeping it. Some report an angelic species with stunning colors and a timid disposition, whereas others baulk at the mere mention of its name, having witnessed it harassing other species to death. Nevertheless, it remains a firm favorite among marine aquarists. A well thought-out stocking plan can help to avoid potential problems.

WHAT size?
Males up to 4 in (10 cm). Females and juveniles will not exceed 2 in (5 cm).

WHAT does it eat?
In the wild, primarily benthic invertebrates, particularly crustaceans. Mysis and brineshrimp make suitable substitutes, but fish accept almost any meaty offering.

WHERE is it from?
Widespread throughout the Red Sea and tropical Indo-Pacific.

WHAT does it cost?
★★☆☆☆
Relatively inexpensive.

▲ *A popular aquarium fish with the potential to be a dream or a nightmare, depending on the individual concerned.*

HOW do I sex it?
Males are larger than females, but otherwise there are no obvious external sexual differences.

WHAT kind of tank?
Fish-only; live rock-based fish-only system; or reef aquarium.

WHAT minimum size tank?
13 gal (50 l) is adequate for a small system housing some live rock and a single sixline wrasse.

HOW do other fish react?
Most marine species, apart from perhaps other members of the genus *Pseudocheilinus,* will not harm this wrasse. Resident mature dottybacks may take exception to it, as they have a similar rock-loving existence.

WHAT to watch out for?
Avoid specimens with discolored patches on the body, as they may have a parasitic infection or still be stressed after importation. Individuals should feed readily.

HOW compatible with inverts and corals?
Will not harm sessile invertebrates or anemones. Individual fish have been known to attack ornamental shrimp.

WHAT area of the tank?
Uses coral branches or porous rockwork as retreats.

HOW many in one tank?
Keep singly or in male/female pairs.

HOW does it behave?
Some territorial individuals are highly aggressive towards new introductions, apparently even to the extent that they attack fish much larger than themselves. Other specimens can be extremely shy, retreating into the rockwork whenever another fish passes. If you should obtain a belligerent individual, then plan any attempt to remove it carefully, as this wily species will not fall for many of the attempts made to catch it.

WILL it breed in an aquarium?
Yes.

Pseudocheilinus octotaenia

Eightline wrasse

FISH PROFILE

The popularity of the eightline wrasse is compromised by the fact that it is a less attractive version of its close relative, the pajama, or sixline, wrasse, *Pseudocheilinus hexataenia*. This is unfortunate, as *P. octotaenia* has much to offer in its own right, not least the fact that it achieves a more robust size and is very hardy in captivity.

WHAT size?
5.5 in (14 cm) maximum. Males are the largest individuals.

WHAT does it eat?
A varied diet consisting mainly of bottom-dwelling invertebrates, plus fish eggs, larvae, and small molluscs. In the aquarium it accepts most foods; mysis, brineshrimp, chopped shellfish, and whole cockles are a good start.

WHERE is it from?
East Africa to Hawaii. Many specimens enter the aquarium hobby through Hawaiian exporters.

WHAT does it cost?
★★☆☆☆
Relatively inexpensive.

▶ *Although safe with corals, eightline wrasses will eat some beneficial creatures.*

HOW do I sex it?
Males are likely to be larger, but otherwise there are no external sexual characteristics.

WHAT kind of tank?
Fish-only; live rock-based fish-only system; or reef aquarium.

WHAT minimum size tank?
48 gal (180 l).

HOW do other fish react?
Conflicts can occur between this and other wrasse species. Dottybacks might also react aggressively towards it, as they often take exception to other fish that want to swim in the same rockwork as they do.

WHAT to watch out for?
Do not be put off by individuals with faded colors, as these may be the result of stress in the dealer's tank or the fact that the fish has been stocked for a long time. After a short period in a home aquarium the colors become brilliant once more.

HOW compatible with inverts and corals?
Should not harm corals but may take small crustaceans, including hermit crabs and small molluscs.

WHAT area of the tank?
Swims among rockwork, thoroughly investigating all available nooks and crannies.

HOW many in one tank?
Keep singly or in male/female pairs.

HOW does it behave?
Although many individuals behave nicely at around 1.5–2.3 in (4–6 cm)—the size at which they are imported—the confidence of this bold species increases as it grows, and it can harass and damage other fish that are unable to escape its attentions. Those that were once aggressors can easily become victims as this fish surpasses them in terms of size and belligerence.

WILL it breed in an aquarium?
Potentially yes.

Wetmorella nigropinnata

Sharpnosed possum wrasse

A shy and secretive species being imported in increasing numbers for the aquarium hobby. As familiarity with this species increases, it will undoubtedly become more popular with aquarists—it is ideal for the peaceful reef aquarium.

▲ *The beautiful possum wrasse is set to become increasingly popular in the hobby.*

WHAT size?
Males to 3¹/₈ in (8 cm); females slightly smaller.

WHAT does it eat?
Wild specimens feed on benthic invertebrates, including copepods, amphipods, and other small crustaceans. In the aquarium they accept brineshrimp, mysis, and chopped shellfish.

WHERE is it from?
Tropical Indo-Pacific.

WHAT does it cost?
★★★☆☆ ★★★★★
Expensive for its size.

HOW do I sex it?
Males are larger and more robust-looking than females. Females have the same coloration as juveniles, namely two pale white vertical bands.

WHAT kind of tank?
A small aquarium with shady areas and plenty of live rock providing many hiding places.

WHAT minimum size tank?
10 gal (40 l), assuming excellent water quality.

HOW do other fish react?
Will not mix well with aggressive fish, including damselfishes and some dottyback species. Not a choice for the busy aquarium.

WHAT to watch out for?
Specimens in dealers' aquariums might be shy and reluctant to venture into the open, but they should feed. Never buy this fish unless you have seen it eat some frozen food, such as brineshrimp.

HOW compatible with inverts and corals?
Completely trustworthy with corals and other invertebrates.

WHAT area of the tank?
In and among rockwork and other decor.

HOW many in one tank?
Keep singly or in pairs. The latter are best acquired as juveniles.

HOW does it behave?
Initially timid, but its confidence will grow, although it seldom ventures far from the refuge of the rocks.

WILL it breed in an aquarium?
Potentially, yes.

Bodianus sp.
Red candystripe hogfish

FISH PROFILE

This newly-discovered hogfish is a beautiful fish currently little known in the hobby. However, its behavior and stunning good looks should guarantee its increased popularity as aquarists become more familiar with its appearance and characteristics.

WHAT size?
Males and females 4.3 in (11 cm).

WHAT does it eat?
The natural diet is likely to resemble that of hogfish that achieve a similar size, such as *B. bimaculatus*, which consumes a wide range of free-living benthic invertebrates. Offer aquarium specimens meaty foods like mysis, brineshrimp, and chopped shellfish initially, gradually introducing more pellet or flaked preparations as the fish becomes more settled.

WHERE is it from?
Central Pacific. Christmas Island, and Indonesia. Aquarium specimens tend to be collected from Bali at present.

WHAT does it cost?
★★★★★
Expensive.

HOW do I sex it?
No known external sexual differences.

WHAT kind of tank?
Fish only; live rock-based fish-only system; or reef aquarium.

WHAT minimum size tank?
53 gal (200 l).

HOW do other fish react?
This hogfish may be bullied by dwarf angelfishes, tangs, or other hogfishes and wrasses.

WHAT to watch out for?
Ignore specimens with a high breathing rate. It is not unusual to see this fish hiding in the corners of the dealer's aquarium when first imported, but it becomes bolder with time.

▼ *This attractive species resembles the rare hogfish* B. opercularis *but is more available in the hobby.*

HOW compatible with inverts and corals?
Should not harm most sessile invertebrates, but can damage or consume ornamental shrimp.

WHAT area of the tank?
Settled fish are active, open water-swimmers, investigating all areas of the aquarium.

HOW many in one tank?
Keep singly.

HOW does it behave?
This fish is likely to be aggressive towards fish with a similar shape or lifestyle to itself. Similar species are known to consume very small fish and this cannot be ruled out in the home aquarium.

WILL it breed in an aquarium?
No.

Bodianus anthioides

Lyretailed hogfish

FISH PROFILE

The lyretailed hogfish is easily recognizable by its orange head and long V-shaped markings on the tail. Juveniles are available when tiny and can prove demanding to keep. However, if provided with good water quality and an aquarium of sufficient size for its long-term requirements, this fish should prove hardy and long-lived.

WHAT size?
Males and females 10 in (25 cm).

WHAT does it eat?
In the wild, a variety of bottom-living invertebrates, such as echinoderms, molluscs, crustaceans, and even small fish. The smallest juveniles (.75–1.25 in/2–3 cm) might need to be fed specially prepared small foods, as even brineshrimp may be too large. Most individuals will accept a variety of meaty foods, including chopped shellfish, mysis, krill, whole clams, and similar.

WHERE is it from?
Widespread in the Indo-Pacific, but never a common species throughout this range. It can be found from the Red Sea to Tuamotu.

WHAT does it cost?
★★★☆☆   ★★★★☆
Moderately expensive.

HOW do I sex it?
No known external sexual differences.

WHAT kind of tank?
Fish-only or live rock-based fish-only system.

WHAT minimum size tank?
106 gal (400 l).

HOW do other fish react?
Juveniles are often tolerated by more aggressive species because they act as cleaners. Mature specimens should be robust enough to look after themselves.

WHAT to watch out for?
Always ensure specimens are feeding before buying them, particularly if they are very small.

HOW compatible with inverts and corals?
Should not harm corals or most sessile invertebrates, but will eat many of the popular ornamental invertebrates stocked as algal grazers or scavengers.

WHAT area of the tank?
An active, open water-swimmer that makes regular visits to the rockwork to hunt for food.

HOW many in one tank?
Keep singly. Males seem to occupy territories covering many square yards, within which will be one or two females. The scale of this makes it almost impossible to recreate in an aquarium situation.

HOW does it behave?
The lyretailed hogfish will assert itself over more retiring species, so stock it with suitably robust fish.

WILL it breed in an aquarium?
No.

▼ *Wild specimens often scour sandy areas for food, blowing away sand with jets of water from the mouth.*

Bodianus mesothorax

Coral hogfish

FISH PROFILE

This species is typical of many hogfish in that it undergoes a major change from juvenile to adult coloration. The juvenile is jet-black with bright yellow spots around the eyes and on the body. The change from juvenile to adult coloration (shown at right) occurs quickly at sizes of around 2 in (5–6 cm). Small specimens in adult coloration tend to be hardier and less timid than juveniles.

WHAT size?
Males and females 10 in (25 cm).

WHAT does it eat?
In the wild, a variety of benthic invertebrates, including echinoderms, polychaetes worms, crustaceans, and molluscs. In the aquarium, any meaty diet should suffice, together with flake and granular food. Recently imported fish usually accept mysis and brineshrimp.

WHERE is it from?
Eastern Indian Ocean and Western Pacific. Imported frequently from the Philippines and Indonesia.

WHAT does it cost?
★★☆☆☆
Inexpensive.

HOW do I sex it?
No known external sexual differences.

WHAT kind of tank?
Fish-only or live rock-based fish-only system.

WHAT minimum size tank?
100 gal (400 l).

HOW do other fish react?
Most fish, other than large wrasses or larger dottybacks, will ignore the coral hogfish. Hogfishes are generally tolerant of aggression from other fish.

WHAT to watch out for?
Newly-imported juvenile specimens are attractive but potentially difficult to maintain. If you must have one, make sure it is feeding well and observe it closely to be sure that it is getting enough to eat.

HOW compatible with inverts and corals?
Will probably not harm corals or other sessile invertebrates, but will attack and eat many of the beneficial detritivores associated

▲ *The adult coloration is markedly different from that of the juvenile.*

with reef aquariums, such as snails and hermit crabs.

WHAT area of the tank?
Juveniles hide in and among rockwork, but once they have undergone their color change they become more confident and swim actively around the aquarium decor, frequently venturing into open water.

HOW many in one tank?
Keep singly.

HOW does it behave?
Hogfishes are sturdy fish with assertive personalities and will dominate less robust tankmates. Do not keep them with very small or sensitive species.

WILL it breed in an aquarium?
Hogfishes have spawned in large-scale laboratory systems, but will probably not do so in a home aquarium.

Bodianus pulchellus

Cuban hogfish

FISH PROFILE

The Cuban hogfish and its close relative, the Spanish hogfish (*Bodianus rufus*), are among the most attractive species from this genus. They are known to spawn together and hybridize in their natural environment. The Cuban hogfish is not commonly seen in Europe but is available, albeit at a premium price. Small juvenile specimens may act as cleaners of other fish.

▲ B. pulchellus *is one of the few vivid red species available for the aquarium.*

WHAT size?
Males and females 11.4 in (29 cm).

WHAT does it eat?
In the wild, a cosmopolitan diet that includes a wide variety of planktonic and benthic invertebrates. In an aquarium, this carnivore should accept most of the commonly available frozen foods, including brineshrimp, mysis, chopped shellfish, and formula foods.

WHERE is it from?
Gulf of Mexico, Caribbean, South America, and isolated areas of the Eastern Atlantic.

WHAT does it cost?
★★★★☆ ★★★★★
Moderate to expensive.

HOW do I sex it?
No known external sexual differences.

WHAT kind of tank?
Fish-only or live rock-based fish-only system.

WHAT minimum size tank?
160 gal (600 l).

HOW do other fish react?
Juveniles may be victimized by larger fish, but are soon able to hold their own among most larger species because they act as cleaner fish. Few fish can bother an adult specimen.

WHAT to watch out for?
Make sure specimens are feeding before buying them and be aware that small individuals develop quickly and soon outgrow the smaller aquarium.

HOW compatible with inverts and corals?
Might be safe with some corals, but not with most ornamental or useful species of invertebrates.

WHAT area of the tank?
An active fish that covers most of the aquarium in its never-ending search for food.

HOW many in one tank?
Keep singly.

HOW does it behave?
A bold fish that often harasses small or more peaceful species. It may even try to eat small gobies, so house it with similar-sized robust fish.

WILL it breed in an aquarium?
No. Some species of hogfish have been spawned in laboratories, but this is unlikely to be practical in most home aquariums.

Choerodon fasciatus

Harlequin tuskfish

FISH PROFILE

A stunning hogfish species that commands a high price due to its scarcity and looks, but proves hardy in the aquarium. Its temperament changes over time, and from a shy, retiring juvenile it becomes a confident, even aggressive, adult.

WHAT size?
Males and females 11.8 in (30 cm).

WHAT does it eat?
In the wild, a variety of benthic invertebrates, including echinoderms, crustaceans, molluscs, and worms. In the aquarium, it will feed initially on brineshrimp and mysis, but offer an increasingly varied diet to satisfy its long-term requirements. Provide chopped shellfish plus frozen formula foods containing a variety of ingredients. Include vitamin supplements.

WHERE is it from?
Indo-Pacific from the Red Sea to Australia.

WHAT does it cost?
★★★★★
Juveniles are the most affordable, but still quite costly for their size. Adults are expensive, particularly those collected from Australian waters, which are perceived to be better colored.

▶ *Australian specimens tend to be the most colorful individuals.*

HOW do I sex it?
No known external sexual differences.

WHAT kind of tank?
Fish-only or live rock-based fish-only system.

WHAT minimum size tank?
120 gal (450 l).

HOW do other fish react?
Any territorial species may assert itself over the juvenile tuskfish and it will often keep out of harm's way where such fish are present. Adults have the confidence to hold their own against boisterous fish, such as mature angelfishes and surgeonfishes.

WHAT to watch out for?
Juveniles may be quite shy when small, and since they hide for extended periods it can be difficult to keep an eye on them in a large aquarium. However, specimens acquired when small and allowed to grow into a system will often be less aggressive than specimens introduced in their adult coloration.

HOW compatible with inverts and corals?
Will not generally harm corals or most sessile invertebrates, but will eat many of the species of invertebrate that comprise the "clean-up crew" of the marine aquarium, namely brachyuran crabs, hermit crabs, and snails. No mobile invertebrate is safe from the attentions of this fish.

WHAT area of the tank?
Juveniles remain close to or behind decor and rockwork. Adults will dominate any open water when not searching every square inch of the aquarium for food.

HOW many in one tank?
Keep singly.

HOW does it behave?
Juveniles are not usually aggressive, but adults can be once settled into their new aquarium. However, with a sensible choice of suitable tankmates, this tuskfish should present few problems.

WILL it breed in an aquarium?
No.

Beautiful but territorial

Tangs from the genera *Zebrasoma* and *Ctenochaetus* and surgeonfishes from the genera *Paracanthurus* and *Acanthurus* are very popular aquarium fish around the world, not only for the outstanding beauty of many species but also because of the useful role they play in the control of nuisance algae. However, these herbivorous fish can be highly territorial and you must take some care when introducing them to an aquarium where some of the more belligerent species are already present. All species possess a pair of modified scales on the caudal peduncle that are scalpel-sharp, hence the name "surgeonfish." These can be used in attack or defense and are capable of inflicting painful wounds to both aquarists and fish. We also include a species of rabbitfish in this section, as many of their aquarium requirements are similar to those of tangs and surgeonfishes.

Price guide

★	$25–$45
★★	$45–$80
★★★	$80–$125
★★★★	$125–$150
★★★★★	$175+

FISH PROFILE

One of two large sailfin tangs with vertical gold and brown bands (the other being *Z. veliferum*). This species can be distinguished by the presence of gold spots on the underside of the body. It is quite a variable species, depending on collection location. Given that the juveniles of the different color morphs can be very similar, it is difficult to anticipate what these fish will look like when they mature.

WHAT size?
Males and females 16 in (40 cm).

WHAT does it eat?
Wild specimens feed on a variety of marine algae and it is important to provide enough green foods, whether as part of specialist formula foods or in dried form. Supplement this with meaty foods, such as chopped shellfish and mysis.

WHERE is it from?
Red Sea to South Africa, India to Java.

WHAT does it cost?
★☆☆☆☆   ★★☆☆☆
Relatively inexpensive.

Zebrasoma desjardinii

Indian Ocean sailfin tang

HOW do I sex it?
No external sexual differences.

WHAT kind of tank?
Fish-only; live rock-based fish-only; or reef aquarium.

WHAT minimum size tank?
132 gal (500 l).

HOW do other fish react?
Tangs can be bullied by other tangs, surgeonfishes, true angelfishes, and dwarf angels. Stocking small individual tangs early on can help to prevent this, but remember that these fish are also very territorial.

WHAT to watch out for?
Avoid skinny specimens and be aware that this tang quickly grows to a large size. A juvenile only a few inches long can reach 12 in (30 cm) in just a couple of years.

HOW compatible with inverts and corals?
Should not harm invertebrates, with the possible exception of the occasional nip at a trailing polyp tentacle.

WHAT area of the tank?
Adults swim in the open areas of the aquarium searching for food. Juveniles are more shy initially, but should settle and become very tame with time.

HOW many in one tank?
Given its eventual large size, keep singly.

HOW does it behave?
All *Zebrasoma* tangs are aggressive to some degree and this species is no exception. Think about the stocking plan before you add the first fish to the aquarium, because this can completely avoid any territoriality problems. It then becomes possible to house this species with other tangs and surgeonfishes, including other *Zebrasoma* spp. and those from the genera *Acanthurus*, *Ctenochaetus* and *Paracanthurus*.

WILL it breed in an aquarium?
No.

▼ *Juveniles like this one are often available when small. Be aware of the size potential of this species before you buy.*

Zebrasoma flavescens

Yellow sailfin tang

The hugely popular yellow sailfin tang is an aquarium icon. It has stunning coloration, achieves a moderate maximum size, and does a useful job in preventing unwanted algae. Of all of the members of the *Zebrasoma* genus—a group that includes several wonderful species—it is perhaps the best.

WHAT size?
Males and females 8 in (20 cm).

WHAT does it eat?
Wild specimens feed on filamentous algae, but graze on many different forms of algae in the home aquarium, including some *Caulerpa* and *Sargassum* species. Where there is no algae present, provide dried forms. (Lettuce is a poor substitute for natural marine algae.) Supplement the algae with mysis, brineshrimp, flaked and pellet foods.

WHERE is it from?
The principal marine fish export from Hawaii. It is endemic to island chains in this Central Tropical Pacific region.

WHAT does it cost?
★★☆☆☆
Relatively inexpensive.

HOW do I sex it?
No external sexual differences.

WHAT kind of tank?
Fish-only; live rock-based fish-only system; or reef aquarium.

WHAT minimum size tank?
80 gal. (300 l).

HOW do other fish react?
Yellow sailfin tangs are capable of looking after themselves, but are unlikely to be able to defend themselves adequately against large surgeonfishes or true angels. Formulate a stocking plan for an aquarium that is to include tangs.

WHAT to watch out for?
Insufficiently fed specimens can appear "pinched" in their pelvic region. Grazing material can help prevent this. Avoid individuals with high breathing rates or any blemishes on the body.

▼ *This tang is one of the most commonly kept marine species.*

HOW compatible with inverts and corals?
Should not harm any invertebrates with the possible exception of some coral polyps. This behavior seems to have more to do with the fish's grazing instincts, rather than finding the polyps palatable.

WHAT area of the tank?
Frequents brightly-lit areas and ventures into the rockwork in its continual search for food.

HOW many in one tank?
Can be kept singly, in pairs, or in small groups. Simultaneous introduction is essential.

HOW does it behave?
Not as aggressive as some members of the genus *Zebrasoma*. It is difficult to be totally sure which species this fish may take exception to. Territorial aggression may be the result of stocking the fish in a system that is too small for its demands.

WILL it breed in an aquarium?
No.

Zebrasoma rostratum

Black (longnose) sailfin tang

FISH PROFILE

With the exception of the hugely expensive *Zebrasoma gemmatum*, the spectacular black sailfin tang is the least common member of the genus available to hobbyists. For this reason alone it is highly prized, but its hardy disposition means it can be successfully maintained in the home aquarium. Its limited availability is determined by the remoteness of its natural range and solitary nature.

WHAT size?
Males and females 8.25 in (21 cm).

WHAT does it eat?
Although a specialist feeder on filamentous algae, it will accept a wide variety of offerings in the aquarium. Provide dried algae, brineshrimp, chopped shellfish, and mysis at least three times a day—more often if it does not seem to be gaining weight.

WHERE is it from?
Found in the Eastern Central Pacific, including the Solomon, Pitcairn, and Tuamotu Islands.

WHAT does it cost?
★★★★★
Very expensive at any size.

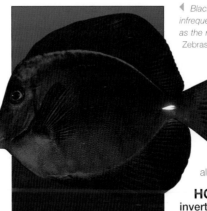

HOW do I sex it?
No external sexual differences.

WHAT kind of tank?
Fish-only, live rock-based fish-only system; or reef aquarium.

WHAT minimum size tank?
132 gal (500 l).

HOW do other fish react?
Other fish will treat the black sailfin tang as they would any other tang. However, its high price is sufficient to ensure that fishkeepers are reluctant to take chances with its introduction, so there is less information about compatibility issues than for more common tangs.

WHAT to watch out for?
Perhaps due to the great distances this species has to travel before it reaches a dealer's tank, it is often quite thin. Small specimens measuring only an

Black tangs are imported infrequently, but are as hardy as the rest of the genus Zebrasoma.

inch or two will need immediate intervention and regular, almost continuous, feeding before they are ready for sale. However tempting, they are best left alone until they have settled.

HOW compatible with inverts and corals?
Should not harm invertebrates. May occasionally nip at polyp tentacles.

WHAT area of the tank?
Initially shy, but settles well. Roams all over the aquarium with the confidence of the genus *Zebrasoma*.

HOW many in one tank?
Best kept singly. Can be maintained in pairs, but introduce these simultaneously.

HOW does it behave?
Will react aggressively to new introductions. Fortunately, this is shortlived and once the new fish knows its place, things should settle down.

WILL it breed in an aquarium?
No.

Zebrasoma scopas

Brown sailfin tang

FISH PROFILE

Perhaps the least desirable of the *Zebrasoma* tangs, but in a genus with so many brightly-colored and spectacular gems to offer, this drabber species is nonetheless an excellent fish for the home aquarium.

◀ *Although less colorful than other tangs, this species is attractive and well-suited to the aquarium.*

WHAT size?
Males and females 7.9 in (20 cm).

WHAT does it eat?
Filamentous algae in the wild, but will graze various species of macro-algae in the home aquarium. Can be useful in preventing some undesirable forms. Offer dried algae that the fish can visit repeatedly to satisfy its grazing instincts, and provide frozen brineshrimp or mysis two or three times daily. With time, this tang should accept flaked or granular foods.

WHERE is it from?
Found throughout much of the Tropical Indo-Pacific, from East Africa to the Tuamotu Islands.

WHAT does it cost?
★☆☆☆☆   ★★☆☆☆
Inexpensive.

HOW do I sex it?
No external sexual differences.

WHAT kind of tank?
Fish-only; live rock-based fish-only system; or reef aquarium.

WHAT minimum size tank?
93 gal (300 l).

HOW do other fish react?
Most fish leave the brown sailfin tang alone. Possible exceptions include other tangs, surgeonfishes, and dwarf angelfishes that might assert themselves over it when it is first introduced into the aquarium.

WHAT to watch out for?
Some specimens may be emaciated by the time they arrive in the dealer's aquarium, and this may prove irreversible in individuals that are reluctant to feed. Small individuals may be quite timid when first introduced; they can remain concealed in rockwork, only venturing out to feed.

HOW compatible with inverts and corals?
Should not harm invertebrates. May occasionally nip at polyp tentacles.

WHAT area of the tank?
Remains close to the rockwork, ready to retreat to safety should danger threaten.

HOW many in one tank?
Best kept singly.

HOW does it behave?
Will react aggressively to new introductions. Fortunately, this is shortlived and once the new fish has been advised who is the boss, things should settle down.

WILL it breed in an aquarium?
No.

Zebrasoma veliferum

Pacific sailfin tang

FISH PROFILE

Juvenile Pacific sailfin tangs have longer dorsal and anal fins than their Indian Ocean relatives (*Zebrasoma desjardinii*) and also lack the gold head and body spots. Otherwise they are very similar, both in terms of appearance and husbandry.

WHAT size?
Males and females 16 in (40 cm).

WHAT does it eat?
Dried forms of algae in a lettuce clip will satisfy the fish's browsing instincts, although it can be quite a messy eater. It should also accept most meaty foods, including brineshrimp (enriched forms containing Omega 3 and spirulina are best) and mysis, together with flake and granular foods.

WHERE is it from?
Tropical Pacific Ocean, from Indonesia to the Hawaiian Islands.

WHAT does it cost?
★☆☆☆☆
★★☆☆☆
Relatively inexpensive.

HOW do I sex it?
No external sexual differences.

WHAT kind of tank?
Fish only; live rock-based fish-only system; or reef aquarium.

WHAT minimum size tank?
132 gal (500 l).

HOW do other fish react?
The long fins of the juveniles can be the target of fin-hippers or take a battering during any territorial disputes.

WHAT to watch out for?
Avoid skinny specimens and be aware that this species quickly grows large. A juvenile specimen measuring only an inch (2.5 cm) can reach 12 in (30 cm) in perhaps only a couple of years at most.

HOW compatible with inverts and corals?
Should not harm invertebrates, with the possible exception of some coral polyps if insufficient dried algae is provided.

WHAT area of the tank?
Small juveniles can spend prolonged periods hiding in caves and crevices, particularly after introduction. Adults are more confident, searching for algae on rockwork or algae-grazing.

HOW many in one tank?
Given its large final size, keep singly.

HOW does it behave?
All *Zebrasoma* tangs are aggressive to some degree and this species is no exception. Mixing it with other tangs is possible with care, and provided the introductions are well researched, any territorial aggression can be minimized. Where potential conflicts are identified, try to add fish of significantly different sizes or, where possible, stock potential aggressors simultaneously.

WILL it breed in an aquarium?
No.

◄ *Juveniles have proportionately long dorsal and anal fins compared with adult specimens.*

Zebrasoma xanthurum

Purple tang

A beautiful and highly desirable Red Sea species. It is available at very small sizes that will develop into hardy specimens. It grows larger than the yellow sailfin tang (*Z. flavescens*), a point to note if you plan to introduce both species. In most situations, and regardless of the other species stocked, this species will become the dominant fish in any aquarium.

▶ A striking species that will often dominate other aquarium inhabitants.

WHAT size?
Males and females 10 in (25 cm).

WHAT does it eat?
Wild specimens favour filamentous algae, and this dietary preference can help to prevent similar undesirable algae in the aquarium. It will also graze on more fleshy forms of macro-algae. Supplement the diet with dried algae, formula foods containing vegetable material and enriched brineshrimp, mysis, and flaked foods. Once settled, this species will accept almost any foods offered.

WHERE is it from?
Red Sea and Persian Gulf. Occasionally reported from the Maldives.

WHAT does it cost?
★★★☆☆ ★★★★☆
A costly species, perhaps due to its Red Sea origins.

HOW do I sex it?
No external sexual differences.

WHAT kind of tank?
Fish-only; live rock-based fish-only system; or reef aquarium.

WHAT minimum size tank?
132 gal (500 l).

HOW do other fish react?
Take care with dwarf angelfishes, other tangs, surgeonfishes, and other boisterous species. However, short-term bickering seldom becomes all-out war and the purple tang is a robust species, able to tolerate unwanted attention, at least in the short term.

WHAT to watch out for?
Pale specimens are generally indicative of individuals that have been in the dealer's tank for some time. Although less attractive than newly-acquired specimens, they can represent good potential purchases as they will be settled and well acclimatized.

HOW compatible with inverts and corals?
Should not harm sessile invertebrates, although it may occasionally nip at coral polyp tentacles. Large specimens have been observed killing and eating ornamental shrimp, but this is rare.

WHAT area of the tank?
Roams around the entire aquarium, asserting itself where necessary over its less dominant tankmates.

HOW many in one tank?
Keep singly.

HOW does it behave?
The behavior of this species can change from quite submissive when small to belligerent when large. Even significantly larger fish can be cowed by this tang, and once it becomes dominant, it is very unwise to introduce any fish larger than a few inches.

WILL it breed in an aquarium?
No.

Ctenochaetus hawaiiensis

Chevron tang

FISH PROFILE

This is the largest species of bristletooth tang, with a marked change between juvenile and adult coloration. Its high price, even as a juvenile specimen, reflects its rarity and the difficulty of collecting it. Juveniles are almost exclusively imported and usually only found in deep-water, coral-rich areas.

WHAT size?
Males and females 10 in (25 cm).

WHAT does it eat?
In the wild, this species uses its brushlike teeth to remove fine algal films and detritus from rock surfaces. Captive specimens should feed on most particulate foods, including mysis and brineshrimp, although they may prefer the latter. Enrich these foods with vitamin supplements for long-term health.

WHERE is it from?
Most specimens hail from the Hawaiian Islands in the Tropical Pacific Ocean, but it is also found throughout Oceania and Micronesia.

WHAT does it cost?
★★★★☆
Perhaps the most expensive bristletooth tang.

HOW do I sex it?
No external sexual differences.

WHAT kind of tank?
Reef aquarium or live rock-based fish-only system.

WHAT minimum size tank?
106 gal (400 l).

HOW do other fish react?
Take care when introducing this species to aquariums with resident *Zebrasoma* spp. tangs or surgeonfishes.

▲ *This species is most commonly available as a juvenile.*

WHAT to watch out for?
Avoid thin or very small juveniles (one inch or less), as well as individuals with washed-out coloration.

HOW compatible with inverts and corals?
Perfectly suited to the reef aquarium.

WHAT area of the tank?
Close to the rockwork on which it browses.

HOW many in one tank?
Keep singly.

HOW does it behave?
In common with all bristletooth tangs, this active species uses its pectoral fins to provide much of its forward momentum. It pauses frequently to feed.

WILL it breed in an aquarium?
No.

▲ *This subadult has lost the juvenile colors.*

Ctenochaetus strigosus

Kole (yellow-eyed) tang

FISH PROFILE

Being a bristletooth tang, this is one of the most useful fish species in any aquarium because it helps to remove detritus from rocky substrates. A close relative, *Ctenochaetus truncatus*, found in the Indian Ocean, also has a gold ring around the eye, but white spots on the body rather than the stripes of *C. strigosus*.

WHAT size?
Males and females 6 in (15 cm).

WHAT does it eat?
Micro-algae and detritus in the wild, yet will readily accept meaty foods, such as mysis and brineshrimp, in the aquarium. Offer dried algae.

WHERE is it from?
Only found in the waters surrounding the Hawaiian Islands and Johnston Islands in the Pacific Ocean.

WHAT does it cost?
★★☆☆☆
Relatively inexpensive.

HOW do I sex it?
No external sexual differences.

WHAT kind of tank?
A reef aquarium with plenty of live rock or live rock fish-only system.

WHAT minimum size tank?
66 gal (250 l).

HOW do other fish react?
Surgeonfishes, dwarf angelfishes, and other tangs present the greatest threat to this fish.

WHAT to watch out for?
Ensure that specimens are feeding well before you buy them. This species is likely to succumb quickly to protozoan parasite infections, so introduce it to a stable aquarium that has been established for a few months.

HOW compatible with inverts and corals?
Will not harm sessile invertebrates or ornamental shrimp.

WHAT area of the tank?
Open water-swimmer that pauses frequently to peck vigorously at the rockwork.

HOW many in one tank?
Keep singly.

HOW does it behave?
Can become territorial towards subsequent fish introductions. Add other tang species simultaneously. Most individuals prove to be fairly benign, but rogue elements are sometimes encountered.

WILL it breed in an aquarium?
No.

▲ The spots on the body of this fish show that it is the Indian Ocean species Ctenochaetus truncatus.

◀ Full of character and highly useful, Ctenochaetus strigosus is an aquarium favorite.

Ctenochaetus tominiensis

Tomini bristletooth tang

FISH PROFILE

One of the least well known species of bristletooth tang, yet with the good points of its close relatives. It is available at relatively small sizes, is hardy and settles well into the home aquarium. It is easy to distinguish from other bristle-tooths by its white tail and the two yellow-orange flashes on the dorsal and anal fins.

◀ *A relatively new species that will increase in popularity as an attractive alternative to C. strigosus.*

WHAT size?
Males and females 5.5 in (13 cm).

WHAT does it eat?
In the wild and in a home aquarium, detritus and algal films, which makes it a highly useful fish species. It will also usually accept dried nori (a seaweed substitute) and particulate frozen foods.

WHERE is it from?
Indonesia, Solomon Islands, and Palau.

WHAT does it cost?
★☆☆☆☆ ★★☆☆☆
Relatively inexpensive. Less often available than *Ctenochaetus strigosus* but similarly priced.

HOW do I sex it?
No external sexual differences.

WHAT kind of tank?
A reef aquarium is best, especially in view of the benefits of introducing this species, but a live rock-based fish-only system is also acceptable.

WHAT minimum size tank?
80 gal (300 l).

HOW do other fish react?
Zebrasoma spp. tangs may react adversely to the introduction of this species, despite the fact that the grazing instincts of both genera complement each other quite nicely.

WHAT to watch out for?
Tomini tangs require excellent water quality and failure to provide this can result in stressed fish that are more likely to pick up protozoan parasite infections.

HOW compatible with inverts and corals?
With the possible exception of the inevitable rogue specimen, tomini tangs will ignore all invertebrates.

WHAT area of the tank?
Open water and close to the rockwork.

HOW many in one tank?
Keep singly.

HOW does it behave?
A busy open-water-swimmer that pauses regularly to peck vigorously at the rockwork using its specialized teeth to "brush" food items from its surface. Although bristletooth tangs are generally less territorial than other tangs or surgeonfishes, take care with subsequent fish introductions.

WILL it breed in an aquarium?
No.

Acanthurus achilles

Achilles surgeonfish

A stunning surgeonfish, regularly imported through Hawaii, but not one of the easier species to maintain in captivity.

WHAT size?
Males and females 19.5 in (24 cm).

WHAT does it eat?
In the wild it browses on filamentous and macroalgae on exposed reefs, but make sure it is taking meaty foods before you buy it. Readily accepts brineshrimp; feed this regularly, enriched with spirulina and Omega 3. With time, it should accept a wider variety of foods. Dried macro-algae is extremely useful in maintaining body weight and also satisfies the fish's grazing instincts.

WHERE is it from?
Southern tip of the Baja Peninsula in Mexico, the Hawaiian Islands and Micronesia.

WHAT does it cost?
★★★☆☆   ★★★★☆
Relatively expensive.

HOW do I sex it?
No external sexual differences.

WHAT kind of tank?
Fish only; live rock-based fish-only system; reef aquarium with care.

WHAT minimum size tank?
120 gal (450 l).

HOW do other fish react?
A territorial species in its own right, the Achilles surgeonfish will be targeted by other surgeonfishes and tangs already in residence.

WHAT to watch out for?
This species is very prone to contracting a protozoan parasite infestation shortly after being introduced to the aquarium, which can be a great problem in reef or live rock-based systems. Try feeding food soaked in commercial garlic extract preparations and using ultraviolet sterilization to help prevent any disease.

HOW compatible with inverts and corals?
May occasionally nip at corals. Will not harm ornamental shrimp.

WHAT area of the tank?
A busy open-water-swimmer that pauses to graze on macro-algae.

HOW many in one tank?
Keep singly.

HOW does it behave?
Will dominate the aquarium and occasionally feels the need to assert itself over its fellow aquarium residents. It will swim with fins erect and flash its tail spines as a sign of annoyance. Such apparent belligerence rarely escalates into a direct assault.

WILL it breed in an aquarium?
No.

▼ *This striking species must be feeding before you acquire it.*

Acanthurus coeruleus

Atlantic blue surgeonfish

FISH PROFILE

The only Atlantic species from this genus that is regularly imported for the aquarium trade. Juveniles have a yellow base color with a pale blue pigment around the pupil of the eye that darkens with age and becomes the characteristic blue coloration of Atlantic and Caribbean surgeonfish.

▶ *The adult coloration of this species is uniformly blue. The juveniles are bright yellow.*

WHAT size?
Males and females maximum 15 in (39 cm), but this is exceptional. A better average is 5–10 in (12–25 cm).

WHAT does it eat?
In the wild, grazes on a variety of seaweeds, other marine algae, and detritus. Captive specimens require plenty of dried marine algae, supplemented with particulate foods such as brineshrimp, mysis, and chopped shellfish.

WHERE is it from?
New York (a seasonal visitor) and Bermuda to the Gulf of Mexico and Brazil. Also found in the Eastern Atlantic at Ascension Island.

WHAT does it cost?
★☆☆☆☆
Relatively inexpensive.

HOW do I sex it?
No external sexual differences.

WHAT kind of tank?
Fish-only; live rock-based fish-only system; or reef aquarium.

WHAT minimum size tank?
106 gal (400 l).

HOW do other fish react?
A. coeruleus will be ignored by most other aquarium species. If trying to introduce it into a system housing *Zebrasoma* tangs, then adding a specimen that is significantly smaller or larger than the existing fish helps to reduce territorial aggression.

WHAT to watch out for?
This fish is capable of adjusting its color intensity, seemingly dependent on its moods. A uniformly dull individual in a dealer's aquarium is not necessarily a low-quality specimen or ailing in some way.

HOW compatible with inverts and corals?
Should not harm sessile invertebrates, corals, or ornamental shrimp. In the absence of sufficient dried algae, the fish's browsing instincts may drive it to nip at polyps.

WHAT area of the tank?
Swims actively in brightly-lit areas of the aquarium.

HOW many in one tank?
Best kept singly. In very large systems it can be maintained in small groups of three to five, a situation that reflects the aggregations it forms in the wild.

HOW does it behave?
Can be highly territorial and harass newly introduced fish to death. The problem appears to center on small individuals stocked as juveniles into tanks that are too small for their long-term maintenance. In large systems the problem is reduced, but this fish should be one of the final larger fish introduced to any aquarium.

WILL it breed in an aquarium?
No.

Acanthurus japonicus

Goldrim surgeonfish

The goldrim surgeonfish is a beautiful species, but not as popular as other surgeonfish species with more vivid coloration. However, it can represent a good alternative to species such as the powder blue (*A. leucosternon)* and Achilles surgeon (*A. achilles).*

▲ *The goldrim is a wonderful alternative to the more available powder blue surgeonfish.*

WHAT size?
Males and females 8.25 in (21 cm).

WHAT does it eat?
Primarily marine algae. Providing the exact type of algae consumed in the wild is not straightforward, so it helps if the fish will accept alternatives such as mysis or brineshrimp until it can be weaned onto dried forms of algae.

WHERE is it from?
Indonesia and the Philippines to Southern Japan.

WHAT does it cost?
★★☆☆☆ ★★★☆☆
Moderately expensive.

HOW do I sex it?
No external sexual differences.

WHAT kind of tank?
Fish-only; live rock-based fish-only system; or reef aquarium.

WHAT minimum size tank?
132 gal (500 l).

HOW do other fish react?
Territorial species such as tangs (*Zebrasoma* spp.) might initially react aggressively, but on the whole, the goldrim surgeonfish is sturdy enough to look after itself. As a general rule, do not mix members of this genus.

WHAT to watch out for?
The reef compatibility of this species is similar to that of the powder blue and Achilles surgeonfish. Individuals commonly contract protozoan infestations within anything from hours to weeks from initial introduction

into the new aquarium. Running an ultraviolet sterilizer is useful during this phase.

HOW compatible with inverts and corals?
Should not harm ornamental shrimp or most sessile invertebrates. May occasionally nip at trailing tentacles of polyps.

WHAT area of the tank?
Swims actively with its pectoral fins, pausing to peck vigorously at rockwork.

HOW many in one tank?
Keep singly.

HOW does it behave?
Aquarium temperament is similar to that of the more aggressive *Acanthurus* species. Stock this species last.

WILL it breed in an aquarium?
No.

Acanthurus leucosternon

Powder blue surgeonfish

FISH PROFILE

The powder blue surgeonfish will always be popular among marine aquarists so long as there are companies prepared to import it. However, despite its wide availability, it is not ideally suited to the marine aquarium. It requires a high degree of care and its temperament makes tankmate selection and stocking regimes critical.

WHAT size?
Most specimens are imported at 3–6 in (8–15 cm). Larger individuals generally settle better than smaller ones. Males and females reach 9 in (23 cm) in length.

WHAT does it eat?
In the wild, feeds almost exclusively on macro-algae. and dried forms are essential for the long-term wellbeing of the powder blue in the aquarium. Also accepts brineshrimp, mysis, chopped shellfish, and dried foods.

WHERE is it from?
East Africa to the Andaman Sea, Indonesia, and Christmas Islands.

WHAT does it cost?
★★☆☆☆
Medium-priced.

HOW do I sex it?
No external sexual differences.

WHAT kind of tank?
Fish-only or live rock-based fish-only system.

WHAT minimum size tank?
120 gal (450 l).

HOW do other fish react?
The powder blue surgeonfish may be targeted by large angelfishes and tangs, but can look after itself. As a general rule, do not mix *Acanthurus* species.

WHAT to watch out for?
The tiny scales on the body show up every blemish, so try to obtain a clean specimen. Individuals should be eating brineshrimp or mysis before you acquire them. Specimens that appear washed out may have been in the dealer's tank for some time. They often represent good buys and will regain their colors once introduced into a larger, less stressful aquarium.

HOW compatible with inverts and corals?
Unlikely to harm any sessile invertebrates or ornamental shrimp. The powder blue can become infested with protozoan parasites shortly after introduction. Where copper medication cannot be used, this can present major problems. For this reason it is difficult to recommend stocking this fish where corals are present.

WHAT area of the tank?
An active swimmer over rockwork. Becomes very tame.

HOW many in one tank?
Keep singly.

HOW does it behave?
Not only is it highly territorial and belligerent, it also has a pair of scalpel-sharp modified scales located at the base of the tail with which it can slice a fish to pieces. The powder blue should be the final fish introduced in any stocking regime.

WILL it breed in an aquarium?
No.

◀ *This is an aggressive species and should ideally be the final large addition to a marine aquarium.*

Acanthurus lineatus

Clown (lined) surgeonfish

FISH PROFILE

This strikingly-colored surgeonfish is one of the most widely available to marine hobbyists, but shares many of the less desirable traits of its close relative the powder blue surgeonfish (*Acanthurus leucosternon*). However, one advantage of *A. lineatus* is that it is often available at much smaller sizes than the powder blue, and therefore the impact of territorial aggression is reduced, at least until it grows.

WHAT size?
Up to 15 in (38 cm; males are larger.

WHAT does it eat?
Feeds primarily on algae, but has been observed taking crustaceans, such as free-swimming shrimp. Usually accepts mysis or brineshrimp. Offer these a few times a day and provide dried algae daily to satisfy the fish's herbivorous requirements.

WHERE is it from?
The Tropical Indo-Pacific from East Africa to the Hawaiian Islands. Not in the Red Sea.

WHAT does it cost?
★☆☆☆☆   ★★☆☆☆
Relatively inexpensive. Small specimens are particularly reasonable.

HOW do I sex it?
Males are usually larger, but this is difficult to ascertain unless you have specimens approaching their maximum wild size. Most fish offered for sale will be juveniles.

WHAT kind of tank?
Fish-only; live rock-based fish-only; or reef aquarium, with care.

WHAT minimum size tank?
200 gal (750 l) or more for long-term maintenance.

HOW do other fish react?
Can be bullied by tangs and dwarf angelfishes when small, but as it grows, its active swimming and belligerent nature will ensure that few fish will ever pester it.

WHAT to watch out for?
Avoid skinny specimens that appear unwilling to feed. The most desirable individuals will be swimming actively and consistently, and have bright colors.

HOW compatible with inverts and corals?
As with all *Acanthurus* species, take care where corals are present, as the fish is prone to infestation by protozoan parasites.

Individuals that are not provided with enough grazing material may peck at polyp tentacles.

WHAT area of the tank?
A small specimen (less than 2.3 in/6 cm) may be shy at first and hide in rockwork. As it settles and grows, it should become an active swimmer over the rockwork, pausing often to graze on algae.

HOW many in one tank?
Keep singly.

HOW does it behave?
Introducing the most benign fish to an aquarium housing a dominant clown surgeonfish can result in disaster, particularly if the resident is a large specimen. The tail spines are capable of inflicting terrible damage and even robust species, such as true angelfishes, can be killed by a territorial surgeonfish.

WILL it breed in an aquarium?
No.

▼ *A stunning species that shares the territorial nature of most other* Acanthurus *surgeonfish.*

Acanthurus pyroferus

Pacific Ocean mimic surgeonfish

FISH PROFILE

A. pyroferus is an amazing fish that mimics two, possibly three species. Where it shares its range with the lemonpeel angelfish *(Centropyge flavissimus)*, the juveniles have the characteristic yellow body with blue eye-ring. If this species is not present then it may mimic the half-black *(C. vroliki)* or herald's angel *(C. heraldi)*. *A. pyroferus* has more attractive adult coloration than *A. tristis* (the Indian Ocean mimic surgeonfish).

◀ *Although not the brightest or most colorful surgeonfish, this species still has many fans in the marine hobby.*

▼ *This juvenile is the form that mimics the lemonpeel angelfish* (Centropyge flavissimus).

WHAT size?
Males and females 10 in (25 cm).

WHAT does it eat?
In the wild, a variety of algae, plus the associated animal life. Offer brineshrimp, mysis, flake, and dried algae to keep this species in good shape.

WHERE is it from?
Despite the common name, this species is Indo-Pacific in origin, being found from the Seychelles in the west to the Great Barrier Reef and Vanuatu.

WHAT does it cost?
★☆☆☆☆ ★★☆☆☆
The price of juveniles can depend on their coloration. Those that mimic the lemonpeel angelfish are the most expensive, while half-black specimens cost the least. None is excessively expensive.

HOW do I sex it?
No external sexual differences.

WHAT kind of tank?
Fish-only; live rock-based fish-only system; or reef aquarium.

WHAT minimum size tank?
120 gal (450 l) for an adult specimen.

HOW do other fish react?
This species can be the subject of bullying by tangs and other surgeonfishes. It is possible to maintain juveniles with the dwarf angelfish species they mimic if you are prepared to endure the occasional skirmish between them.

WHAT to watch out for?
This species usually settles and feeds well, even in a retailer's tank. Avoid skinny specimens.

HOW compatible with inverts and corals?
Should not harm corals, other sessile invertebrates, or ornamental shrimp.

WHAT area of the tank?
Although juveniles may be quite shy at first and spend extended periods in spaces in the rockwork, they soon settle and begin to scour the rockwork for algae or other tasty morsels.

HOW many in one tank?
Keep singly.

HOW does it behave?
For those aquarists who like the shape and activity of the surgeonfish but cannot stock a fish with aggressive tendencies, the Pacific mimic is ideal. It has subtle yet beautiful markings and is one of the most peaceful representatives of this otherwise territorial genus.

WILL it breed in an aquarium?
No.

Acanthurus sohal

Sohal (Arabian) surgeonfish

A large, active species of surgeonfish that proves very hardy in an aquarium situation. As a fish of shallow reef surge zones, it is very at home in a brightly-lit aquarium, but due to its substantial potential size it should only be stocked in a suitably large tank.

WHAT size?
Males and females 16 in (40 cm).

WHAT does it eat?
Wild specimens prefer brown macro-algae and also some filamentous forms. In general, this is not a useful fish for tackling blooms of hair-algae in the home aquarium. Feed aquarium fish a combination of meaty foods and dried forms of algae. They also accept frozen preparations containing vegetable material.

WHERE is it from?
Endemic to the Red Sea and Arabian Gulf.

WHAT does it cost?
★★★☆☆   ★★★★☆
As a fish confined to the Red Sea and Arabian Gulf, it is subject to the premium that all fish collected in these waters seem to demand, and is one of the more expensive surgeonfishes as a result.

HOW do I sex it?
No external sexual differences.

WHAT kind of tank?
Fish-only; live rock-based fish-only system; or reef aquarium.

WHAT minimum size tank?
200 gal (750 l).

HOW do other fish react?
Most fish, with the possible exception of large tangs or angelfishes, will not react adversely to the introduction of the sohal surgeonfish. Introducing a specimen significantly larger or smaller than the existing aquarium occupants can help to minimize any conflict.

WHAT to watch out for?
Always observe the fish feeding before buying. Those that do not feed in the dealer's tank are the exception rather than the rule.

HOW compatible with inverts and corals?
May occasionally nip at button polyps (Zoanthids) or large-polyp stony corals. Will not harm other sessile invertebrates or ornamental shrimp.

WHAT area of the tank?
An active swimmer over rockwork and aquarium decor.

HOW many in one tank?
Keep singly.

HOW does it behave?
Highly aggressive towards new introductions, especially those that are similar in size to itself. It should be the final introduction to the aquarium wherever possible.

WILL it breed in an aquarium?
No.

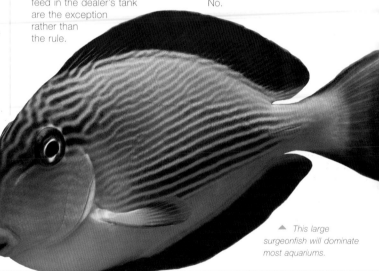

▲ *This large surgeonfish will dominate most aquariums.*

Acanthurus tristis

Indian Ocean mimic surgeonfish

FISH PROFILE

The adult coloration is nothing exceptional: at best it is something a bit different. The appeal of this species lies in the juvenile specimens, which mimic the pattern of the dwarf angelfish *Centropyge eibli* almost perfectly. It is thought that by the time the juvenile surgeonfishes settle out onto the reef from their planktonic existence to coexist with the similar-sized dwarf angelfishes, the latter have been settled out for quite a few weeks. Through experience and attrition, they have therefore become difficult for predators to catch and are therefore worth mimicking.

WHAT size?
Males and females 10 in (25 cm).

WHAT does it eat?
Feeds readily on a variety of meaty foods. Offer chopped shellfish, brineshrimp, mysis, and dried algae.

WHERE is it from?
Indian Ocean, from India to Indonesia.

WHAT does it cost?
★☆☆☆   ★★☆☆☆
Only juveniles are usually offered for sale and are moderately priced.

HOW do I sex it?
No external sexual differences.

WHAT kind of tank?
Fish-only; live rock-based fish-only system; or reef aquarium.

WHAT minimum size tank?
80 gal (300 l).

HOW do other fish react?
Most fish will leave this species alone. Possible exceptions include dwarf angelfishes (it is difficult to know whether their aggression is because they think *A. tristis* is another dwarf angelfish or whether they recognize it as a surgeonfish) and *Zebrasoma* spp tangs. It is possible to house this fish with the dwarf angelfish it mimics.

WHAT to watch out for?
Specimens approaching 3.5–4 in (9–10 cm) and still showing their juvenile coloration are likely to change into the drab brown livery of the adult sooner rather than later.

▲ *A juvenile mimic surgeonfish (top) mimics a* Centropyge eibli *below it.*

HOW compatible with inverts and corals?
Should not harm sessile invertebrates or ornamental shrimp.

WHAT area of the tank?
This species can be shyer than others from the genus, but a settled specimen makes regular excursions into more brightly-lit areas of the aquarium to peck at rockwork and browse on algae.

HOW many in one tank?
Keep singly.

HOW does it behave?
One of the most laid-back and tolerant surgeonfishes. The only fish under any direct threat are members of the same species.

WILL it breed in an aquarium?
No.

Naso lituratus

Orangespine unicornfish

A large species of unicornfish often encountered on tropical reefs in male/female pairs. The Indian Ocean and Red Sea form was once thought to be *N. lituratus*, but has recently been renamed *Naso elegans*. *N. lituratus* can be distinguished quite easily by its brown-black dorsal fin, whereas in *N. elegans* it is bright yellow. Husbandry is the same for each.

WHAT size?
Males and females 18 in (45 cm).

WHAT does it eat?
In the wild, it grazes primarily on brown macro-algae, including *Sargassum*, often found growing on live rock from Fiji. Captive specimens can be successfully weaned onto mysis and brineshrimp and should take dried foods with time. Be sure to provide dried algae for long-term maintenance and feed the fish several times each day.

WHERE is it from?
Much of the tropical Pacific Ocean.

WHAT does it cost?
★★☆☆☆ ★★★★★
A medium-priced species unless available when very small. Usually less expensive than *Naso elegans*.

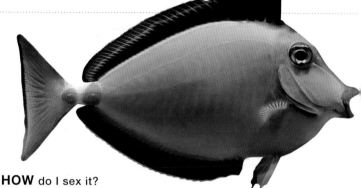

▲ *A beautiful and peaceful fish.*

HOW do I sex it?
Large male specimens have long trailing streamers arising from each corner of the tail fin.

WHAT kind of tank?
Fish-only; fish-only with live rock; or a large reef aquarium with plenty of swimming space.

WHAT minimum size tank?
210–238 gal (800–900 l) is suitable for all but the very largest specimens.

HOW do other fish react?
Despite its very large and well-developed caudal spines, the orangespine unicornfish is not particularly able to defend itself against more aggressive species, such as large *Acanthurus* spp. surgeonfishes or larger tangs. It will cohabit with these species, but should be introduced first to minimize potential problems.

WHAT to watch out for?
Only buy specimens that you know are feeding. Look for signs of weight loss, which is common in underfed specimens of this active species. Large individuals are capable of moving unsecured pieces of rockwork or coral base rock as they browse on the algae growing there.

HOW compatible with inverts and corals?
May occasionally nip at corals.

WHAT area of the tank?
An open water-swimmer that frequently pauses to browse on algae growing on the rockwork.

HOW many in one tank?
Most aquariums will only be large enough for a single individual, but its relaxed temperament means that a very large aquarium could house pairs or even groups.

HOW does it behave?
Peaceful. Often partners with other species as they search for food.

WILL it breed in an aquarium?
Pairs have been observed spawning in the wild, but this has not been recorded in captivity.

Paracanthurus hepatus

Regal (Pacific blue) tang

FISH PROFILE

This is the only species within the genus. The regal tang is one of the most popular marine fish due to its striking coloration and ready availability. However, this does not mean that it is ideally suited to every aquarium that it finds itself in.

WHAT size?
Wild males and females 12 in (30 cm), but nearer 8 in (20 cm) in captivity.

WHAT does it eat?
Juveniles feed on zooplankton. Adults incorporate plenty of algae into their diet and readily accept dried forms.

WHERE is it from?
A wide-ranging species from the tropical Indo-Pacific, found from East Africa to Samoa.

WHAT does it cost?
★☆☆☆☆   ★★★☆☆
Very small specimens are likely to be expensive by the standards of most other tang species, but still within the range of most pockets.

HOW do I sex it?
No external sexual differences.

WHAT kind of tank?
Fish-only; live rock-based fish-only system; or a reef aquarium.

WHAT minimum size tank?
To house this species long term, the minimum size aquarium is 130 gal (500 l) and preferably larger. Small specimens will very quickly outgrow a small aquarium.

HOW do other fish react?
Small juveniles may be targeted by damselfishes or small tangs.

WHAT to watch out for?
The regal tang is prone to contracting protozoan parasite infestations shortly after introduction. This is a problem in itself, but even more so in a live rock-based system or one in which corals are present.

▼ *The solid blue coloration can fade if the water quality is poor.*

Offering foods soaked in garlic preparations can help prevent an outbreak.

HOW compatible with inverts and corals?
Many aquarists successfully keep regal tangs with corals. However, rogue individuals can nip at the polyps of sessile invertebrates and clam mantles. Offering dried forms of algae to satisfy the fish's browsing instincts may control such behavior.

WHAT area of the tank?
Open-water-swimmers.

HOW many in one tank?
House large specimens singly or in pairs. Small juveniles school naturally and can be kept in large numbers.

HOW does it behave?
Less aggressive or territorial than most tangs and surgeonfishes, but will dominate less assertive species. Small specimens will bicker among themselves and the smallest and weakest may die. Regal tangs are lively and active unless stressed or threatened, in which case they wedge themselves into any available crevice.

WILL it breed in an aquarium?
No.

Siganus vulpinus

Foxface rabbitfish

A peaceful, algae-grazing
species that makes a
reasonable alternative to
surgeonfishes or tangs,
although perhaps
not quite as
good-looking as
some of those
species.

WHAT size?
Males and females 9.5 in
(24 cm).

WHAT does it eat?
Most frozen foods and flake.
Provide dried algae for grazing.
Wild specimens feed primarily
on algae and zooplankton.

WHERE is it from?
Tropical Western Pacific.

WHAT does it cost?
★☆☆☆☆   ★★☆☆☆
Small specimens are very
cheap and specimens of most
sizes are very affordable.

▲ *Take care when introducing this
species—it has venomous spines.*

HOW do I sex it?
No external sexual differences.

WHAT kind of tank?
Fish-only; live rock-based fish-
only; a reef system only with care.

WHAT minimum size tank?
66 gal (250 l) should be sufficient
for all but the largest single
specimen.

HOW do other fish react?
Territorial tangs and surgeonfishes
are unlikely to react well to the
introduction of this species, but
after the initial aggressive welcome
they should settle down.

WHAT to watch out for?
Venomous spines can inflict painful
injuries if handled carelessly.

HOW compatible with inverts
and corals?
Individuals will not harm crabs or
shrimp, but may very occasionally
nip at sessile invertebrates.
Satisfying their grazing instincts
may solve this problem.

WHAT area of the tank?
Open water but close to rockwork.
Specimens become extremely
tame in a short period of time.

HOW many in one tank?
Can be kept in pairs or small
groups, but provide a large
aquarium (120 gallons/450 liters
or more) if housing more than one
specimen.

HOW does it behave?
Peaceful. Not a strongly territorial
species.

WILL it breed in
an aquarium?
No.

Zanclus cornutus

Moorish idol

FISH PROFILE

An attractive, unique species, often acquired by aquarists with little realistic chance of maintaining it successfully for any length of time. However, it is not as impossible to keep as some aquarists suggest. Before buying a specimen, consider very carefully whether you can commit the time and effort needed to maintain it long-term.

WHAT size?
Males and females 9 in (23 cm).

WHAT does it eat?
Accepts zooplankton and its aquarium substitutes. Enrich the diet with vitamin supplements. Entice the fish with as many different offerings as possible. Proprietary formulations for sponge-browsing marine fish are also helpful. Be sure to feed the fish several times a day.

WHERE is it from?
Found throughout the Tropical Indo-Pacific, from East Africa to the Hawaiian Islands, the Gulf of California and Peru.

WHAT does it cost?
★★★☆☆ ★★★★★
Depends on the point of origin. Many of the better-quality specimens are exported via Hawaii and may be more expensive than individuals collected elsewhere.

HOW do I sex it?
No external sexual differences.

WHAT kind of tank?
A mature, live rock-based system is essential.

WHAT minimum size tank?
132 gal (500 l).

▼ *An aquarium with plenty of live rock is best for this species.*

HOW do other fish react?
Take care when introducing this species into an aquarium containing territorial tangs or surgeonfishes. Keeping it with other species that browse on sponges will reduce the amount of naturally-occurring food available to it.

WHAT to watch out for?
Never buy a specimen without observing it feeding and being confident that you have the skills to maintain it successfully. Avoid specimens that appear emaciated and try to source individuals that have been in the dealer's aquarium for more than a few days.

HOW compatible with inverts and corals?
Likely to consume any of the encrusting animals that make up its natural diet. It will ignore non-sessile invertebrates.

WHAT area of the tank?
An active, open-water species that investigates the rockwork for any morsels of food to peck at.

HOW many in one tank?
Can be maintained in twos or threes in a very large aquarium. Best kept singly if in any doubt.

HOW does it behave?
Becomes very tame and feeds boldly once settled.

WILL it breed in an aquarium?
No.

Treat with respect

Triggerfishes are named for their short, curved dorsal spine that can be used to anchor the fish into rocky crevices from which they cannot be removed unless they intentionally release their locking mechanism. The group contains many genera with a wide variety of temperaments and dietary preferences and should not be purchased unless the aquarist has a system capable of holding an individual in the long term. Species that feed largely on zooplankton tend to be less aggressive or destructive in an aquarium.

Price guide

★	$25–$45
★★	$45–$70
★★★	$70–$115
★★★★	$115–$175
★★★★★	$175+

Pufferfishes are able to inflate their bodies by sucking in water, making themselves appear larger and more intimidating to potential aggressors. Some, like species from the genus *Diodon*, are covered with spines that become erect when they inflate, making them even less appealing to predators. Some species have skin or internal organs that are toxic.

FISH PROFILE

This beautiful triggerfish is not sensitive or difficult to keep, but tankmates robust enough to withstand its opportunistic aggression are hard to find. As a result, it is often returned to the dealer after killing all its tankmates. However, in the right setting it will become very tame, rewarding the aquarist with fascinating behavior and longevity.

WHAT size?
Males and females 12 in (30 cm).

WHAT does it eat?
In the wild, echinoderms, corals, fish, algae crustaceans, and worms. A captive individual will accept shellfish, mysis, and brineshrimp, plus dead fish such as lancefish or sand eels. Offering molluscs with their shells on can help distract the fish from its otherwise aggressive behavior, if only temporarily. It will also nibble at dried algae in a lettuce clip.

WHERE is it from?
Red Sea and the Indo-Pacific. Some authorities maintain that specimens obtained from the Red Sea are far more benign than their Indo-Pacific relatives.

WHAT does it cost?
★☆☆☆☆   ★★☆☆☆
Inexpensive.

Balistapus undulatus

Undulate triggerfish

HOW do I sex it?
No known external sexual differences.

WHAT kind of tank?
Fish-only aquarium.

WHAT minimum size tank?
145 gal (550 l).

HOW do other fish react?
Naturally aggressive fish can be aggressive towards this triggerfish, at least in the days following its introduction. However, its confidence grows as its size increases and the aggressors often become the victims of this powerful fish.

WHAT to watch out for?
There is little to worry about when selecting this species. It is not unusual for small individuals to appear timid, but they will usually feed after a few minutes.

HOW compatible with inverts and corals?
Do not house with any invertebrates.

WHAT area of the tank?
Juveniles can spend large amounts of time in hiding, but as they settle and grow they will dominate all areas of the aquarium.

HOW many in one tank?
Keep singly.

HOW does it behave?
Aggression in all but a few specimens is the norm rather than the exception. For the fewest problems, it is best to maintain this fish in an aquarium on its own.

WILL it breed in an aquarium?
No.

▼ *This beautiful species is often available when small. Keep it only if you are prepared to forgive its aggressive behavior.*

Balistoides conspicillum

Clown triggerfish

FISH PROFILE

A beautiful fish that deserves the popularity it has earned among marine aquarists. However, before acquiring a specimen, it is important to appreciate its rapid growth rate and dominant personality. Aquarists who can satisfy the long-term demands of this species will be rewarded by a long-lived, gorgeous and highly entertaining marine fish.

▲ *This adult specimen clearly shows why this fish is such an aquarium favourite.*

WHAT size?
Males and females 18 in (45 cm).

WHAT does it eat?
In the wild, mainly hard-shelled invertebrates such as crabs, sea urchins, and molluscs, which it crushes with its large and powerful teeth. Aquarium specimens will accept a range of meaty foods. Be sure to offer a varied diet and provide shell-on foods regularly.

WHERE is it from?
East Africa to Indonesia in the Tropical Indo-Pacific.

WHAT does it cost?
★★☆☆☆   ★★★★★
An expensive triggerfish at any size. Some collectors charge more for small individuals than larger specimens, reflecting the desirability of each in the hobby.

HOW do I sex it?
No obvious external differences.

WHAT kind of tank?
Fish-only aquarium. May be safe in a live rock-based system, but will gradually gnaw away the rock.

WHAT minimum size tank?
132 gal (500 l).

HOW do other fish react?
Most fish will ignore the introduction of a clown triggerfish, even when it is only a few inches long. Small territorial wrasses and damselfishes might represent the greatest threat, but will back off as the specimen grows.

WHAT to watch out for?
Do not be tempted to buy a highly attractive small specimen unless you have the means to care for it long term. Individuals for sale should have solid colors, be bold, and feed readily. Careless aquarists may experience nasty bites!

HOW compatible with inverts and corals?
Cannot be housed with corals, sessile invertebrates, or ornamental shrimp.

WHAT area of the tank?
Newly-introduced specimens may spend prolonged periods close to rockwork or even in hiding, but as they become more settled and confident they will dominate the entire aquarium and investigate it thoroughly in search of food.

HOW many in one tank?
This species is a natural loner and should be housed singly.

HOW does it behave?
Assume that this fish will become quite aggressive and potentially lethal towards its tankmates. Although this transition from a relatively peaceful juvenile does not seem to take place in every case and there are no advance warnings, choose tankmates at the outset in anticipation of the likely outcome.

WILL it breed in an aquarium?
No.

Odonus niger
Blue triggerfish

FISH PROFILE

Another appealing species of triggerfish that usually proves problematic in the long term. It is available for sale at temptingly small sizes and its attractive swimming motion means that it is often bought by aquarists who are unable to meet its requirements.

WHAT size?
Males and females 18 in (45 cm).

WHAT does it eat?
In the wild, zooplankton and sponges. Will accept most of the foods readily available to marine aquarists. Try to provide a variety of meaty foods and feed the fish regularly—at least three times per day.

WHERE is it from?
Indo-Pacific, from the Red Sea and East Africa to Australia and Micronesia.

WHAT does it cost?
★☆☆☆☆ ★★☆☆☆
Inexpensive.

HOW do I sex it?
No external sexual differences.

WHAT kind of tank?
Fish-only; live rock-based fish-only system.

WHAT minimum size tank?
132 gal (500 l).

HOW do other fish react?
Most fish completely ignore *O. niger* when it is first introduced.

WHAT to watch out for?
Some individuals behave in an exemplary manner, whereas others are almost inconceivably difficult. Individual fish have been known to target the eyes of other fish, removing them quickly and efficiently. However,

▼ *This species needs plenty of swimming space and very robust tankmates.*

many specimens present few problems, other than their large maximum size.

HOW compatible with inverts and corals?
Likely to nibble at most corals. Offering dried algae and feeding it regularly can help to prevent this behavior, but it cannot be considered trustworthy.

WHAT area of the tank?
An active, open water-swimming species that pauses regularly to inspect the rockwork and/or other decor in its never-ending search for food.

HOW many in one tank?
Can be kept in pairs or small groups, provided you appreciate the demands a number of these large fish will put on an aquarium's water quality.

HOW does it behave?
May be too aggressive for many small species of fish, some of which might even be eaten. Its temperament with similar-sized or larger fish will depend on the individual concerned; it could be aggressive or submissive.

WILL it breed in an aquarium?
No.

Pseudobalistes fuscus

Blue jigsaw triggerfish

FISH PROFILE

The beautiful juvenile blue jigsaw triggerfish will undoubtedly tempt many aquarists who do not suspect that it will achieve huge proportions and has the capacity to destroy any aquarium decor. However, other aquarists value this species for exactly the same reasons!

WHAT size?
Males and females 22 in (55 cm).

WHAT does it eat?
In the wild, echinoderms, crustaceans, corals, and almost anything meaty into which it can sink its well-developed teeth. Aquarium specimens eat almost anything offered. Juveniles can be more finicky than older individuals and may need brineshrimp or mysis.

WHERE is it from?
Red Sea and Indian Ocean. Less common, but present, in the Pacific Ocean.

WHAT does it cost?
★★☆☆☆
Moderately expensive. Juveniles are almost exclusively available, as they have the attractive neon-blue lines on the body.

HOW do I sex it?
No known external differences.

WHAT kind of tank?
Fish-only aquarium.

WHAT minimum size tank?
238 gal (900 l).

HOW do other fish react?
Juveniles can be susceptible to aggression from other fish, but they tend to hide and can be quite shy for prolonged periods until they grow large enough to hold their own.

WHAT to watch out for?
Avoid fish with cloudy eyes or that are not feeding. It is normal for this species to be quite reclusive, but its appetite usually gets the better of it and it will feed in the dealer's tank.

HOW compatible with inverts and corals?
Do not maintain with any invertebrates.

WHAT area of the tank?
Will dominate the entire aquarium.

HOW many in one tank?
Keep singly.

HOW does it behave?
Although not particularly belligerent, its size, appetite, and robust nature demand that it is maintained with suitably sturdy species. Large angelfishes and pufferfishes are suitable.

WILL it breed in an aquarium?
No.

▼ *The yellow base color of this juvenile will become blue as it matures.*

Rhinecanthus aculeatus

Picasso triggerfish

FISH PROFILE

One of the most familiar marine fish species and certainly one of the most commonly kept triggerfishes. The Picasso is named for the delicate pigment markings on the body that look as though they have been applied with a paintbrush.

▶ *Maintain this species with other hardy marine fish that are able to look after themselves.*

WHAT size?
Males and females 12 in (30 cm).

WHAT does it eat?
This fish is a true omnivore, consuming anything and everything that could be remotely construed as edible. Provide it with plenty of meaty foods, including shell-on molluscs and crustaceans. The types of food offered are less important than providing variety.

WHERE is it from?
Eastern Atlantic, tropical Indo-Pacific to Hawaiian Islands.

WHAT does it cost?
★☆☆☆☆   ★★☆☆☆
Inexpensive.

HOW do I sex it?
No obvious external differences.

WHAT kind of tank?
Fish-only or live rock-based fish-only systems.

WHAT minimum size tank?
132 gal (500 l).

HOW do other fish react?
Most fish will ignore the Picasso, with the possible exception of larger or similar triggerfishes.

WHAT to watch out for?
Small (1 in/3 cm) specimens are very tempting, but do not buy this fish unless you are sure you can satisfy its long-term demands, particularly a sufficiently large aquarium. Heater guards are recommended.

HOW compatible with inverts and corals?
Will harm many corals, sessile invertebrates, and crustaceans. Should not be trusted in any aquarium housing invertebrates.

WHAT area of the tank?
Investigates every square centimetre of the aquarium.

HOW many in one tank?
Best kept singly.

HOW does it behave?
Boisterous when small, becoming increasingly aggressive as it grows. Specimens mature at around 5.5 in (14 cm) and will relentlessly bully any slightly delicate species.

WILL it breed in an aquarium?
No.

Xanthichthys auromarginatus

Blue throat triggerfish

FISH PROFILE

Given its natural zooplankton-feeding instincts, rather than the decor-wrecking characteristics of many of its relatives, this is arguably the species of triggerfish most suited for introduction into a reef aquarium.

WHAT size?
Males and females 12 in (30 cm).

WHAT does it eat?
In time, aquarium specimens will accept most foods, including frozen and prepared diets. Offer a variety, with occasional vitamin supplements.

WHERE is it from?
Indo-Pacific. Most specimens are imported through Hawaii.

WHAT does it cost?
★★☆☆☆ ★★★☆☆
A middle-priced fish. Often available in pairs or trios, but these command a premium.

HOW do I sex it?
Males have a blue throat patch and a bright yellow edge to the tail, dorsal and ventral fins.

WHAT kind of tank?
Superb in fish-only or live rock-based fish-only systems, as they can be maintained long-term without ever becoming very aggressive. Can be stocked into a reef aquarium with care.

WHAT minimum size tank?
120 gal (450 l) when small; up to 200 gal (750 l) if fully grown.

HOW do other fish react?
May not prosper where other large, more aggressive species of open-water fish are housed.

WHAT to watch out for?
Despite its size, this can be a shy species, particularly when first introduced into the aquarium.

HOW compatible with inverts and corals?
Should not harm any sessile invertebrates, but may not be completely trustworthy with all species of ornamental shrimp. Appears to ignore most larger *Lysmata* spp.

WHAT area of the tank?
Once settled, this species enjoys swimming in open water above rocky or sandy substrates.

HOW many in one tank?
Can be kept singly; in male/female pairs; or in trios of two females to one male.

HOW does it behave?
Unlike many triggerfishes, it is very rarely aggressive towards other fish, although it will have occasional disputes with members of the same species.

WILL it breed in an aquarium?
Potentially. Eggs are laid in a rudimentary nest and guarded by the male.

▲ *Only the male has the blue throat patch and yellow edges to the ventral, dorsal, and tail fins.*

Arothron nigropunctatus
Blackspotted pufferfish

FISH PROFILE

The genus *Arothron* contains species generally referred to as "dog-faced" pufferfish. The blackspotted is commonly imported and will become as tame as its namesake family pet, rewarding the aquarist with hardiness and longevity. Some authorities suggest that this is the same species as the Red Sea-endemic *A. diadematus* (masked pufferfish). Husbandry for both species is identical.

▼ *Hardy and full of character, this species is a delight to keep.*

WHAT size?
Males and females 13 in (33 cm).

WHAT does it eat?
A true omnivore that consumes hard coral tips, crustaceans, molluscs, and algae. It is easy to feed in a home aquarium, but be sure to provide an equally varied diet. Dried algae on a lettuce clip can satisfy the browsing instincts of this pufferfish, in addition to providing essential nutrition.

WHERE is it from?
Tropical Indo-Pacific, from East Africa to Micronesia.

WHAT does it cost?
★★★☆☆
One of the least expensive *Arothron* species, unless it is predominantly yellow, as these fish command a premium.

HOW do I sex it?
No known external differences.

WHAT kind of tank?
Fish-only or live rock-based fish-only system.

WHAT minimum size tank?
120 gal (450 l).

HOW do other fish react?
Most large pufferfishes are ignored by all but the largest and most belligerent species. Mature angelfishes may chase newly-introduced specimens, but generally speaking, this pufferfish is able to look after itself.

WHAT to watch out for?
The best specimens may appear shy at first, but will definitely feed in the dealer's tank. Well-acclimatized, settled individuals approach the glass when people pass by, expecting to be fed.

HOW compatible with inverts and corals?
Not reef-safe. Will harm ornamental crustaceans.

WHAT area of the tank?
Spends extended periods of time hovering motionless or even resting on sand or rockwork. Otherwise it swims slowly over rock and sand looking for food.

HOW many in one tank?
Keep singly.

HOW does it behave?
This largely peaceful species can be maintained with many other types of fish with few problems.

WILL it breed in an aquarium?
No.

Canthigaster jactator

Hawaiian spotted pufferfish

Sharpnosed pufferfishes, sometimes known as tobies, are generally smaller and more benign than other pufferfishes, such as those from the genera *Arothron* and *Diodon*. They are therefore better suited to the average-sized home aquarium. The Hawaiian spotted pufferfish is a small, subtly beautiful species, well suited to the smaller setup.

WHAT size?
Males and females up to 3.5 in (9 cm).

WHAT does it eat?
A true omnivore that feeds on a wide range of invertebrates and algae. Offer shellfish, brineshrimp, mysis, and any other meaty foods that it will accept. Dried algae on a lettuce clip helps to satisfy the fish's browsing instincts.

WHERE is it from?
Endemic to the Hawaiian Islands.

WHAT does it cost?
★☆☆☆☆
Inexpensive.

HOW do I sex it?
Males are slightly larger than females.

WHAT kind of tank?
Fish-only or live rock-based fish-only system with plenty of swimming space.

WHAT minimum size tank?
53 gal (200 l).

HOW do other fish react?
Most fish ignore pufferfishes, but this species will not thrive where particularly boisterous fish are present. Do not house it with large predatory species, such as groupers or morays.

WHAT to watch out for?
Avoid fish with cloudy eyes and specimens that sulk in the corner of the tank, as they may be showing signs of distress associated with recent importation. Ensure that potential purchases are feeding.

▼ *This small Hawaiian endemic looks angelic but can nip the fins of more sedentary species.*

HOW compatible with inverts and corals?
Although this fish does not eat corals, it may nip at their soft tissue. Do not house it with ornamental shrimp, other crustaceans, or invertebrates used as cleaners in live rock-based systems.

WHAT area of the tank?
Should swim close to rockwork in search of food.

HOW many in one tank?
Best kept singly.

HOW does it behave?
In common with many sharpnosed pufferfishes, this Hawaiian species has a reputation for nipping at the fins of larger fish. Its audacity seemingly knows no bounds and it will even target the most robust species. However, many individuals are quite peaceful and never present a threat to other fish, provided they are well fed.

WILL it breed in an aquarium?
No.

Canthigaster valentini

Valentini pufferfish

FISH PROFILE

A small and attractive species of sharpnosed pufferfish that is widely available in the hobby and will suit many aquariums. Most large fish will ignore it due to its ability to inflate its body. Likely to be distasteful rather than lethal to anything trying to bite a chunk from it.

▶ *Do not keep this attractive fish with long-finned species— it may nip them.*

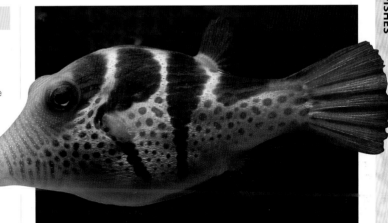

WHAT size?
Males 4.3 in (11 cm); females about 3 in (7.5 cm).

WHAT does it eat?
In the wild, this omnivore's diet includes filamentous algae, crustaceans, polychaete worms, corals, and echinoderms. To meet its nutritional needs in captivity, be sure to provide a variety of different foods. Dried algae, enriched brineshrimp, mysis, chopped and whole shellfish are all useful.

WHERE is it from?
Widespread in the tropical Indo-Pacific, from the Red Sea to Eastern Australian coast.

WHAT does it cost?
★☆☆☆☆
Inexpensive.

HOW do I sex it?
Males are larger and less tolerant of members of the same species.

WHAT kind of tank?
Fish-only or live rock-based fish-only.

WHAT minimum size tank?
40 gal (150 l).

HOW do other fish react?
Small fish can be troublesome; territorial damselfishes, tangs, and boisterous wrasses will probably cause the most problems.

WHAT to watch out for?
Avoid fish that do not feed or are not swimming actively.

HOW compatible with inverts and corals?
Cannot be trusted with corals or other sessile invertebrates.

May consume small ornamental shrimp and tubeworms, and nip at bivalves.

WHAT area of the tank?
Remains close to the rockwork as it searches for food.

HOW many in one tank?
Keep in pairs or small groups of one male and several females. If you cannot reliably determine the sex of individuals, keep them singly.

HOW does it behave?
May occasionally nip at small or delicate fish or those with tempting trailing fin edges, such as lionfishes.

WILL it breed in an aquarium?
Potentially. Males are reported to dominate harems of females, spawning with each in turn.

Chilomycterus antillarum

Honeycomb spiny burrfish

FISH PROFILE

This attractive pufferfish is sometimes erroneously described as a boxfish on account of its angular body shape, especially when small. Small specimens are desirable, but can be a problem to maintain in an aquarium due to their apparent reluctance to feed on the commonly available marine foods.

WHAT size?
Males and females 112 in (30 cm).

WHAT does it eat?
In the wild, mainly benthic crustaceans. Provide similar foods in captivity. Give small individuals brineshrimp and mysis until they are feeding readily, then increase the range of foods offered. Anything shellfish-based should be fine.

WHERE is it from?
Western Atlantic, straying into sub-tropical and even temperate waters.

WHAT does it cost?
★★☆☆☆   ★★★☆☆
Usually more expensive than the porcupine pufferfish, but not very costly.

▶ *This fish is more delicate than Diodon spp. pufferfishes and may prove initially reluctant to feed.*

HOW do I sex it?
No known external differences.

WHAT kind of tank?
Fish-only aquarium.

WHAT minimum size tank?
120 gal (450 l).

HOW do other fish react?
Most fish ignore this well-defended species unless it is very small, in which case it can be molested by larger, inquisitive species, such as angelfishes, triggerfishes, or wrasses. *C. antillarum* may not be robust enough to hold its own against larger or more belligerent fish.

WHAT to watch out for?
Specimens that feed readily are usually small and should be highly prized, as they are the exception rather than the rule. Most larger individuals will not settle at all and you may need to entice them to feed with large live shrimp. Leave newly-imported fish to settle before you buy.

HOW compatible with inverts and corals?
Do not house with any invertebrates. Some will be actively pursued and eaten and others nibbled out of curiosity.

WHAT area of the tank?
May spend some of the day resting on sandy or rock substrates. This is typical of its natural behavior; divers report seeing the same individual occupying the same resting place day after day. It becomes more active when searching for food.

HOW many in one tank?
Keep singly. Can be kept with others of its own kind in an aquarium over 160 gal (600 l).

HOW does it behave?
C. antillarum is a threat to any fish small enough to be consumed. Otherwise it is unlikely to present too many problems to other fish.

WILL it breed in an aquarium?
No.

Diodon holocanthus

Porcupine pufferfish

FISH PROFILE

Its entertaining behavior and bizarre appearance make this a popular marine fish. It is commonly available at quite small sizes (less than 4.75 in/12 cm), but be aware that specimens grow quickly and put heavy demands on the filtration of the aquarium.

▶ *This tempting species requires a system that can meet its long-term requirements.*

WHAT size?
Males and females 18 in (45 cm).

WHAT does it eat?
In the wild, this fish includes sea urchins, hard-shelled molluscs, and various crustaceans in its natural diet. It is important to provide meaty foods, including whole shellfish, prawns, shrimp, and bivalve molluscs. Leaving the shells on such items benefits the digestion of the pufferfish, but can lead to lots of mess that you will need to clean up.

WHERE is it from?
Exported from almost every major collection region in the world.

WHAT does it cost?
★☆☆☆☆   ★★☆☆☆
Moderately priced.

HOW do I sex it?
No external differences.

WHAT kind of tank?
Fish-only or live rock-based fish-only systems.

WHAT minimum size tank?
120 gal (450 l).

HOW do other fish react?
Most fish ignore *D. holocanthus*, although it can be targeted by triggerfishes or large mature angelfishes. It can suck water into its body and inflate into a prickly ball when threatened.

WHAT to watch out for?
Avoid specimens with cloudy eyes and fish that seem reluctant to feed. The best individuals will be less than 4 in (10 cm) long and eagerly approach the aquarist as they anticipate being fed.

HOW compatible with inverts and corals?
Not safe with any invertebrates. May nip at sessile invertebrates, including corals. Shrimp, hermit crabs, and bivalve molluscs are all part of its natural diet.

WHAT area of the tank?
Small juveniles (less than 2.75 in/7 cm) swim actively in the water column. As this species is nocturnal, it often finds somewhere to rest during the day, becoming more active at night. However, as aquarists usually "train" it to receive food during the day, it often becomes more active at this time.

HOW many in one tank?
Best kept singly due to the demands the fish puts on the aquarium filtration when fully grown. Pairs or groups can be maintained in sufficiently large systems (more than 200 gal/ 750 l).

HOW does it behave?
Will attack and sometimes catch and eat smaller fish. It is capable of holding its own with larger fish, and will not present a threat to any tankmates, provided they are large enough not to be eaten.

WILL it breed in an aquarium?
No.

Colorful and compact

▶ Most people think of groupers as large predatory fish—which is true for most species, but they have close relatives that are quite easy to care for long term in the aquarium. Grammas are small, elongated fish and are included with the dottybacks in this section because they occupy similar niches; both groups are found close to and among rockwork and have brightly-colored representative species. Both groups can be considered miniature predators, so take care when selecting suitable tankmates— even smaller fish and invertebrates can fall victim to their carnivorous tendencies. Their very modest final size does mean that they are suitable for the small aquarium and can breed, given suitable conditions. Where pairs of the less aggressive dottybacks are housed together, they are almost guaranteed to spawn. This group also contains the basslets.

Price guide

★	$15–$25
★★	$25–$45
★★★	$45–$70
★★★★	$70–$95
★★★★★	$95–$150

FISH PROFILE

A secretive species with much to offer the aquarist prepared to observe it only infrequently. Also commonly known as the marine betta because its fins resemble those of the freshwater Siamese fighting fish, *Betta splendens*. It is closely related to the golden forktail *(Assessor flavissimus)*.

WHAT size?
Males and females 7.4 in (20 cm).

WHAT does it eat?
In the wild, small fish and crustaceans. In an aquarium, most meaty frozen foods. Mysis, brineshrimp, and a variety of shellfish should keep it in excellent health.

WHERE is it from?
Widespread in the tropical Indo-Pacific, ranging from the Red Sea in the West to Tonga in the East.

WHAT does it cost?
★★★☆☆ ★★★★☆
Fairly expensive but not unreasonable.

▶ *The comet grouper is a gorgeous fish that specializes in preying on small crustaceans.*

Calloplesiops altivelis

Comet grouper

HOW do I sex it?
Some authors maintain that male and female specimens show differences in the size and distribution of the spots over the body.

WHAT kind of tank?
A system with plenty of hiding places, but this can be a fish-only setup, live rock-based fish-only, or a reef aquarium with care.

WHAT minimum size tank?
66 gal (250 l).

HOW do other fish react?
Will not thrive in the presence of very busy or territorially aggressive fish. Do not house with fish that are small enough to be swallowed whole.

WHAT to watch out for?
Try to ensure that this fish is getting enough to eat. Due to its secretive nature it will not necessarily feed in an obvious manner. Sometimes, introducing food under blue, or "moon," lights encourages the fish out into the open.

HOW compatible with inverts and corals?
Will eat smaller species of ornamental shrimp.

WHAT area of the tank?
Close to rockwork, often remaining behind aquarium decor for prolonged periods.

HOW many in one tank?
Best kept singly or in mated pairs.

HOW does it behave?
The comet grouper is said to mimic the head of moray eels, as illustrated when it dives into rockwork, exposing the large eye spot and "gaping mouth" formed by the rounded fins. However, the large tail and eye spot also have a role in predation. When the fish locates a potential prey item, it curls its tail in front of the unfortunate victim, thus distracting it and enabling the comet to get within striking distance.

WILL it breed in an aquarium?
Yes. Specimens have been raised in captivity.

Chromileptes altivelis

Snowflake (panther) grouper

FISH PROFILE

A widely available, instantly recognizable species. However, it is not suitable for most aquariums as it reaches a very large maximum size and is, after all, a predator. Tank-bred specimens may command a premium over specimens obtained from the wild. However, responsible aquarists should pay the higher price, since this species is under great pressure from collectors and fishermen alike.

▼ *This juvenile has a lower density of spots than can be seen in adult fish.*

WHAT size?
Males 27.5 in (70 cm); females smaller.

WHAT does it eat?
Juveniles take small crustaceans and fish larvae, while large specimens feed on a wide variety of smaller fish. Captive specimens are easy to feed on shellfish, whole fish, and similar meaty foods.

WHERE is it from?
Western Pacific and Eastern Indian Ocean.

WHAT does it cost?
★★☆☆☆
Relatively inexpensive.

HOW do I sex it?
Males are usually larger than females. Note that all specimens are female when first hatched. They remain this way as juveniles and only when adult will the dominant female become a male.

WHAT kind of tank?
Fish-only or live rock-based fish-only system.

WHAT minimum size tank?
238 gal (900 l).

HOW do other fish react?
Will be ignored by most fish. The growth rate of *C. altivelis* is slow but steady, so issues may arise with other predatory fish outgrowing this species and it falling victim to their appetites.

WHAT to watch out for?
Attractive, hardy juveniles are often available at about 2 in (5–6 cm) long. However, unless you have an aquarium large enough to house them, you will experience problems later on.

HOW compatible with inverts and corals?
May harm ornamental shrimp but should not touch coral. Unsuited to a reef aquarium due to its large size and inevitably high waste production.

WHAT area of the tank?
Usually swims in the open, but also spends long periods motionless among rockwork.

HOW many in one tank?
Best kept singly or in pairs.

HOW does it behave?
The fish's distinctive swimming style appears ritualized and labored.

WILL it breed in an aquarium?
Specimens farmed in captivity have been sporadically available to those in the hobby. Spawnings do occur, but are infrequently reported by home aquarists due to the small number of people with systems large enough to house pairs or harems of mature fish.

Assessor flavissimus

Golden forktail

FISH PROFILE

An often-overlooked species that makes an interesting alternative to other open water-swimming fish such as anthias and chromis. Colors intensify with age and a shoal of well-settled individuals makes for a stunning display.

WHAT size?
Males 2.4 in (6 cm); females 2.2 in (5.5 cm).

WHAT does it eat?
Zooplankton in the wild. Offer captive specimens a variety of foodstuffs, including most meaty frozen foods. With time and persistence, they may take granular and flaked foods.

WHERE is it from?
The Great Barrier Reef, Australia.

WHAT does it cost?
★★☆☆☆
Most specimens are obtained through a small number of sources, so prices are fairly constant and relatively modest.

HOW do I sex it?
Males are larger and more territorial.

WHAT kind of tank?
A reef aquarium is absolutely ideal, although a live-rock, fish-only system is also suitable.

WHAT minimum size tank?
26 gal (100 l) for a small group.

HOW do other fish react?
Resident open water-swimming fish will often not tolerate the presence of other fish in this zone. These may include anthias (*Pseudanthias* spp.), chromis (*Chromis* spp.), fairy wrasses (*Cirrhilabrus* spp.) and swallowtail angelfishes (*Genicanthus* spp.). Territorial damselfishes are also unlikely to welcome this species.

WHAT to watch out for?
Larger individuals within the shoal may bicker with one another, but this is rarely serious.

HOW compatible with inverts and corals?
Will not harm invertebrates, sessile or otherwise.

WHAT area of the tank?
Open water above or in front of rockwork. Individuals sometimes swim upside-down in caves or beneath overhangs, a trait shared with other grammas.

HOW many in one tank?
Keep in small groups, added simultaneously.

HOW does it behave?
Peaceful towards other fish.

WILL it breed in an aquarium?
Yes, the male incubates eggs in his mouth. The fry are quite small but have been raised in captivity. Where groups of this species are housed together in a peaceful aquarium, spawning probability is very high.

▶ More often than not, assessors swim upside-down rather than the "right" side up.

Gramma loreto

Royal gramma

FISH PROFILE

One of the all-time favorite marine fish due to its stunning coloration and ease of keeping. The royal gramma is an exquisite species, but over-collection has resulted in the banning of its export from some countries.

▶ *The pink pigment dominating the front portion of the body appears blue at depth.*

WHAT size?
Males and females 3.2 in (8 cm) maximum.

WHAT does it eat?
Wild specimens feed on zooplankton and small shrimps; offer similar food items in the aquarium. Weaning this species onto flake or granular preparations can be difficult.

WHERE is it from?
The Western Caribbean and Central and South America.

WHAT does it cost?
★★☆☆☆
Reasonably priced.

HOW do I sex it?
Males are usually slightly larger and more aggressive towards intruders into their territory. In the absence of a dominant male specimen, females become males.

WHAT kind of tank?
Will thrive in almost any system that does not house more aggressive fish.

WHAT minimum size tank?
13 gal (50 l) or more.

HOW do other fish react?
Large territorial damselfishes may attack the royal gramma.

WHAT to watch out for?
This shy species often hides for sustained periods in the rockwork and decor. In the presence of many boisterous tankmates it may need target feeding, as it may not feel confident enough to compete.

HOW compatible with inverts and corals?
Has the potential to harm ornamental shrimp, although this is unusual with the usual *Lysmata* spp. "cleaner" shrimp.

WHAT area of the tank?
Stays close to a refuge, which can mean any available nook or cranny.

HOW many in one tank?
Keep singly or in pairs.

HOW does it behave?
Often hovers with its ventral surface just above the rockwork. Where caves and overhangs are present, it swims upside-down.

WILL it breed in an aquarium?
Yes. Males are nest builders and often tend the eggs laid by the female. This species has been successfully raised in captivity.

Gramma melacara

Blackcap gramma

FISH PROFILE

This species is closely related to the royal gramma, but as it is found in deeper water and presents more problems for collectors it commands a high price. As it is often found at depths below 00 ft (30 m), it often takes time to adjust to a brightly lit reef aquarium, and may become more active under artificial moonlight or blue actinic light. An ideal subject for a low-light, specialist aquarium.

WHAT size?
Males and females 4 in (10 cm) maximum.

WHAT does it eat?
A variety of small animals, including shrimp, amphipods, polychaetes and sometimes very small fish species. In the aquarium, will accept most shrimp- or shellfish-based frozen preparations.

WHERE is it from?
The Western Caribbean and Central America.

WHAT does it cost?
★★★☆☆ ★★★★☆
G. melacara is relatively expensive, often costing two to three times the price of its very close relative, the royal gramma (*G. loreto*).

▶ *This expensive species is shy and reclusive and needs a peaceful aquarium.*

HOW do I sex it?
Males are usually slightly larger, with a more robust appearance. Otherwise, sexing individuals is difficult.

WHAT kind of tank?
Will thrive in almost any system that does not house more aggressive fish.

WHAT minimum size tank?
13 gal (50 l) or more.

HOW do other fish react?
The blackcap gramma is extremely shy and will be dominated by any slightly aggressive species when first introduced into the aquarium.

WHAT to watch out for?
Make sure specimens are feeding before buying them. They should not be the last fish introduced into an aquarium stocked with boisterous fish.

HOW compatible with inverts and corals?
Unlikely to present a threat to most ornamental shrimps, with the possible exception of the most delicate or smallest species. It will not harm corals.

WHAT area of the tank?
Stays close to rockwork, never straying too far from its favorite bolthole.

HOW many in one tank?
Best kept singly or in pairs. Groups are possible where budget and a large (132 gallons/500 liter plus) aquarium permit.

HOW does it behave?
Will swim with its ventral surface facing the rockwork and can be seen swimming upside-down in caves. Very small goby species may be eaten by this species.

WILL it breed in an aquarium?
Yes, it has been successfully spawned and raised in captivity. To experience some spawning behavior, acquire small juvenile specimens where possible to avoid any territorial disputes between males.

Liopropoma rubre

Swissguard basslet

A highly sought-after species that is common in its natural range, yet infrequently encountered within the marine aquarium hobby.

WHAT size?
Males and females 3.2 in (8 cm).

WHAT does it eat?
In the wild, benthic organisms. In the aquarium most specimens eagerly accept meaty frozen foods, including brineshrimp, mysis, and chopped shellfish, enriched with vitamins.

WHERE is it from?
Subtropical and tropical regions of North and South America, including Southern Florida, the western Caribbean and Central American coasts.

WHAT does it cost?
★★★★★
Expensive, but worth every penny.

HOW do I sex it?
No obvious external differences.

WHAT kind of tank?
A peaceful system with plenty of retreats is essential. The fish will thrive where live rock is stocked.

WHAT minimum size tank?
A small (6.6-gallon/25-liter) aquarium suits smaller specimens and arguably offers the best chance for regular sightings. However, water quality must be excellent and highly maintained, which is difficult with such small water volumes without prior experience.

HOW do other fish react?
Resident damselfishes may react adversely to the introduction of this basslet.

WHAT to watch out for?
Specimens for sale are likely to be quite shy and usually either hiding or cowering because they are in a completely alien environment. The majority settle well and feed readily if stocked into a suitable aquarium.

HOW compatible with inverts and corals?
Ideal with sessile invertebrates. Small, delicate shrimp may be attacked, but the Swissguard can be confidently stocked into most invertebrate aquariums.

WHAT area of the tank?
Close to rockwork. Rarely ventures too far from refuge.

HOW many in one tank?
Keep singly or in pairs. Be aware that an aquarium larger than 26 gal (100 l) is necessary for numbers, and only then with care. One individual may become dominant over time. Try to stock individuals of the same size and at the same time where possible.

HOW does it behave?
Although generally very peaceful, it may clash with species with a similar fondness for rock crevices, such as grammas and dottybacks.

WILL it breed in an aquarium?
Yes.

◀ The Swissguard is one of the smallest members of a large genus of basslets.

Liopropoma swalesi

Candyline basslet

FISH PROFILE

This species is becoming increasingly available within the hobby and makes an interesting alternative to the Swissguard basslet *(Liopropoma rubre)* or the even more elusive Caribbean candy basslet *(L. carmabi)*. Many members of the genus *Liopropoma* are large predators and therefore unsuitable for most home aquariums, but this species is a jewel that will grace most peaceful aquariums.

WHAT size?
Males and females 2 in (5 cm).

WHAT does it eat?
In the wild, a variety of small animals, from zooplankton to benthic populations. Offer a variety of frozen foods with regular vitamin supplementation to maintain bright colors.

WHERE is it from?
Indonesia. Many specimens appear to be collected from Bali.

WHAT does it cost?
★★★★★
Commands a high price for its size.

HOW do I sex it?
No external visual differences.

WHAT kind of tank?
Reef or live rock-based aquarium with plenty of hiding places.

WHAT minimum size tank?
12 gal (45 l) is large enough, assuming excellent water quality.

HOW do other fish react?
Damselfishes, dottybacks, and similar fish may react adversely to the introduction of this species and contribute to its reclusive tendencies.

WHAT to watch out for?
Ensure that specimens are feeding before you buy them and be prepared for the often elusive nature of this fish.

HOW compatible with inverts and corals?
A coral-rich environment is ideal as it affords plenty of hiding places. The fish may harm the

▲ *The lack of black pigment on the tail of this species distinguishes it from the Caribbean species* L. carmabi.

most delicate ornamental shrimp.

WHAT area of the tank?
In and among rockwork, rarely straying far from cover.

HOW many in one tank?
It should be possible to maintain this fish in groups, but being so new to the hobby reports of success are sketchy.

HOW does it behave?
This very peaceful, shy species inhabits various retreats and a settled specimen may be territorial towards species that share this mode of existence, such as dottybacks or grammas.

WILL it breed in an aquarium?
No known reports, but success is highly likely in the future.

Plectranthias inermis

Red blotched perchlet

FISH PROFILE

A little-known recent introduction to the aquarium hobby that will almost certainly become extremely popular as its attributes achieve wider recognition. Despite its close resemblance to the hawkfish family (Cirrhitidae) in both appearance and behaviour, the red blotched perchlet is actually a species of basslet (Serranidae).

◀ *This beautiful fish settles well when housed in a peaceful aquarium.*

WHAT size?
Males and females 1.8 in (4.5 cm) maximum.

WHAT does it eat?
In the wild, amphipods and other small crustaceans. Readily accepts most frozen preparations in the aquarium.

WHERE is it from?
Indonesia and the Philippines. Most specimens in the UK originate from Balinese waters.

WHAT does it cost?
★★★★★
Still an expensive species, but the high price may reduce as more fish are collected.

HOW do I sex it?
No known external differences.

WHAT kind of tank?
Live rock-based, fish-only system or a small reef aquarium.

WHAT minimum size tank?
13 gal (50 l).

HOW do other fish react?
Any larger, aggressive fish may bully *P. inermis*.

WHAT to watch out for?
This deep-water species may shun the bright lights of a reef aquarium. Systems with moonlight or blue actinic lighting may offer the perchlet more opportunities to become more adventurous.

HOW compatible with inverts and corals?
Will not harm any commonly maintained invertebrates.

WHAT area of the tank?
Occupies the rockwork and very rarely ventures into open water.

HOW many in one tank?
More than one could be housed in a larger aquarium (40 gal/150 l or more).

HOW does it behave?
This timid species needs plenty of time and effort invested in it if it is to reveal its true potential. Specimens are not difficult to maintain in captivity, but their secretive nature and preference for the more dimly-lit areas of the aquarium mean that they will not be one of the more obvious aquarium inhabitants.

WILL it breed in an aquarium?
Not recorded but certainly potentially possible, particularly in larger aquariums.

Serranus tabacarius

Tobacco basslet

FISH PROFILE

Although not as colorful as its close relative the chalk basslet, the tobacco basslet is nonetheless an attractive fish and one that will do well in quite boisterous aquariums. A good subject to grow with large fish species purchased as juveniles.

WHAT size?
Males and females 8.7 in (22 cm).

WHAT does it eat?
Accepts any meaty foods, including mysis, brineshrimp, and chopped shellfish. Larger specimens require correspondingly large foods.

WHERE is it from?
Western Atlantic, including Caribbean reefs and Southern Florida.

WHAT does it cost?
★☆☆☆☆
Relatively inexpensive.

HOW do I sex it?
Individuals are simultaneous hermaphrodites, meaning that they are functional males and females at the same time.

WHAT kind of tank?
Ideal in fish-only or live rock-based fish-only systems.

WHAT minimum size tank?
66 gal (250 l) for a single individual, larger for multiple additions.

HOW do other fish react?
Tobacco basslets are shy when first introduced to the aquarium and may fall victim to large territorial damselfishes or aggressive wrasses, angelfishes, and species with similar behavior. As it grows, it becomes more confident and robust.

WHAT to watch out for?
Avoid fish that refuse to feed or are particularly reclusive, since these may be recent imports.

HOW compatible with inverts and corals?
Should not harm corals or other sessile invertebrates, but its large final size and taste for ornamental or cleaning invertebrates make it unsuitable for most reef systems.

WHAT area of the tank?
Prefers to remain close to sand or rock substrates.

HOW many in one tank?
Larger systems can support small groups.

HOW does it behave?
Has the potential to consume smaller fish, so do not stock it with anything that might become a mouthful as this species grows. Not particularly territorial. It has been reported following fish that disturb the substrate as part of their feeding activity, such as goatfishes. The tobacco basslet snaps at anything that tries to escape from it.

WILL it breed in an aquarium?
Yes. In larger systems it has the potential to do so.

◀ Brown and cream colors combine well in this subtly beautiful species.

Serranus tortugarum

Chalk basslet

FISH PROFILE

A small, shy species from the Caribbean, akin to the *Pseudochromis* dottybacks of the Indo-Pacific, but generally far more peaceful than the majority of the latter species.

WHAT size?
Males and females 13.2 (8 cm).

WHAT does it eat?
Accepts any meaty foodstuffs, including chopped shellfish, mysis, and brineshrimp.

WHERE is it from?
Western Atlantic, including Caribbean reefs and Southern Florida.

WHAT does it cost?
★☆☆☆☆
Relatively inexpensive.

HOW do I sex it?
Individuals are simultaneous hermaphrodites, meaning that they are functional males and females at the same time.

WHAT kind of tank?
Ideal for a peaceful reef or live rock-based aquarium.

WHAT minimum size tank?
13 gal (50 l) for a single individual, but larger for multiple additions.

HOW do other fish react?
Will not do well in the presence of more aggressive species. Avoid territorial damselfishes.

WHAT to watch out for?
Specimens appear restless, often nipping at each other. This perfectly natural behavior occurs in the wild as well as in the aquarium.

HOW compatible with inverts and corals?
May attack very small, non-cleaning species of shrimp, including the sexy anemone shrimp, *Thor amboinensis*. Will not harm corals or other sessile invertebrates.

WHAT area of the tank?
A few inches above the rockwork, rarely venturing far from cover.

HOW many in one tank?
Small groups can be maintained with few problems.

HOW does it behave?
Although initially shy, this species should settle well into most aquariums, providing they do not house too many large or boisterous species.

WILL it breed in an aquarium?
Yes.

▼ *The chalk basslet is a beautiful fish from the Western Atlantic.*

Cypho purpurescens

Flame dottyback

FISH PROFILE

One of the few dottyback species available in the hobby that is not a member of the genus *Pseudochromis*. The flame dottyback is a stunning species, ideal for the larger live-rock-based system in which it can remain unmolested. It is not a fish to stock if you want its colors on permanent display, since it spends as much time hunting behind the rockwork as in front.

WHAT size?
Males and females 3 in (7.5 cm).

WHAT does it eat?
A miniature predator that feeds voraciously on small polychaete worms and crustaceans. In the aquarium it should not prove difficult to feed. Offer brineshrimp, mysis, chopped shellfish, and any alternative meaty foods.

WHERE is it from?
Papua New Guinea, Great Barrier Reef east to Tonga in the central Pacific.

WHAT does it cost?
★★☆☆☆   ★★★☆☆
One of the more expensive members of this family.

HOW do I sex it?
Males are bright red; females have a dark purple head and pink body.

WHAT kind of tank?
Best suited to a live rock-based aquarium or small reef system.

WHAT minimum size tank?
106 gal (400 l) for a pair, with plenty of rockwork to provide retreats and hiding places.

HOW do other fish react?
Many species can act adversely to this fish; it is quite a shy species in any system, but particularly so where larger, more boisterous fish are present.

WHAT to watch out for?
As male fish are quite stunning and desirable due to their crimson coloration, the females are not imported with anything like the same regularity. This is a shame, as pairs are easy to identify and make fascinating additions to a small aquarium, where it is possible to observe their breeding behavior.

▲ *The male flame dottyback gives the species its common name.*

HOW compatible with inverts and corals?
May harm ornamental shrimp or other small crustaceans. May also consume tubeworms.

WHAT area of the tank?
In and among rockwork or hunting around rubble or decor with plenty of holes and crevices.

HOW many in one tank?
Can be kept singly, in pairs, or in trios, where one male is introduced with two females.

HOW does it behave?
Do not keep with delicate species, including those that resemble it in form or behavior. It can kill diminutive fish that it takes a dislike to. It will thrive with sturdy schooling species such as damsels (*Chrysiptera taupou* is ideal) and larger tangs.

WILL it breed in an aquarium?
Yes.

Ogilbyina queenslandiae

Queensland dottyback

FISH PROFILE

A large dottyback that combines stunning coloration with a belligerent attitude. It may be reclusive in many aquariums, but woe betide any fish that are not strong enough to defend themselves against this territorial beauty.

WHAT size?
Males and females 6 in (15 cm).

WHAT does it eat?
Wild fish favor small benthic crustaceans, small fish, and worms. Almost any meaty foods will entice them in the aquarium, and as they grow, offer correspondingly large items. Brineshrimp and mysis can be replaced by larger chunks of shellfish flesh.

WHERE is it from?
Endemic to the coastal reefs of Queensland in Australia.

WHAT does it cost?
★★☆☆☆　★★★☆☆
Moderately expensive; on a par with many species of Red Sea-endemic dottybacks.

HOW do I sex it?
Females have yellow-brown flanks and a grey-colored head. Males are more striking, but without the same variety of colors.

WHAT kind of tank?
Best suited to a live rock-based aquarium or small reef system.

WHAT minimum size tank?
100 gal (400 l) is adequate for a pair, with plenty of rockwork in place to offer retreats and hiding places.

HOW do other fish react?
Most fish will ignore or avoid the Queensland dottyback, particularly because it is fond of hiding in and among rockwork, even in the most peaceful aquariums.

WHAT to watch out for?
Prone to color loss in the aquarium. Supplementing food with color-enhancing additives and offering a wide variety of different foodstuffs can help prevent this.

HOW compatible with inverts and corals?
May harm ornamental shrimp or other small crustaceans. May also consume tubeworms.

WHAT area of the tank?
In and among rockwork or hunting around rubble or decor with plenty of holes and crevices.

HOW many in one tank?
Keep singly, in pairs, or in trios, where one male is introduced with two females.

HOW does it behave?
Do not keep with delicate species, including those similar in form or behavior. Should not be underestimated; may kill and eat small gobies, damselfishes, and blennies. Will thrive with sturdy schooling species, such as larger specimen damsels (*Chrysiptera taupou* is ideal) and larger tangs.

WILL it breed in an aquarium?
Yes. It has been successfully reared in captivity.

▶ *This beautiful species can be quite pugnacious. This specimen is a female.*

Pseudochromis aldabraensis

Arabian (orange) dottyback

FISH PROFILE

Most specimens on sale are captive bred. Juveniles can be maintained together, but often have a slightly washed-out appearance. Their growth rate in the aquarium is prodigious, and juveniles quickly differentiate into males and females.

▶ *The benign nature of this dottyback is said to be typical only of captive-bred individuals.*

WHAT size?
Males 4 in (10 cm); females 3.2 in (8.5 cm).

WHAT does it eat?
In the wild, small benthic invertebrates, including errant polychaetes and crustaceans. Aquarium specimens accept mysis, brineshrimp, and chopped shellfish.

WHERE is it from?
Persian Gulf, Oman, Pakistan, and Sri Lanka.

WHAT does it cost?
★★★☆☆ ★★★★☆
One of the most expensive commonly available dottyback species.

HOW do I sex it?
Males have a more elongated body shape, females are more rounded and smaller. Two juveniles will differentiate into a male and female specimen, albeit after some initial bickering.

WHAT kind of tank?
Live rock-based fish-only aquarium or reef system.

WHAT minimum size tank?
40 gal (150 l) system for a pair.

HOW do other fish react?
Similar species may not tolerate it, but it usually lurks in the rockwork until the immediate threat disappears. Small *Pseudocheilinus* wrasse can be a problem, particularly if introduced before the dottybacks.

WHAT to watch out for?
This species resembles *Pseudochromis dutoiti*, which has a reputation for belligerence. Some authorities maintain that the Arabian dottyback is similarly behaved, but that captive-bred specimens are unusually benign.

HOW compatible with inverts and corals?
May attack tubeworms and attack and eat ornamental shrimp. Should not harm corals or other sessile invertebrates.

WHAT area of the tank?
Investigates rockwork for worms, shrimp or crabs. Rarely ventures into open water except to take food offered by the aquarist.

HOW many in one tank?
Keep singly or in pairs.

HOW does it behave?
Smaller fish, such as gobies, blennies, anthias, etc., may be bullied or driven out of the immediate location. Rarely a long-term or terminal problem.

WILL it breed in an aquarium?
Yes. If a mature male disappears for prolonged periods of time, he is probably incubating the egg ball laid in a suitable hole. The male checks out the potential nesting site before encouraging the female to visit and deposit her eggs. This can happen regularly in the home aquarium.

Pseudochromis diadema

Flashback (diadema) dottyback

FISH PROFILE

There are two main types of dottyback: the generally good and the generally bad. Many aquarists have fallen afoul of the fact that many of the less-suitable species are beautiful and reasonably priced. Unfortunately, the flashback dottyback is one of these.

WHAT size?
Males 2.3 in (6 cm); females a little smaller.

WHAT does it eat?
Wild specimens include a variety of benthic crustaceans in their diet. Aquarium fish will eat almost any food offered, but are particularly fond of mysis and brine shrimp.

WHERE is it from?
Western Pacific. The majority of aquarium specimens are exported from the Philippines.

WHAT does it cost?
★☆☆☆☆
Inexpensive by any standards for tropical marine fish.

HOW do I sex it?
Males appear larger and more robust, females more rounded.

WHAT kind of tank?
Live rock-based fish-only aquarium or reef system.

WHAT minimum size tank?
26 gal (100 l).

HOW do other fish react?
Stock small wrasse from the genus *Pseudocheilinus* after this species, as territorial individuals can be aggressive towards the dottyback.

WHAT to watch out for?
P. diadema could potentially be confused with the orchid dottyback (*P. fridmani*), but the latter has a prominent black stripe through the eye pigment in the tail fin.

HOW compatible with inverts and corals?
May attack and eat ornamental shrimp. Should not harm corals or other sessile invertebrates.

▲ *The beauty of this fish belies its nature and it should be stocked with care.*

WHAT area of the tank?
Tends to hover an inch or two above the substrate and in open water on the lookout for planktonic and benthic invertebrates.

HOW many in one tank?
Keep singly or in pairs in sufficiently large systems.

HOW does it behave?
Will often not tolerate similarly-sized species, including gobies, other dottybacks, dartfishes, grammas, and small hawkfish—essentially anything that is not large or belligerent enough to look after itself. The really bad news is that these are the very fish that aquarists on a limited budget or with smaller systems want to keep.

WILL it breed in an aquarium?
Yes.

Peudochromis flavivertex

Sunrise dottyback

FISH PROFILE

Many aquarists overlook the sunrise dottyback due to its diminutive size, but an established individual is extremely attractive. Given plenty of rocky cover, a pair will behave perfectly naturally in the home aquarium and provide plenty of entertainment for the aquarist. It is possible to maintain *P. flavivertex* with other dottyback species given a sufficiently large aquarium (106 gal/400 l or more).

WHAT size?
Males 3 in (7.5 cm); females 2.5 in (6.5 cm).

WHAT does it eat?
In the wild, a variety of benthic worms and crustaceans. In the aquarium, it accepts most small meaty food particles, including brineshrimp, mysis, and chopped shellfish. May have a role in controlling small polychaete bristleworms.

WHERE is it from?
Red Sea and the Gulf of Aden.

WHAT does it cost?
★★★☆☆
Moderately expensive for what is a quite small fish.

HOW do I sex it?
Males are more elongated, females more rounded, often with a blue-green color on the head and forward body section and a pale yellow back end. Keeping two juveniles in male coloration together for a prolonged period can cause one individual to differentiate into a female.

WHAT kind of tank?
Live rock-based fish-only or reef aquarium.

WHAT minimum size tank?
26 gal (100 l).

HOW do other fish react?
Larger species may cause this fish prolonged anxiety, with the result that it hides away for much of the time and needs target feeding. In an aquarium with plenty of live rock to provide crevices and hiding places, the dottyback grows in confidence.

▼ *Although this species is often very shy, its stunning good looks justify its inclusion in the home aquarium.*

WHAT to watch out for?
Fish that have been bullied in a dealer's tank will have split fins or marks on the body. Avoid these. Try to acquire a male/female pair so that you can witness their fascinating behavior.

HOW compatible with inverts and corals?
May attack and eat ornamental shrimp. Will not harm corals or other invertebrates.

WHAT area of the tank?
Seldom moves far from cover.

HOW many in one tank?
Keep singly or in pairs.

HOW does it behave?
Seldom aggressive, other than to defend its nest site.

WILL it breed in an aquarium?
Yes, it has been successfully reared in captivity. If a mature male disappears for prolonged periods of time, he is likely to be incubating the egg ball laid in a crack or hole in the rockwork.

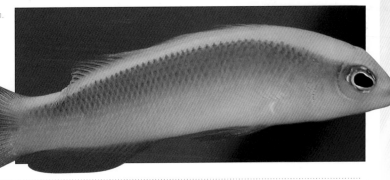

Pseudochromis fridmani

Orchid dottyback

A small yet stunningly-colored species that settles well into the aquarium. Specimens will behave naturally in all but the smallest system.

WHAT size?
Males and females 2.75 in (7 cm).

WHAT does it eat?
Any meaty foods, including frozen mysis and brineshrimp. Rarely accepts dried foods.

WHERE is it from?
Only found in the Red Sea. Tank-raised specimens are available.

WHAT does it cost?
★★★☆☆
Expensive for its size.

HOW do I sex it?
Males are more elongated, with a longer lower lobe to the tail fin. Females appear quite stout, especially when about to spawn.

WHAT kind of tank?
Best kept in a reef or live rock-based fish-only aquarium.

WHAT minimum size tank?
12 gal (45 l) is sufficient if well filtered.

HOW do other fish react?
Unlikely to thrive and behave naturally when introduced to an aquarium containing territorial damselfishes. Otherwise, its close affinity with the rockwork means that it can often avoid more belligerent fish quite easily.

WHAT to watch out for?
Males disappear for periods of time when they are guarding recently laid eggs.

▼ *Two juveniles should differentiate into male and female specimens that form a pair.*

HOW compatible with inverts and corals?
Dottybacks present no threat to corals but may harm ornamental shrimp.

WHAT area of the tank?
Close to the rockwork, only rarely venturing into open water.

HOW many in one tank?
Pairs can be kept with few problems even in a small aquarium, while large systems will accommodate more than two specimens. Individuals can change sex, but each system will only have one male and the rest will be female.

HOW does it behave?
Aggressive towards similarly shaped species, although nowhere near as problematic as similar species from the Indo-Pacific.

WILL it breed in an aquarium?
Yes, pairs will spawn frequently. Males guard the eggs laid in caves and crevices. Planktonic larvae are difficult, although not impossible, to raise.

Pseudochromis paccagnellae

False gramma (royal) dottyback

FISH PROFILE

Few people could dispute the obvious beauty of this species, but do not be fooled into thinking that it could not possibly be as aggressive or problematic as its reputation suggests. If anything it's worse. This should be the fundamental consideration when deciding whether to introduce this species. Is it desirable enough to dictate the temperament and species to be stocked with it?

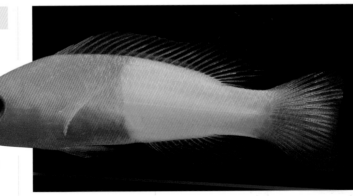

▲ *A much more aggressive fish than Gramma loreto, which it resembles.*

WHAT size?
Males 2.75 in (7 cm); females 2.8 in (8 cm).

WHAT does it eat?
In the wild, small benthic animals, such as small crustaceans and polychaete worms. In the aquarium most individuals readily accept frozen formula foods, mysis, brineshrimp, and other meaty foods.

WHERE is it from?
From Indonesia to Vanuatu off the Eastern coast of Australia. Also found in Palau.

WHAT does it cost?
★☆☆☆☆ ★★☆☆☆
Slightly more expensive than other small *Pseudochromis* species collected from this region, but still well within the range of most budgets.

HOW do I sex it?
Males are more elongated, females appear more rounded.

WHAT kind of tank?
Fish-only; live rock-based fish-only system; or reef aquarium.

WHAT minimum size tank?
26 gal (100 l).

HOW do other fish react?
Most fish of a similar size will not tangle with this species. Larger fish will chase it occasionally, but it is agile enough to escape into rockwork and hide.

WHAT to watch out for?
If you absolutely must have this species or it is suited to your boisterous, live rock-based fish-only system, then choose specimens with no damage to the fins, clear eyes, and no discoloration on the body.

HOW compatible with inverts and corals?
Likely to attack and kill ornamental shrimp. Will not harm corals or other sessile invertebrates.

WHAT area of the tank?
When allowed to settle and "do its own thing," it hovers above the rockwork. This may not be possible when stocked into an aquarium with large, hardy fish species, as is recommended.

HOW many in one tank?
Keep singly.

HOW does it behave?
Any similar-sized species is under threat from this fish. Even larger, docile individuals may be harassed by the royal dottyback.

WILL it breed in an aquarium?
Yes, if the aquarium is large enough to house a pair, i.e. 278 gal (900 l) or more.

Pseudochromis porphyreus

Strawberry (magenta) dottyback

FISH PROFILE

A cheap and readily available species that can prove problematic in the marine aquarium due to its belligerent nature. Its beauty attracts many aquarists, but those seeking such color in their aquarium might be better advised to introduce the more benign, if expensive, Red Sea endemic *Pseudochromis fridmani*.

WHAT size?
Males and females 2.3 in (6 cm).

WHAT does it eat?
In the wild, mainly crustaceans. Captive specimens accept most meaty foods, including chopped shellfish, mysis, brineshrimp. Vitamin additives assist in color retention.

WHERE is it from?
Western Pacific: Philippines to Samoa.

WHAT does it cost?
★☆☆☆☆
Inexpensive.

HOW do I sex it?
No external visual differences.

WHAT kind of tank?
Fish-only; live rock-based fish-only system; reef aquarium.

WHAT minimum size tank?
26.5 gal (100 l).

HOW do other fish react?
Damselfishes, territorial wrasses, and other dottybacks present the greatest threat to this species, as they resent the encroachment of other fish onto their area. Otherwise, this fish can look after itself.

WHAT to watch out for?
Avoid excessively pale specimens. Some color loss is not unusual in specimens that have been kept in a dealer's aquarium long-term, but it can also signify a newly imported, stressed specimen.

HOW compatible with inverts and corals?
Will not harm corals, but cannot be trusted with ornamental crustaceans. Should be safe with echinoderms and molluscs.

WHAT area of the tank?
Close to rockwork and refuge.

HOW many in one tank?
Best kept singly in most systems to avoid territorial aggression. (120 gal/450 l is required for a pair.)

HOW does it behave?
May attack and kill smaller or less robust species. Even damselfishes and similar hardy fish can be harassed to death by the strawberry dottyback if they are introduced to an aquarium with this fish in residence.

WILL it breed in an aquarium?
Potentially, yes. It has been successfully raised in captivity.

▶ *Pseudochromis porphyreus is very similar to the orchid dottyback, but does not have any pigment in the pectoral fins and lacks the black eye stripe of its Red Sea relative.*

Pseudochromis sankeyi

Sankey's dottyback

FISH PROFILE

This is an interesting species of dottyback, mainly due to the fact that the vast majority of specimens available to aquarists are captive-bred. This means that there are few problems associated with purchasing it, although its price reflects the difficulties involved in its captive rearing. Although not as striking as other members of the genus endemic to the Red Sea, it is just as easy to maintain and very rewarding to keep.

◄ *This unusually-patterned fish shares the more benign disposition of the other Red Sea-endemic species of dottybacks available.*

WHAT size?
Males 2.75 in (7 cm); females 2.5 in (6.5 cm).

WHAT does it eat?
For best results, offer meaty foods, including brineshrimp, mysis, and frozen formula foods. The fish will supplement this diet with naturally occurring food items, such as amphipod crustaceans.

WHERE is it from?
Southwestern Red Sea and the Gulf of Aden.

WHAT does it cost?
★★★☆☆
Moderately expensive.

HOW do I sex it?
Males are more elongated in body shape. Females appear more rounded, but this is less apparent than in other members of the genus.

WHAT kind of tank?
Live rock-based fish-only system or reef aquarium.

WHAT minimum size tank?
26 gal (100 l).

HOW do other fish react?
Although secretive, this species is hardy enough to hold its own in the presence of much larger and more boisterous fish, provided it can find plenty of hiding places in the rockwork.

WHAT to watch out for?
Check for signs of damage caused by infighting, which can occur where a number of individuals have been housed together in a small aquarium.

HOW compatible with inverts and corals?
May attack and eat ornamental shrimp. Will not harm corals. Reported to consume small polychaete fireworms.

WHAT area of the tank?
Individuals swim jerkily over rockwork constantly on the lookout for small shrimp or the other crustaceans it loves to eat.

HOW many in one tank?
Keep singly or in pairs for the fewest problems. This species occurs in colonies in its natural range and this situation can be replicated in the larger home aquarium (120 gal/450 l or more).

HOW does it behave?
When first introduced, many dottybacks may disappear for a few days, even weeks. This is particularly true in a large aquarium with no similar species stocked. It is nothing to worry about; the fish are cleaning up the large number of naturally occurring worms and crustaceans that can proliferate in the absence of predators.

WILL it breed in an aquarium?
Yes, it has been successfully reared in captivity. If a mature male disappears for prolonged periods of time, he is likely to be incubating the egg ball laid in a crack or hole in the rockwork.

Pseudochromis springeri

Springer's (bluestreak) dottyback

FISH PROFILE

A wonderful dottyback species that can be maintained in pairs in quite a small aquarium. In common with many of the more colorful dottybacks endemic to the Red Sea, it is moderately expensive, but very rewarding to keep.

WHAT size?
Males 2.1 in (5.5 cm); females 1.8 in (4.5 cm).

WHAT does it eat?
Wild specimens feed on a variety of benthic worms and crustaceans. May have a role in the control of small polychaete bristleworms in the home aquarium. Accepts most small meaty food particles, including brineshrimp, mysis, and chopped shellfish.

WHERE is it from?
Red Sea.

WHAT does it cost?
★★☆☆☆   ★★★☆☆
Moderately expensive for what is a quite small fish.

HOW do I sex it?
Males are more elongated, females more rounded and smaller. Two juveniles will differentiate into a male and female specimen, albeit after some initial bickering.

WHAT kind of tank?
Best suited to a live rock-based fish-only system or reef aquarium.

WHAT minimum size tank?
26 gal (100 l).

HOW do other fish react?
Most species ignore dottybacks, but royal grammas might react adversely in the short term. In general, dottybacks are able to hide in rockwork until an aggressive fish calms down. In the absence of suitable cover, dwarf and true angelfish present the greatest threat to them as a whole.

WHAT to watch out for?
Avoid fish that have been bullied in a dealer's tank and have split fins or marks on the body. Try to acquire a male/female pair so that you can witness their behavior.

HOW compatible with inverts and corals?
May attack and eat ornamental shrimp. Will not harm corals or other invertebrates.

WHAT area of the tank?
Has close ties to rocky substrates and seldom moves far from cover. Behaves perfectly naturally in the aquarium and provides plenty of entertainment for the aquarist.

HOW many in one tank?
Keep singly or in pairs.

HOW does it behave?
May bully or drive off smaller fish such as gobies, blennies, etc., but does not present many problems in most tanks.

WILL it breed in an aquarium?
Yes. If a mature male disappears for prolonged periods, he is likely to be incubating the egg ball laid in a hole in the rockwork. It has been successfully reared in captivity.

▼ *This dottyback is full of character and its inquisitive nature means that it rapidly endears itself to many aquarists.*

Pseudanthias pleurotaenia

Square spot wreckfish

FISH PROFILE

One of the largest of the active fairy basslets commonly available in the aquarium hobby. It is seldom available in small sizes and therefore more likely to be considered by aquarists with larger aquariums. Being a fish of deeper water, recorded at depths between 30 and 540 feet, it will take some time to adapt to brightly-lit systems. Often most active under blue actinic lighting.

WHAT size?
Males and females 8 in (20 cm).

WHAT does it eat?
A typical Anthias diet of animals suspended in the water column, such as zooplankton. Offer food several times per day to prevent weight loss in this species. Mysis, brineshrimp, and chopped shellfish are all suitable.

WHERE is it from?
Indo-Pacific, from Rowley Shoals to Samoa.

WHAT does it cost?
★★☆☆☆ ★★★☆☆
Expensive. The cost reflects difficulties associated with collection and the fish's overall size. Collectors may add a premium for male fish.

▶ *Only the male sports the pink blotch that gives this fish its common name.*

HOW do I sex it?
Males have the normal square-shaped pigmentation on the body and are more brightly colored. Pink and purple are the usual color combinations. Females are usually yellow-orange.

WHAT kind of tank?
Fish only; live rock-based fish-only; or reef aquarium. Ideal for the deepwater biotope aquarium.

WHAT minimum size tank?
106 gal (400 l).

HOW do other fish react?
Unless the aquarium is very spacious, do not stock this fish with other large zooplankton-feeders. Species to avoid can include full-grown fairy wrasses, *Genicanthus* spp. angelfishes and other wreckfishes.

WHAT to watch out for?
Try to ensure specimens are feeding before you buy. Individuals with an unusual swimming motion may have problems associated with the collection and retrieval of fish from deep water.

HOW compatible with inverts and corals?
Safe with corals and ornamental free-living invertebrates.

WHAT area of the tank?
Once settled, will swim actively in open water.

HOW many in one tank?
Keep singly unless the aquarium is large enough to accommodate a harem of several females with a single male (185 gal/700 l or more).

HOW does it behave?
Should not be aggressive to any fish other than very similar anthias or individuals from its own species.

WILL it breed in an aquarium?
No.

Pseudanthias squamipinnis

Golden wreckfish

One of the commonest
and most obvious fish
species on many tropical
reefs in the Indo-Pacific,
yet surprisingly, it has
only achieved moderate
popularity among marine
aquarists.

▲ *This male shows the typical vibrant color compared to the orange female.*

WHAT size?
6 in (15 cm) males would be
exceptional in the aquarium,
with females significantly
smaller at 5 in (10 cm) or so.

WHAT does it eat?
On tropical reefs this species
will feed for prolonged
periods on zooplankton. In
the aquarium, a varied diet
is mandatory. Offering mysis
rather than brineshrimp can
help the fish retain or even
gain body mass. It is vital to
feed this species several times
each day to simulate its natural
behavior and nutritional and
energy requirements.

WHERE is it from?
Red Sea, Indian Ocean, and
the Western Pacific Ocean.

WHAT does it cost?
★★☆☆☆   ★★★☆☆
Expensive. The cost reflects
difficulties associated with
collection and the fish's overall
size. Collectors sometimes add
a premium for male fish.

HOW do I sex it?
Males are purple and have a long
first dorsal fin ray. They also have
purple patches on the tips of the
pectoral fins.

WHAT kind of tank?
A live rock-based fish-only
system or reef aquarium, provided
richly oxygenated water can be
guaranteed.

WHAT minimum size tank?
48 gal (180 l) for a single individual,
200 gal (750 l) or more for a shoal.

HOW do other fish react?
This fish may be targeted by other
open water-swimming species, e.g.
parrot wrasse (*Cirrhilabrus* spp).

WHAT to watch out for?
Avoid specimens that do not
feed in dealers' tanks because
they may have been bullied by
conspecifics. Individuals that have
been harassed often hide away or
show signs of damage.

HOW compatible with inverts and corals?
Will not harm sessile invertebrates
or larger ornamental crustaceans.

WHAT area of the tank?
Settled specimens swim in open
water during the aquarium's
daylight hours.

HOW many in one tank?
Can be kept singly, but stunning
when kept in a large aquarium with
a single male and a shoal of up to
a dozen females.

HOW does it behave?
Dominant males may boss smaller
fish species that also swim in open
water. Otherwise, it is fascinating
to watch members of this species
interacting with each other.

WILL it breed in an aquarium?
May scatter spawn into the
water column, but has not been
successfully raised in captivity.

Serranocirrhitus latus

Fathead (hawkfish) anthias

FISH PROFILE

Many aquarists fail with this unusual species of fairy basslet because they treat it in the same way as one of the more commonly available *Pseudanthias* species. Bear in mind that *S. latus* often shuns the brightly-lit waters of coral reefs for overhangs and caves or lives among the branching corals themselves.

WHAT size?
Males 5 in (13 cm); females only 4 in (10 cm) or so.

WHAT does it eat?
Wild specimens feed almost exclusively on zooplankton, an easy diet to simulate in the marine aquarium. However, this species can be quite finicky and you may need to tempt a fish with several different types of food before it will eat. Feed it several times a day on meaty particulate food, such as enriched brineshrimp, mysis, or similar.

WHERE is it from?
Western Pacific including the Great Barrier Reef, Fiji, and Tonga.

WHAT does it cost?
★★★★☆
This is one of the more expensive species of anthias available to hobbyists.

HOW do I sex it?
Males are larger than females.

WHAT kind of tank?
A peaceful reef aquarium.

WHAT minimum size tank?
66 gal (250 l).

HOW do other fish react?
Other planktonivores can attack this fish and it is not wise to house it with more aggressive or boisterous species.

WHAT to watch out for?
Some fish require intense effort to coax them into feeding, but once they are taking food they settle quickly.

HOW compatible with inverts and corals?
Will not harm corals or any sessile invertebrates. Safe with ornamental shrimp and other crustaceans.

WHAT area of the tank?
Inhabits the lower-light areas of a normally lit reef aquarium, sometimes becoming more active under blue actinic lighting.

HOW many in one tank?
In most instances, best kept singly. Aquariums over 120 gal (450 l) will house a male/female pair.

HOW does it behave?
Reserves aggressive behavior almost exclusively for other members of its own species, particularly those of the same sex. In common with many marine fish found under ledges or overhangs, it often swims upside down.

WILL it breed in an aquarium?
No.

▼ *This fish often swims with its underside pointing towards the substrate. Thus, where caves are present, it can be found swimming upside-down.*

Endearing characters

▶ Despite being only distantly related, gobies and blennies are grouped here because the majority of species occupy similar habitats, often being found on, or close to, sand, rubble, or rock substrates. Gobies tend to have large heads and mouths and cylindrical bodies. They often have a sucker on their underside, formed from the fusion of the pelvic fins, that enables them to perch on vertical surfaces. Many species form commensal relationships with shrimps of the genus *Alpheus* and make a fascinating feature in any aquarium. The goby family is the largest group of marine fish, numbering over 2,000 species. Blennies are a less diverse group, with most species favoring a rock-dwelling existence. Their bodies are more laterally compressed than those of gobies and they tend to prefer rocky habitats to rubble or sand. Some species are venomous and are mimicked by their harmless relatives.

Price guide

★	$12–$20
★★	$20–$35
★★★	$35–$45
★★★★	$45–$55
★★★★★	$55–$70

FISH PROFILE

One of the real characters of the fish world and readily available to marine aquarists. Not the most colorful or active species in the aquarium hobby, but endearing. Three different color morphs are found around the Indo-Pacific, of which the half-black and half-yellow one is most regularly imported and prized by aquarists. The other phases have a horizontal white band, with or without a yellow tail, or resemble the Red Sea species, *E. gravieri*.

WHAT size?
Males 4.3 in (11 cm); females a little smaller.

WHAT does it eat?
In its natural environment, feeds primarily on algae, and readily accepts dried algae in the aquarium. Offer small-particle meaty foods, such as brineshrimp and chopped mysis. Should also accept flaked foods when settled.

WHERE is it from?
Tropical Indo-Pacific. Specimens are frequently imported via Sri Lanka, Indonesia, and the Philippines.

WHAT does it cost?
★★☆☆☆
Relatively inexpensive.

Ecsenius bicolor

Bicolor blenny

HOW do I sex it?
Determining the sex of bicolor blennies is not easy. Males are likely to be larger and dominant. The vigilant aquarist may be lucky enough to encounter two individuals cohabiting peacefully in a dealer's aquarium that may be a mated pair. Males will usually fight in such circumstances.

WHAT kind of tank?
Any aquarium is suitable, but this species prefers a system with live rock present.

WHAT minimum size tank?
7 gal (25 l) is sufficient, assuming excellent water quality.

HOW do other fish react?
Most fish will ignore this blenny and it should be "streetwise" enough to keep out of trouble.

WHAT to watch out for?
Do not buy specimens that appear thin or emaciated, and ensure that any potential introduction is feeding before you buy it.

HOW compatible with inverts and corals?
Not a threat to corals or other invertebrates, but similar-looking species are known coral-grazers, so be sure of the identity of the specimen you are buying.

WHAT area of the tank?
Typically on rockwork or decor.

HOW many in one tank?
Keep singly or in mated pairs.

HOW does it behave?
Usually found observing the daily routine of the aquarium from a suitable vantage point, often a hole. Will swim actively into the water column in pursuit of food. Do not keep this species with other blenny species. Despite its endearing nature, this territorial fish will vigorously defend its crevice or hole.

WILL it breed in an aquarium?
Potentially, yes.

▼ *The bicolor blenny often observes the hustle and bustle of aquarium life from a well-placed crevice.*

Ecsenius gravieri

Red Sea mimic blenny

FISH PROFILE

A wonderful species of blenny endemic to the Red Sea. It can be found swimming in open water together with the species of fish that it mimics in color pattern and behavior—another species of blenny called *Meiacanthus nigrolineatus*. This fang-tooth blenny is capable of inflicting painful bites. It is not necessary to maintain the two species together.

WHAT size?
Males and females 3.1 in (8 cm).

WHAT does it eat?
Grazers of algae and consumers of zooplankton in coral-rich areas of tropical reefs. Quite easy to feed in the aquarium. Even very small (10 mm) specimens are able to take brineshrimp easily. Offering some dried algae helps to keep the fish in tiptop condition.

WHERE is it from?
Endemic to the Red Sea and Western Reaches of the Gulf of Aden.

WHAT does it cost?
★★☆☆☆   ★★★☆☆
Relatively inexpensive.

HOW do I sex it?
No external visual differences.

WHAT kind of tank?
Best kept in a reef aquarium with plenty of cover, although a peaceful fish-only system with live rock would also be suitable.

WHAT minimum size tank?
A 13-gal (50-l) aquarium is sufficient, assuming very high quality water can be consistently maintained.

HOW do other fish react?
Avoid stocking with other species from the genus *Ecsenius*.

WHAT to watch out for?
Without a balanced diet, the exquisite coloration of this species can sometimes fade in captivity.

HOW compatible with inverts and corals?
Perfectly compatible with corals and invertebrates.

WHAT area of the tank?
In the absence of the mimicked species, this fish will remain almost exclusively on the rockwork. Individuals commonly occupy a small hole or crevice that serves as a suitable vantage point from which to observe the aquarium and also acts as a refuge.

HOW many in one tank?
Can be kept in numbers when small, but take care when the specimens mature.

HOW does it behave?
An endearing species with a large personality.

WILL it breed in an aquarium?
No.

▼ *This beautiful fish is an occasional import from the Red Sea. It mimics the venomous blenny,* Meiacanthus nigrolineatus.

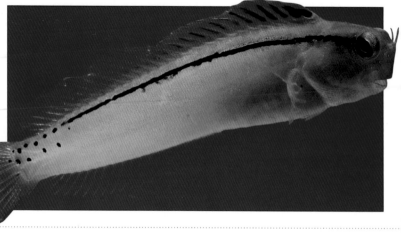

Ecsenius midas
Midas blenny

FISH PROFILE

A fascinating species that mimics the lyretail anthias *(Pseudanthias squamipinnis)*, swimming into open water with them and feeding on zooplankton. The species has separate color forms that are visible when it is resting, but these change when it is shoaling with the anthias. The Indonesian form is the most variable in color, from yellow-orange to green-brown.

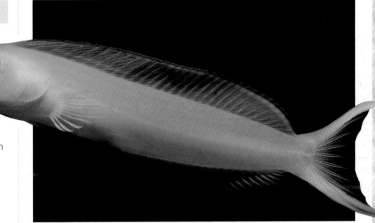

WHAT size?
Males and females 5.1 in (13 cm).

WHAT does it eat?
Zooplankton forms the majority of its diet on coral reefs, but aquarium fish accept most small meaty foods, such as mysis, brineshrimp, and chopped shellfish. With time, they may accept flake.

WHERE is it from?
A wide-ranging species found throughout the Tropical Indo-Pacific.

WHAT does it cost?
★★☆☆☆   ★★★☆☆
Relatively inexpensive.

HOW do I sex it?
No external visual differences.

WHAT kind of tank?
Almost any type of aquarium is suitable, but provide ample swimming space and plenty of live rock. Lyretail anthias are not necessary to maintain this species successfully.

WHAT minimum size tank?
40 gal (150 l).

HOW do other fish react?
Do not keep with other blennies.

WHAT to watch out for?
Some specimens prove reluctant to feed in captivity and require much care and attention to entice them to feed. This is best done by the dealer.

▲ *The Midas blenny is not afraid of swimming in open water but is equally at home on the rockwork.*

HOW compatible with inverts and corals?
Should not harm sessile or free-living invertebrates.

WHAT area of the tank?
Alternates an open-water, highly active swimming style with prolonged periods of rest on the rockwork, watching the world go by.

HOW many in one tank?
Keep singly.

HOW does it behave?
May harass open-water swimmers such as small wrasse.

WILL it breed in an aquarium?
Potentially, yes.

Meiacanthus nigrolineatus

Blue head canary blenny

FISH PROFILE

The genus *Meiacanthus* contains a number of species known as "fang blennies" on account of the very large canine teeth, with a venom gland at their base, found on the lower jaw. These fish tend to be open-water-swimming species and a number of them are mimicked by harmless species. The blue head canary blenny is mimicked by *Ecsenius gravieri*, and the very similar Indo-Pacific species, *Meiacanthus atrodorsalis,* is mimicked by a yellow and blue form of the bicolor blenny, *Ecsenius bicolor.*

WHAT size?
Males and females 3.7 in (9.5 cm).

WHAT does it eat?
Zooplankton in the wild. Many fish that feed on organisms suspended in the water column are easy to cater to in the aquarium, but it can prove difficult to provide these blennies with sufficient food. Offer brineshrimp and chopped mysis several times per day.

WHERE is it from?
Red Sea and Gulf of Aden.

WHAT does it cost?
★★☆☆☆
Inexpensive.

HOW do I sex it?
No external visual differences.

WHAT kind of tank?
Live rock-based fish-only system or reef aquarium with plenty of swimming space.

WHAT minimum size tank?
26 gal (100 l).

HOW do other fish react?
Due to its venomous nature, many fish do not hassle this blenny and it swims confidently in most aquariums. The greatest threat to its comfort comes from territorial damselfishes.

WHAT to watch out for?
Avoid skinny individuals or those with evidence of aggression caused by other fish. It is usual for the colors to fade markedly shortly

▲ *Be sure to observe the blue head canary blenny feeding before you buy it.*

after importation or when fish have been kept long-term in a dealer's tanks.

HOW compatible with inverts and corals?
Should not harm corals or other sessile or ornamental invertebrates.

WHAT area of the tank?
An open water-swimming species.

HOW many in one tank?
Best kept singly.

HOW does it behave?
Quite peaceful; should not bite any tankmates unless it is provoked.

WILL it breed in an aquarium?
No.

Salarius fasciatus

Algae blenny

FISH PROFILE

A hardy, intertidal species of blenny that endears itself to many aquarists due to its interesting behavior and its consumption of certain forms of filamentous algae and detritus. Given its large adult size, do not be tempted to acquire a small specimen for a small aquarium unless you can relocate it to a larger system when it outgrows the original one.

WHAT size?
Males 4.7 in (14 cm); females usually a little smaller.

WHAT does it eat?
Algae and detritus in the wild, but when introduced into the aquarium, many specimens accept mysis and brineshrimp along with other meaty foods. Provide dried algae on a daily basis for the best results with this blenny.

WHERE is it from?
A wide-ranging species found in most of the coral-rich areas of the Tropical Indo-Pacific, including the Red Sea.

WHAT does it cost?
★★☆☆☆
Inexpensive.

HOW do I sex it?
Males tend to be larger.

WHAT kind of tank?
Reef aquarium or live rock-based fish-only system.

WHAT minimum size tank?
At least 66 gal (250 l).

HOW do other fish react?
Take care when introducing this species into an aquarium housing other blenny species. It may also have problems with other substrate-dwelling species, such as hawkfish.

WHAT to watch out for?
Avoid skinny specimens or those that refuse to feed.

HOW compatible with inverts and corals?
Will not harm most corals or other invertebrates and safe with shrimp. Has been recorded biting clam mantles, but offering it some grazing material can alleviate this problem.

WHAT area of the tank?
Usually perches on the rockwork.

HOW many in one tank?
Best kept singly in all but the largest aquariums.

HOW does it behave?
Can display conflicting personality traits. If a larger, more dominant fish is in its immediate vicinity it acts shyly, but once that fish retreats, the algae blenny then bullies a fish smaller than itself. Its aggression comes to the fore in a small aquarium.

WILL it breed in an aquarium?
Potentially, yes. Male blennies tend to be larger than females and defend a nest site where the eggs are laid. Some color changes may be observed in the male during courtship and spawning.

▼ *What this fish lacks in color it makes up for in personality.*

Amblyeleotris aurora

Suntail goby

FISH PROFILE

A beautiful goby that shares its life with an equally stunning pistol shrimp, *Alpheus randalli*. Although the fish is not difficult to maintain in the home aquarium, it is one of the most demanding of the genus *Amblyeleotris* and has certain requirements that must be met if it is to thrive.

WHAT size?
Males and females 4.3 in (11 cm).

WHAT does it eat?
In the wild, small benthic and zooplanktonic invertebrates. Can prove initially reluctant to feed in the aquarium, particularly if it is unable to find refuge. Offer enriched brineshrimp, mysis, chopped shellfish, and similar particulate foods.

WHERE is it from?
Western Indian Ocean, including the Maldives and East Africa.

WHAT does it cost?
★★☆☆☆   ★★★☆☆
A mid-priced goby species.

▶ *This beautiful goby can be nervous and does best when a partner shrimp is present.*

HOW do I sex it?
No significant differences between males and females.

WHAT kind of tank?
Peaceful fish-only; live rock-based fish-only; or reef aquarium.

WHAT minimum size tank?
26 gal (100 l).

HOW do other fish react?
Do not keep with any aggressive species unless it's stocked with its partner shrimp and has been given plenty of time to settle. Even so, some hawkfishes, dottybacks, and wrasses will harass it to the extent that it is never seen.

WHAT to watch out for?
This fish is well known for jumping out of an uncovered aquarium, particularly when not stocked with an Apheid shrimp or in the hours and days after introduction. Minimize problems by stocking it with a partner shrimp and selecting specimens that feed readily.

HOW compatible with inverts and corals?
Perfectly trustworthy in the most diverse reef aquariums.

WHAT area of the tank?
Remains on or very close to sandy or gravel-based substrates.

HOW many in one tank?
Keep singly or in male/female pairs.

HOW does it behave?
Suntail gobies generally tolerate most other commonly kept marine fish. It is not a good idea to keep more than one species from this genus.

WILL it breed in an aquarium?
Potentially, yes.

Amblyeleotris randalli
Randall's shrimp goby

FISH PROFILE

Many *Amblyeleotris* species are suitable for inclusion in the marine aquarium. Of these, Randall's is probably one of the most striking. It can be housed together with any of the Alpheid shrimp known to live with partner gobies.

WHAT size?
Males and females 3.5 in (9 cm).

WHAT does it eat?
Feeds mainly on zooplankton and small benthic invertebrates such as copepods. In the aquarium, offer small specimens enriched brineshrimp and chopped mysis initially, increasing the variety of foods as they grow.

WHERE is it from?
Western Central Pacific, including the Great Barrier Reef and Micronesia.

WHAT does it cost?
★★☆☆☆   ★★★☆☆
One of the more expensive *Amblyeleotris* species, but still within the budget of most marine aquarists.

HOW do I sex it?
All specimens possess the large, rounded dorsal fin. It is likely that pairs will consist of very similar-looking individuals. When groups are kept in a dealer's tank, they often begin to form pairs.

WHAT kind of tank?
Fish-only; live rock-based fish-only; or reef aquarium.

WHAT minimum size tank?
13 gal (50 l).

HOW do other fish react?
A. randalli is fairly shy and will be targeted by more aggressive species. Dwarf angelfishes, wrasses, and other gobies may single it out for bullying.

WHAT to watch out for?
Make sure that specimens are feeding well before you buy them. They need to be target-fed with a basting pipette or similar device when first introduced, as they can be quite reclusive and reluctant to venture into open water to compete for food.

HOW compatible with inverts and corals?
Will not harm any invertebrates, including small ornamental shrimp.

WHAT area of the tank?
This substrate-dwelling fish does not venture far from sand or gravel surfaces.

HOW many in one tank?
Keep singly or in true male/female pairs.

HOW does it behave?
A peaceful species that usually tolerates all other fish. It has even been known to share its shrimp with other goby species.

WILL it breed in an aquarium?
Potentially, yes.

▶ *The large dorsal fin of this species is thought to be used in communication between individuals.*

Amblygobius phalaena

Dragon goby

FISH PROFILE

The dragon goby is a medium-large species that makes an interesting alternative to the more popular gobies from the genus *Valenciennea*. It shares their sand-sifting behavior, but is less prone to weight loss in the aquarium.

WHAT size?
Males and females 6 in (15 cm).

WHAT does it eat?
This goby takes mouthfuls of sandy substrate and expels them through its gills as it searches for small crustaceans, worms, and algae. In the absence of a substrate rich in suitable food, it will usually accept most meaty offerings, mysis and brineshrimp being the most popular. It may also consume filamentous algae where present; provide dried algae in a lettuce clip.

WHERE is it from?
Western Pacific. Most aquarium specimens come from the Philippines and Indonesia.

WHAT does it cost?
★★☆☆☆
Inexpensive.

▲ *This female dragon goby has a single black spot on the tail fin.*

HOW do I sex it?
Females generally have one black spot (ocellus) on the tail fin. Males have a number of spots.

WHAT kind of tank?
Fish-only; live rock-based fish-only; or reef aquarium.

WHAT minimum size tank?
63 gal (240 l).

HOW do other fish react?
Most fish tolerate the presence of this species, but large wrasse and other substrate-dwelling gobies represent the greatest threat to its wellbeing. Where aggression is anticipated, introducing pairs simultaneously can help reduce any harm to one individual goby.

WHAT to watch out for?
Avoid skinny specimens or those that prove reluctant to feed. If males are kept together, one will dominate and harass the other, often preventing it from feeding.

HOW compatible with inverts and corals?
Will not directly harm invertebrates, but its sifting behavior can irritate sessile species that may be showered with sand grains. Generally less of a nuisance than gobies of the genus *Valenciennea*.

WHAT area of the tank?
On sandy or gravel-based substrates.

HOW many in one tank?
Keep singly or in male/female pairs where space allows.

HOW does it behave?
Might take exception to the introduction of other goby species that prefer a substrate-dwelling existence, but otherwise peaceful.

WILL it breed in an aquarium?
Yes. Lays many eggs, but the larvae are quite difficult to rear.

Amblygobius rainfordi
Court jester (old glory)

FISH PROFILE

A sand-sifting goby that stays small and has a very attractive patterning. Pay careful attention to its requirements as it is prone to starving in a home aquarium. This is a shy species and you may not observe it regularly enough to notice any deterioration in its condition.

WHAT size?
Males and females 2.5 in (6.5 cm).

WHAT does it eat?
In the wild, this fish sifts sand and mud in search of burrowing invertebrates. Individuals have very small mouths, so chop food finely. Also known to feed on filamentous algae, so offer dried algae for grazing.

WHERE is it from?
Philippines, Great Barrier Reef, and Micronesia.

WHAT does it cost?
★★☆☆☆
A medium-priced goby.

▶ *This small but beautifully-patterned goby needs plenty of food if it is to thrive.*

HOW do I sex it?
No obvious external differences.

WHAT kind of tank?
Due to the availability of natural foodstuffs, this fish is best kept in a live rock-based fish-only or reef aquarium.

WHAT minimum size tank?
13 gal (50 l).

HOW do other fish react?
Regardless of the size of the aquarium, do not keep this goby with any species more territorial or belligerent than small territorial wrasses, hawkfishes, dottybacks, and similar.

WHAT to watch out for?
Avoid skinny specimens and ensure that fish can obtain sufficient food of the right size. Many individuals will not swim into open water to take food, preferring instead to pick it from the substrate, so a system with a very high flow rate might not be suitable.

HOW compatible with inverts and corals?
Should not harm any ornamental invertebrates, including clams, corals, anemones or crustaceans.

WHAT area of the tank?
On, or close to, the bottom of the aquarium. Occasionally over rockwork looking for algae.

HOW many in one tank?
Best kept singly, unless a true pair can be obtained.

HOW does it behave?
Peaceful, except towards members of its own species.

WILL it breed in an aquarium?
Potentially, yes. Other members of this genus have bred in a home aquarium.

Cryptocentrus cinctus

Yellow prawn goby

FISH PROFILE

The most widely available of all the gobies known to live in the burrows made by pistol shrimp (genus *Alpheus*). This species is also one of the most variable in appearance, ranging from brilliant yellow to gray and even brown forms or combinations of each coloring. All specimens should have four or five faint vertical bands on the body and blue spots on the head.

WHAT size?
Males and females 3 in (7.5 cm).

WHAT does it eat?
In the wild, a variety of small invertebrates taken from the water column, including crustaceans and larval organisms. Aquarium fish have deceptively large mouths and consume most foods. Mysis, enriched brineshrimp, chopped shellfish, and similar foods are all welcomed. Some specimens will even take large mouthfuls of dried marine algae.

WHERE is it from?
Widespread in the Tropical Western Pacific. Many specimens are imported via the Philippines and Indonesia.

WHAT does it cost?
★☆☆☆☆
Inexpensive, especially when small (1 in [2.5 cm] or so).

▲ *This inexpensive, yet beautiful and hardy goby should prove long-lived given suitable care.*

HOW do I sex it?
No known external differences.

WHAT kind of tank?
Fish-only; live rock-based fish-only; or reef aquarium.

WHAT minimum size tank?
20 gal (75 l).

HOW do other fish react?
If added to a system without a burrowing shrimp, this fish can be bullied by wrasses, hawkfishes, dottybacks, and similar aggressive species. Even when it can use the shrimp's burrow, repeated attacks can mean that it remains hidden most, if not all, day.

WHAT to watch out for?
Avoid skinny specimens or those that have been fighting due to being housed together. This fish also has a reputation for jumping out of the aquarium when alarmed.

HOW compatible with inverts and corals?
Perfect for most reef aquariums, except those containing small ornamental shrimp, such as peppermint shrimp (*Lysmata wurdemanni*).

WHAT area of the tank?
This substrate-dwelling species perches on sand or gravel.

HOW many in one tank?
Keep singly or in male/female pairs.

HOW does it behave?
Tends to reserve its aggression for same-sex members of its own species. Should any fish show too much interest in it, the goby inflates its head and opens its jaws to make itself appear a much more menacing proposition.

WILL it breed in an aquarium?
Potentially, yes.

Cryptocentrus caeruleopunctatus

Red Sea harlequin goby

FISH PROFILE

The harlequin goby is a large species that lives in a symbiotic relationship with pistol shrimp from the genus *Alpheus*. Small specimens are seldom available, so it tends to be stocked in large aquariums. In common with many of its close relatives, it has a large, fleshy pelvic sucker that it uses as a perching platform, raising its head to obtain a much better vantage point from which to check for predators.

WHAT size?
Males and females up to 5 in (13 cm).

WHAT does it eat?
In the wild, benthic and planktonic organisms. In the aquarium, it may initially prove reluctant to feed. Usually settles quickly, especially where its partner shrimp is already stocked, taking a variety of meaty foods such as enriched brineshrimp, mysis, and chopped shellfish. Some individuals accept dried algae.

WHERE is it from?
Only known from the Red Sea.

WHAT does it cost?
★★★★☆ ★★★★★
Expensive due to its limited range.

HOW do I sex it?
No external visual differences.

WHAT kind of tank?
Live rock-based fish-only system or reef aquarium, preferably together with a species of burrowing alpheid shrimp.

WHAT minimum size tank?
66 gal (250 l).

HOW do other fish react?
Most fish ignore this goby if it is ensconced with its partner shrimp. Large wrasses, angels, or dottybacks may target it when it is first introduced.

WHAT to watch out for?
Ignore non-feeding specimens or those showing signs of lethargy or emaciation. Individuals housed in same-sex pairs may show signs of damage due to fighting.

HOW compatible with inverts and corals?
May consume smaller species of ornamental shrimp. Otherwise, compatible with sessile invertebrates and most aquarium scavengers.

WHAT area of the tank?
Rarely strays far from sandy or gravel-based substrates.

HOW many in one tank?
Keep singly or in male/female pairs.

HOW does it behave?
Can show aggression towards any small fish that it deems to stray too close to it or its burrow. This problem is exacerbated if it is maintained in an aquarium that is too small. Otherwise, most of its aggression centers on members of its own or similar species.

WILL it breed in an aquarium?
Potentially, yes.

▼ *The rounded head and protruding eyes are typical of the genus Cryptocentrus.*

Ctenogobiops tangaroai

Spangled shrimp goby

FISH PROFILE

A small species of goby that lives with Alpheid "pistol" shrimp in burrows on sandy substrates. It is an interesting and hardy alternative to the more commonly-encountered shrimp gobies from the genera *Stonogobiops, Amblyeleotris,* and *Cryptocentrus.*

▲ *This diminutive goby might need time to settle in the aquarium before it begins to show its exquisite patterning.*

WHAT size?
Males and females 2.3 in (6 cm).

WHAT does it eat?
In the wild, small planktonic and benthic invertebrates such as copepods and amphipods. In the aquarium it should readily accept any meaty foods small enough to fit into its mouth. Chopped mysis and brineshrimp are best. May accept flake and granular food with time.

WHERE is it from?
The Pacific Ocean. Detailed information is sketchy but it is certainly collected in Indonesia and may be much more widespread than this.

WHAT does it cost?
★★☆☆☆   ★★★☆☆
A mid-priced species.

HOW do I sex it?
No known visual differences.

WHAT kind of tank?
Live rock-based fish-only system or reef aquarium.

WHAT minimum size tank?
26 gal (100 l).

HOW do other fish react?
Other gobies, damselfishes, and dottybacks may present a threat.

WHAT to watch out for?
If housing this fish with a pistol shrimp, be aware that the goby will cohabit with it no matter where the shrimp excavates its burrow, even if this happens to be at the back of the aquarium rather than the front.

HOW compatible with inverts and corals?
Will not harm corals or ornamental invertebrates.

WHAT area of the tank?
On sandy or gravel-based substrates.

HOW many in one tank?
Keep singly or in male/female pairs. Numbers can be maintained in a sufficiently large aquarium (80 gal/300 l or more).

HOW does it behave?
Peaceful; should not bother any of its tankmates. However, in the smaller aquarium, it is best to maintain a single species of substrate-dwelling goby.

WILL it breed in an aquarium?
Potentially, yes, but not recorded.

Elacatinus multifasciatus

Multibanded (greenbanded) goby

FISH PROFILE

A small and very desirable rarity within the aquarium hobby. Most specimens currently available are tank-raised. This is a beautiful species to observe at first hand. In its natural environment, it is often found among the spines of sea urchins.

WHAT size?
Females 2 in (5 cm); males usually smaller.

WHAT does it eat?
In the wild, small benthic invertebrates. In the aquarium, provide chopped mysis and brineshrimp, as well as the finer commercial preparations.

WHERE is it from?
Bahamas, Central America, and tropical South American waters.

WHAT does it cost?
★★★☆☆
Fairly expensive for its size. Up to double the price of the blue neon goby, *Elacatinus oceanops*.

HOW do I sex it?
Females are usually the larger and more dominant individuals in a group.

WHAT kind of tank?
Fish-only with live rock or a reef aquarium.

WHAT minimum size tank?
A pair can be easily housed in a 10-gallon (40-liter) aquarium, assuming excellent water quality.

HOW do other fish react?
Do not keep with predatory fish species. Gobies of a similar size or shape may prove aggressive towards this species.

WHAT to watch out for?
Avoid specimens with torn fins or body damage; they may have been fighting among themselves. Although the wounds will heal, this is the responsibility of the dealer.

HOW compatible with inverts and corals?
Perfectly compatible with corals and other invertebrates.

WHAT area of the tank?
A rockwork-dwelling species.

HOW many in one tank?
Can be kept singly, in pairs or small groups given plenty of space.

HOW does it behave?
Peaceful, generally minds its own business, and rarely ventures into open water except when feeding.

WILL it breed in an aquarium?
Yes. Larvae have been successfully raised in captivity.

▼ *Multibanded gobies may be hard to find but are worth waiting for, as they are hardy and peaceful.*

Elacatinus oceanops

Blue neon goby

A diminutive and ever-popular species. It is part of a fairly large genus in which many species have been successfully bred in captivity, some to the extent that they are widely available within the trade.

▶ *The aquarium requirements of this species are much the same as for the rest of the genus* Elacatinus.

WHAT size?
Females 2 in (5 cm); males a little smaller.

WHAT does it eat?
Wild specimens feed on benthic invertebrates, plus parasites and necrotic skin picked from other fish species. Most aquarium specimens accept a variety of foods, but the fish has a tiny mouth, so be sure to provide morsels small enough for it to cope with.

WHERE is it from?
Gulf of Mexico and tropical Central and the northerly coasts of South America.

WHAT does it cost?
★☆☆☆☆   ★★☆☆☆
Relatively inexpensive.

HOW do I sex it?
Females are larger and more dominant than males. They are capable of changing sex, so if you intend keeping more than one individual, buy small specimens or try selecting two fish with a significant size difference.

WHAT kind of tank?
Fish-only; live rock-based fish-only system; or reef aquarium.

WHAT minimum size tank?
A 7-gallon (25-liter) microreef is not too small for this species, but excellent water quality must be maintained.

HOW do other fish react?
Similarly sized gobies may not react well to the blue neon goby. Conversely, larger species with a reputation for territorial aggression will often completely ignore it, unless it is to take advantage of its cleaning abilities.

WHAT to watch out for?
Avoid specimens with dark marks or torn fins, as these are likely to have been the victims of intraspecific aggression. Such individuals may also appear skinny and will require care and attention if they are to recover.

HOW compatible with inverts and corals?
Will not harm invertebrates or corals.

WHAT area of the tank?
Prefers to perch on corals or rocks than swim into open water.

HOW many in one tank?
Keep singly or, better still, in pairs. Groups can be maintained in larger aquariums.

HOW does it behave?
As a cleaner fish, the blue neon goby uses the fused pelvic fins (that form a sucker in many goby species) to hold onto the fish it is cleaning. It then hops over the surface of the fish's body in search of dead skin or foreign bodies.

WILL it breed in an aquarium?
Yes.

Fusigobius longispinus

Orange-spotted sand goby

FISH PROFILE

The genus *Fusigobius* contains a small number of attractive yet robust species suitable for the marine aquarium. They have evolved to live on sandy or rubble substrates. All are very similar in appearance and have the same maintenance requirements in the aquarium.

WHAT size?
Males and females 3.1 in (8 cm).

WHAT does it eat?
In the wild, a variety of crustaceans, worms, and other benthic creatures, including small fish. In an aquarium, it readily consumes almost any meaty foods. Offer mysis, brineshrimp, chopped shellfish. May also accept granular and flaked foods.

WHERE is it from?
Red Sea and East Africa to the Great Barrier Reef and Western Pacific.

WHAT does it cost?
★★☆☆☆   ★★★☆☆
Relatively inexpensive.

HOW do I sex it?
Males have an elongated first dorsal spine that is obvious when it is erect, but it can also be seen reaching beyond the base of the hindmost dorsal fin ray when laid flat.

WHAT kind of tank?
Fish-only or live rock-based fish-only system.

WHAT minimum size tank?
40 gal (150 l).

HOW do other fish react?
This fish is likely to encounter aggression from other sand-dwelling goby species, as well as from normally territorial species.

WHAT to watch out for?
May jump from an uncovered aquarium.

HOW compatible with inverts and corals?
Should not harm corals or most invertebrates, with the possible exception of small ornamental shrimp.

WHAT area of the tank?
Perches on sandy or gravel-based substrates.

HOW many in one tank?
Keep singly or in male/female pairs.

HOW does it behave?
Can be territorial towards similar species or conspecifics. Do not house with very small fish, as it is likely to hunt and eat them.

WILL it breed in an aquarium?
Potentially, yes.

▶ *The orange-spotted sand goby is an attractive but predatory species that may consume small fish and shrimp in the aquarium.*

Lythrypnus dalli

Catalina goby

FISH PROFILE

The most commonly available member of a small genus of attractive gobies found in the tropical and subtropical waters of the Americas. The Catalina goby is most likely to be encountered as a tank-raised specimen. It is a beautiful fish, but strictly speaking is sub-tropical in origin, being found in waters no warmer than 72°F (22°C).

WHAT size?
Males and females 2.3 in (6 cm).

WHAT does it eat?
In the wild, a small predator of zooplanktonic and benthic animals, particularly crustaceans. Tank-raised individuals accept most small particulate food, including granular forms, but chopped mysis and brineshrimp are best, particularly for smaller specimens.

WHERE is it from?
Eastern Pacific around Southern California and the Baja Peninsula in Mexico.

WHAT does it cost?
★★☆☆☆   ★★★★☆
Moderately expensive for a small species of goby.

HOW do I sex it?
Individuals are simultaneous hermaphrodites and therefore have male and female reproductive organs that differ in the extent of their development at the time of spawning.

WHAT kind of tank?
Survives well in a tropical marine aquarium, provided it does not get too warm. Aquariums without chillers are not suitable, as they may achieve temperatures that will cause this fish discomfort or potentially kill it.

WHAT minimum size tank?
13 gal (50 l).

HOW do other fish react?
Thrives with most other species of fish, which usually react with indifference to its presence.

WHAT to watch out for?
Avoid faded or excessively skinny specimens. They have probably not been fed on sufficiently small food items and need some intensive care and attention if they are to be revived.

HOW compatible with inverts and corals?
Will not harm corals or ornamental invertebrates.

WHAT area of the tank?
Rockwork close to refuges and on sandy substrates.

HOW many in one tank?
Keep singly, in pairs or in small groups.

HOW does it behave?
Not aggressive at all. May occasionally bicker with members of its own species.

WILL it breed in an aquarium?
Yes. It has been successfully raised in captivity.

▼ *This beautiful fish might not be able to withstand the higher temperatures experienced in a marine aquarium.*

Stonogobiops nematodes

Antenna (hi-fin banded) goby

FISH PROFILE

This widely-available species of partner goby lives with *Alpheus* spp. shrimp in its natural range, particularly the stunning *A. randalli*. The prospect of maintaining a shrimp goby with pistol shrimp attracts many aquarists and they are very rewarding to keep. The fish uses its large, well-developed eyes to watch for potential aggressors. The shrimp has terrible eyesight but is able to build a burrow. Thus, the goby has a purpose-built retreat to shelter from predators, and the shrimp has a lookout it can trust while it is otherwise employed in its mining operations.

WHAT size?
Males and females 2 in (5 cm).

WHAT does it eat?
A zooplankton feeder in its natural environment. Accepts any meaty particulate food in the aquarium. The mouth is deceptively large and it is amazing what this fish can cram into it.

WHERE is it from?
Most specimens come into the trade from Bali in Indonesia and the Philippines, but it is also found in the Indian Ocean around the Seychelle Islands.

WHAT does it cost?
★★☆☆☆   ★★★☆☆
A mid-priced goby species.

HOW do I sex it?
Almost impossible, even when observing a mated pair.

WHAT kind of tank?
Best suited to a very peaceful, live rock-based fish-only system or reef aquarium.

WHAT minimum size tank?
Best housed in a smaller aquarium to increase the chances of observing it and its behavior.

HOW do other fish react?
Many other species of substrate-dwelling goby will not tolerate antenna gobies. Ironically, the closely related white-rayed shrimp goby (*Stonogobiops yasha*) seemingly coexists quite peacefully with this fish.

WHAT to watch out for?
Try to establish whether an individual is feeding before buying it and check for any signs of torn fins or marks on the body that may be signs of bullying.

▲ *This goby is a common import that should be readily available.*

HOW compatible with inverts and corals?
Perfectly compatible with corals and other invertebrates.

WHAT area of the tank?
Sand or rubble areas.

HOW many in one tank?
Maintain singly or in male/female pairs. The antenna goby will not tolerate same-sex individuals. Rivals grapple with their jaws and the victor will often kill the loser.

HOW does it behave?
When settled, antenna gobies hover above a burrow or similar refuge. This natural behavior is more likely when an Alpheid shrimp is present.

WILL it breed in an aquarium?
Potentially yes, but may be difficult to confirm because egg-laying is likely to take place inside the burrow.

Stonogobiops yasha

White-rayed shrimp goby

This highly sought-after species was once thought to be extremely rare, but individuals are now relatively easy to obtain. A stunning fish with interesting characteristics, not least the large mouth that gapes when this fish is threatened. There are few more fascinating sights than a partner goby and its shrimp. The shrimp digs a burrow and the goby stands guard over the entrance. Should danger threaten, both will retreat quickly into the tunnel. Industrious shrimp can create a whole network of interconnected chambers, so be sure to secure rockwork firmly.

WHAT size?
Males and females 2.3 in (6 cm).

WHAT does it eat?
May be reluctant to feed when first acquired. Fish often begin feeding more readily in an aquarium that is also home to their partner shrimp. Offer small foods, such as brineshrimp, mysis, or chopped shellfish.

WHERE is it from?
Tropical Western Pacific.

WHAT does it cost?
★★★★★
One of the most expensive shrimp gobies.

▶ *Although a relative newcomer to the hobby, this species is becoming increasingly popular with aquarists.*

HOW do I sex it?
Where groups are kept with symbiotic shrimp, males and females will form pairs.

WHAT kind of tank?
Although not essential, a sand or gravel substrate is recommended, particularly if you want to observe the fascinating natural relationship between this species and its partner shrimp, *Alpheus randalli*.

WHAT minimum size tank?
7 gal (25 l) would not be too small, given good conditions.

HOW do other fish react?
Other sand-dwelling gobies may not tolerate this species.

WHAT to watch out for?
Avoid lethargic or emaciated specimens. In the absence of a pistol shrimp, fish may not feed.

HOW compatible with inverts and corals?
Will not harm any sessile invertebrates or ornamental shrimp.

WHAT area of the tank?
Exclusively bottom-dwelling.

HOW many in one tank?
Provided enough shrimp are available, this species seems very tolerant of other individuals. Keeping a small group is the best way to obtain pairs.

HOW does it behave?
In the wild, the fish forms a symbiotic relationship with the stunning alpheid pistol shrimp, *Alpheus randalli*.

WILL it breed in an aquarium?
Not yet recorded, but almost inevitable.

Trimma cana

Candycane pygmy goby

FISH PROFILE

Formally described as recently as 2004, this pretty goby is set to become a firm favorite as aquarists become more familiar with it. It is one of three or four closely-related species with strong physical similarities; all require the same care. If you wish to acquire a group of one species, it is best to buy them at the same time, as subsequent imports may be a different species.

WHAT size?
Males 1 in (2.5 cm); females fractionally smaller.

WHAT does it eat?
In the wild, zooplankton and benthic invertebrates. Some of the smaller particle frozen foods marketed as invertebrate foods are suitable, together with finely chopped shellfish. Brineshrimp are usually small enough to be consumed. Do not presume that because you are feeding the aquarium, this species is getting enough to eat.

WHERE is it from?
Pacific Ocean, including Fiji, Palau, Marshall Islands, and the Caroline Islands, but most aquarium specimens are exported from the Philippines.

WHAT does it cost?
★★☆☆☆   ★★★☆☆
Fairly inexpensive.

HOW do I sex it?
Males are larger than females.

WHAT kind of tank?
Should do well in a reef or live rock-based fish-only aquarium.

WHAT minimum size tank?
7 gal (25 l) is adequate, assuming excellent water quality.

HOW do other fish react?
Appears tolerant of other small gobies, including *Elacatinus*, *Eviota* and other *Trimma* species, although individuals from these genera may not view the goby in the same way. Avoid any predatory species, including hawkfish and larger dottybacks.

WHAT to watch out for?
Avoid emaciated specimens or particularly small individuals.

HOW compatible with inverts and corals?
Perfectly compatible with corals and other sessile invertebrates. Will not harm even the smallest ornamental shrimp.

▲ *This recently-described fish is set to become a very popular choice with marine aquarists.*

WHAT area of the tank?
Prefers to rest on the bottom.

HOW many in one tank?
Can be kept singly, but probably does best in pairs or groups. The upper limit will depend more on the capacity of the aquarium and other inhabitants than problems within this species.

HOW does it behave?
The experience of the home aquarist will be crucial when compiling information about this newly introduced species. We can derive some useful knowledge from looking at similar species within the genus, but it will have some unique traits.

WILL it breed in an aquarium?
Not recorded but highly likely.

Trimma rubromaculatus

Red splash pygmy goby

FISH PROFILE

This is one of the large number of pygmy goby species currently described. It is becoming increasingly available and ever more popular within the marine hobby. It is very easy to maintain and should not present any problems.

WHAT size?
Males and females .8 in (2 cm).

WHAT does it eat?
Zooplankton in the wild, but takes any meaty foods offered, provided they are small enough to be easily consumed. Enriched brineshrimp, chopped mysis, and chopped mussel are suitable.

WHERE is it from?
Papua, New Guinea.

WHAT does it cost?
★★☆☆☆   ★★★☆☆
Their small size and apparent abundance in the collection areas makes them inexpensive.

HOW do I sex it?
Males are likely to be the largest individuals within a group, but there are no definite distinguishing features between males and females.

WHAT kind of tank?
This species will be at home in the very smallest reef or live rock-based aquarium, provided good water quality can be maintained.

WHAT minimum size tank?
8–12 gal (30–45 l), assuming excellent water quality.

HOW do other fish react?
Avoid larger predatory species, such as hawkfish or larger grammas and dottybacks.

▼ *A small shoal makes a wonderful display in a peaceful marine aquarium.*

WHAT to watch out for?
There are few problems with this robust species. Avoid specimens that show signs of bullying.

HOW compatible with inverts and corals?
Perfectly at home in a coral-rich environment and will not present a threat to any invertebrates.

WHAT area of the tank?
On the rockwork or hovering in open water a few inches above the bottom of the aquarium.

HOW many in one tank?
Keep in pairs or small groups to observe their natural behavior.

HOW does it behave?
Males dominate a harem of females, but otherwise peaceful.

WILL it breed in an aquarium?
Not recorded but highly likely.

Tryssogobius colini

Tiny dartfish

FISH PROFILE

A tiny fish that is surprisingly hardy and ideally suited to the smaller, peaceful reef aquarium. It is likely that several closely-related species exist, some of which are yet to be described by science.

▲ *This species may be available as small as .4 in (10 mm) in length.*

WHAT size?
Males and females 1.4 in (3.5 cm).

WHAT does it eat?
Zooplankton in the wild, but accepts most particulate foods in the home aquarium, provided they are small enough to be easily consumed.

WHERE is it from?
Tropical Western Pacific.

WHAT does it cost?
★☆☆☆☆ ★★☆☆☆
Inexpensive.

HOW do I sex it?
No obvious external differences, but males are likely to be more aggressive than females towards individuals of the same species.

WHAT kind of tank?
Perfect for the small reef aquarium or a system that includes plenty of live rock.

WHAT minimum size tank?
8 gal (30 l).

HOW do other fish react?
Do not keep with aggressive fish.

WHAT to watch out for?
This diminutive dartfish is much more resilient to the attentions of other fish than its size and beauty suggest, but do not take this for granted. Its small size will make it an easy target for predators such as hawkfish.

HOW compatible with inverts and corals?
Will not harm ornamental shrimp or corals.

WHAT area of the tank?
Over sand or rockwork but rarely strays too far from refuge.

HOW many in one tank?
Can be kept singly, in pairs or small groups where aquarium space allows.

HOW does it behave?
Doesn't do much except hover above the rockwork looking pretty for most of the time. However, keep a group of these dartfish and you should be treated to social interactions including the establishment of a pecking order and, potentially, courtship and breeding.

WILL it breed in an aquarium?
Not recorded but likely.

Valenciennea strigata

Blue cheek sleeper goby

FISH PROFILE

To succeed with this popular aquarium fish, you must be able to provide its nutritional requirements. It belongs to a specialized group of gobies that sift mouthfuls of sand or gravel in their mouths, sorting out edible particles from the inedible and expelling the latter through the gills.

WHAT size?
Males 7 in (18 cm); females slightly smaller at 6 in (15 cm).

WHAT does it eat?
In the wild, it sorts small worms, crustaceans, fish eggs, and even small fish from the substrate. Provide plenty of food in the aquarium; feed the fish regularly several times per day with high-energy mysis shrimp or chopped shellfish. Brineshrimp may entice specimens to feed, but has little use as a long-term feed.

WHERE is it from?
Widespread in the tropical Indo-Pacific, from East Africa to Australia.

WHAT does it cost?
★★★☆☆ ★★★★★
True pairs from the Coral Sea tend to be the most costly.

▶ *Pairs seem to do better in the aquarium than single individuals.*

HOW do I sex it?
Sexing specimens is difficult unless you can observe a pair. In this situation, the male will be significantly larger than the female.

WHAT kind of tank?
Fish-only; live rock-based fish-only system; or reef aquarium.

WHAT minimum size tank?
66 gal (250 l).

HOW do other fish react?
Do not house with large wrasses, boisterous species such as some triggerfishes, or other sand-dwelling gobies.

WHAT to watch out for?
Avoid non-feeding fish and/or excessively skinny specimens. It has been suggested that emaciated fish might harbor gut parasites that are difficult to treat.

HOW compatible with inverts and corals?
Should not directly harm ornamental shrimp or any invertebrates, but its digging can undermine rockwork and corals. Its sifting behavior can irritate corals that have sand dumped on them.

WHAT area of the tank?
On sandy or gravel substrates, sometimes rising into mid-water in search of food.

HOW many in one tank?
Can be kept singly, but increased survival rates are reported for male/female pairs.

HOW does it behave?
Resident fish seldom tolerate the introduction of other substrate-dwelling species, such as other *Valenciennea* species or prawn gobies from the genera *Cryptocentrus* or *Amblyeleotris*.

WILL it breed in an aquarium?
Yes, but it can be difficult to confirm as this often takes place in a cave out of the aquarist's sight.

Valenciennea wardii

Ward's sleeper goby

FISH PROFILE

One of the most attractive of the many species of goby that use their mouths to separate morsels of food from inedible sand. Ward's sleeper gobies are extremely susceptible to bacterial infections, particularly those that affect the mouth. Check the entire goby for signs of inflammation before buying. Ward's sleeper goby is only available sporadically in the hobby and is considered very rare in its natural environment.

WHAT size?
Males 5.1 in (13 cm); females about 4 in (10 cm).

WHAT does it eat?
Sifts edible creatures from sandy substrates in the wild and this behavior continues in the aquarium, albeit with less success. Accepts most frozen foods, but requires regular feeding 5-10 times per day if it is to thrive.

WHERE is it from?
Various isolated localities in the tropical Indian Ocean and Western Pacific.

WHAT does it cost?
★★★☆☆ ★★★★☆
Moderately expensive, particularly when compared with most other members of this genus that are widely available in the trade.

HOW do I sex it?
Males are usually larger than females, but this is not apparent unless you can observe a pair.

WHAT kind of tank?
Best housed in a live rock-based fish-only system. Many aquarists introduce it into a reef aquarium, but conflicts can occur when you consider the amount of food the fish requires and the need to maintain excellent water quality for coral health.

WHAT minimum size tank?
53 gal (200 l).

HOW do other fish react?
Other sand-dwelling species are unlikely to tolerate this goby. These can include other large gobies of the genera *Cryptocentrus* and *Amblyeleotris* and also medium-sized and large wrasses from the genera *Thalassoma* and *Coris*.

WHAT to watch out for?
Avoid emaciated individuals, as these are unlikely to recover even with the best intensive care.

▲ *Give this striking fish time to settle in the dealer's aquarium before buying it.*

HOW compatible with inverts and corals?
Will not directly harm any corals or ornamental crustaceans and echinoderms, but can cause problems by depositing sand onto sessile invertebrates.

WHAT area of the tank?
On, or hovering over, sand and gravel.

HOW many in one tank?
Male/female pairs appear to do better than single individuals.

HOW does it behave?
Can react aggressively towards similar species, but on the whole very peaceful, even shy.

WILL it breed in an aquarium?
Other members of this genus have been reported spawning in home aquariums, and as more people provide the needs of this delicate species, the likelihood of Ward's sleeper goby doing so will improve.

Curious novelties

Cowfishes and boxfishes are very similar groups that are characterized by species in which the skeleton has become fused into a rigid structure containing all the internal organs. Cowfishes tend to enhance this protection with long spines, and both cowfishes and boxfishes secrete noxious venom from their skin. However, they are not invulnerable and should not be housed with aggressive species. Tiny individuals offered for sale are particularly tempting. These fish cannot deal very well with high water flow and need plenty of specialized attention if they are to thrive. Filefishes are included in this section for convenience, although they are very closely related to triggerfishes. Their aquarium temperament is usually far more benign than that of their often-belligerent cousins, but some species have strict dietary requirements that can be difficult to provide in the aquarium.

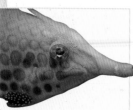

Price guide

★	$20–$35
★★	$35–$60
★★★	$60–$70
★★★★	$70–$90
★★★★★	$140–$175

FISH PROFILE

A remarkable species, readily identifiable by its two pairs of long spines, one pointing forward and one to the rear. The body becomes more elongated with age and reaches quite an impressive maximum size, even in the home aquarium.

WHAT size?
Males and females 18 in (46 cm).

WHAT does it eat?
This specialized feeder blows jets of water from its mouth to expose food items in sandy substrates. These may include small burrowing molluscs, worms, and crustaceans. Although it will attempt this behavior in the aquarium, it will also accept food from the water column. Offer dried algae, mysis, brineshrimp, enriched formula foods, and vitamin supplements.

WHERE is it from?
Indo-Pacific, from the Red Sea to Australia.

WHAT does it cost?
★☆☆☆☆   ★★★☆☆
Small juveniles are inexpensive. Adults certainly cost more, but are not too expensive.

Lactoria cornuta
Longhorn cowfish

▲ *This cowfish's common name refers to the paired hornlike projections over each eye. The pectoral fins are used for propulsion and the tail as a rudder.*

HOW do I sex it?
No known external differences.

WHAT kind of tank?
Fish-only or live rock-based fish-only system.

WHAT minimum size tank?
120 gal (450 l).

HOW do other fish react?
Boisterous species, such as large wrasses or hawkfishes, may bother the cowfish when it is small. However, it is largely ignored by other fish, not least on account of its impressive, spiky armaments. Furthermore, the toxin it exudes when stressed or threatened is lethal to all aquarium inhabitants if not quickly removed.

WHAT to watch out for?
Small specimens are very tempting, but be aware of their substantial maximum size. Any suitable specimen will be feeding and alert and often "follows" people as they pass the aquarium.

HOW compatible with inverts and corals?
Cannot be trusted in a reef aquarium as it may target any or all of the species present.

WHAT area of the tank?
An open-water-swimmer that scours the rockwork and sand in search of food.

HOW many in one tank?
Juveniles can be kept in groups but adults are solitary. Best kept singly.

HOW does it behave?
A largely peaceful species that does best when housed with equally tolerant tankmates.

WILL it breed in an aquarium?
No.

▼ *Attractive juveniles are tempting, but be aware of the large final size of this fish.*

Ostracion cubicus

Yellow boxfish

FISH PROFILE

A beautiful species and very popular with marine aquarists due to its interesting appearance and affordability. However, small juveniles the size of sugar cubes require specialist care. This is not an easy fish to maintain in any aquarium; if you are thinking of buying a boxfish, be prepared to stock tankmates that will complement it.

▶ *Boxfishes are often available when individuals are still the size of small sugar lumps.*

WHAT size?
Males and females 18 in (45 cm).

WHAT does it eat?
In the wild, mainly marine algae, supplemented with worms, crustaceans, molluscs, and small fish. In the aquarium, it is important to offer meaty foods or enriched formula diets at least three times a day. The fish also needs continual access to dried algae on which to browse at will.

WHERE is it from?
Indo-Pacific, from the Red Sea to the Hawaiian Islands.

WHAT does it cost?
★☆☆☆☆   ★★★☆☆
Small juveniles are inexpensive. Adults are more costly, but less commonly seen.

HOW do I sex it?
Males may be larger, but can only be distinguished from females when observing a pair together.

WHAT kind of tank?
Fish-only or live rock-based fish-only system.

WHAT minimum size tank?
145 gal (550 l).

HOW do other fish react?
Small specimens may be bullied by aggressive fish of any size, but this boxfish can emit a defensive secretion called ostracitoxin to repel potential aggressors. In some circumstances, this may be enough to rid itself of the unwanted attentions of bullying fish, but usually the victim will be damaged or killed in such situations. Provide plenty of hiding places so that the boxfish can avoid aggressive species without resorting to toxin production.

WHAT to watch out for?
Small specimens are particularly difficult to maintain no matter how tempting they may be.

HOW compatible with inverts and corals?
Cannot be trusted in a reef aquarium, as it may target any or all of the species present. In any case, small individuals do not do well in the high-flow systems favored by reef aquarists.

WHAT area of the tank?
Tends to hover in open water, except when browsing from rocks or algae provided by the aquarist.

HOW many in one tank?
Juveniles can be kept in groups but adults are solitary. Single specimens are best.

HOW does it behave?
Yellow boxfishes are not overtly aggressive but will dominate other fish in the aquarium, particularly more docile species. Suitable tankmates should be robust in their own right but unlikely to bother the boxfish.

WILL it breed in an aquarium?
No.

◀ *This specimen demonstrates nicely the origins of the common name "boxfish."*

Ostracion meleagris

Black boxfish

FISH PROFILE

A beautiful marine fish that requires more care than most other commonly available species. There are two distinct subspecies from the Hawaiian Islands and Eastern Pacific; the closely-related species *O. cyanurus* is found in the Red Sea. This is one of the few boxfish species that can be regularly purchased in male/female pairs.

WHAT size?
Males 10 in (25 cm); females usually under 6 in (15 cm).

WHAT does it eat?
Specializes in benthic invertebrates and algae and may prove difficult to feed in the home aquarium. A wide variety of offerings is essential, with regular vitamin supplements. Offer mysis, enriched brineshrimp, formula foods containing sponge material, and dried algae.

WHERE is it from?
Tropical Indo-Pacific, from East African to Mexico.

WHAT does it cost?
Single female specimens are modestly priced (★). Males (★★★). True pairs are expensive (★★★★★).

HOW do I sex it?
Males are larger, with blue-purple flanks and yellow stripes along the uppermost edge of the flanks. Females are uniformly dark brown or black with white spots.

WHAT kind of tank?
Fish-only or live rock-based fish-only system with plenty of swimming space. This fish cannot usually cope with the high flow rates in reef aquariums.

WHAT minimum size tank?
80 gal (300 l).

HOW do other fish react?
Like many boxfishes, this species can secrete a potent toxin when threatened or stressed, meaning that most larger fish will ignore it. The greatest threat to this species comes from smaller territorial or nippy species.

WHAT to watch out for?
Although it may mean rejecting many of the specimens seen in dealers' tanks, ignore non-feeding individuals. When considering a pair, the male will usually be the less well acclimatized individual; before buying, check it for signs of an increased breathing rate and cloudiness of the skin.

HOW compatible with inverts and corals?
May nip at sessile invertebrates and smaller ornamental shrimp.

WHAT area of the tank?
Swims in open water, descending to the rockwork or decor in search of food.

HOW many in one tank?
Keep singly or in pairs.

HOW does it behave?
Not an aggressive species; settles well into most aquariums.

WILL it breed in an aquarium?
Must have the potential to do so where true pairs are stocked.

▼ *The male black boxfish is exquisitely colored and larger than the female.*

Chaetoderma pencilligera

Tasselled filefish

An unusual fish that is often available when quite small (two inches or so) and very tempting to marine aquarists. As with many fish that rely on their physical appearance for camouflage, they do not appreciate being kept in an aquarium with few hiding places. The extensions of the skin help this fish to blend in with the seaweeds found in its natural environment.

WHAT size?
Males and females 12 in (30 cm).

WHAT does it eat?
In the wild, assorted benthic invertebrates, including encrusting forms and corals. In the aquarium it should feed readily on mysis, brineshrimp, chopped shellfish, and similar foods.

WHERE is it from?
Indian Ocean and Western Pacific, including Indonesia, Malaysia and Australia.

WHAT does it cost?
★☆☆☆☆   ★★★☆☆
The very smallest specimens are not particularly expensive, but their price increases significantly in direct proportion to their size at sale.

▶ *The frondlike extensions of the skin of this fish help it to remain concealed in weedy areas.*

HOW do I sex it?
No external visual differences.

WHAT kind of tank?
Fish-only or live rock-based fish-only system with plenty of swimming space.

WHAT minimum size tank?
120 gal (450 l). The fish has a prodigious growth rate and will need plenty of space.

HOW do other fish react?
The largely benign filefish can be picked on by any more aggressive species, including triggers, puffers and angelfish, particularly when it is small.

WHAT to watch out for?
Try to avoid non-feeding specimens. The best fish will have clear eyes and feed greedily in the dealer's aquarium.

HOW compatible with inverts and corals?
Not suitable for inclusion in any reef aquarium due to its fairly large final size and cosmopolitan tastes.

WHAT area of the tank?
Juveniles can spend significant periods of time in hiding and certainly will not stray too far from the rockwork. Settled specimens or those sharing their aquarium with peaceful species will be more active in open water.

HOW many in one tank?
Keep singly.

HOW does it behave?
Reserves its aggression for other members of the same species.

WILL it breed in an aquarium?
No.

Oxymonacanthus longirostris

Harlequin filefish

FISH PROFILE

This delicate filefish species is very difficult to feed. Indeed, it is arguable whether it should be collected for the aquarium trade at all. However, good specimens do exist and given the availability of many specialized foods and vitamin supplements, marine enthusiasts have never had a better chance of success with this fish.

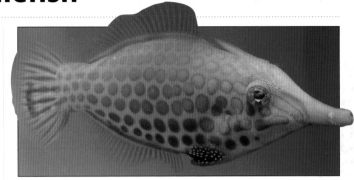

▲ *This male individual shows the beauty of the species.*

WHAT size?
Males and females 4 in (10 cm).

WHAT does it eat?
Good specimens accept brineshrimp, but their small mouths cannot accept anything much bigger. Apply paste foods to rockwork and incorporate shellfish meat into artificial and dead corals for the fish to pick at. Feed small amounts at least 7 or 8 times daily and treat food regularly with vitamin supplements. Even this amount of care and attention to feeding may not guarantee success.

WHERE is it from?
Indo-Pacific, from East Africa to Samoa.

WHAT does it cost?
★★☆☆☆   ★★★☆☆
Can be unfairly expensive given the poor survival rate. Many dealers refuse to stock it on ethical grounds, but it is still collected and therefore available.

HOW do I sex it?
Males have a black patch with white spots surrounding the orange pigment on the pelvic flap. Black pigment may be present in females, but not overlaid with white dots.

WHAT kind of tank?
A peaceful live rock-based fish-only system or reef aquarium.

WHAT minimum size tank?
66 gal (250 l).

HOW do other fish react?
Do not house the harlequin filefish with any species that may react aggressively towards it. Peaceful tankmates are best.

WHAT to watch out for?
Avoid excessively thin specimens. This fish is difficult enough to maintain without having to try to reverse the effects of long-term starvation. Selecting specimens that feed readily will mean a greater chance of success.

HOW compatible with inverts and corals?
Will eat the polyps of various species of hard coral. Will ignore ornamental shrimp.

WHAT area of the tank?
In and among corals and rockwork. Needs plenty of hiding places.

HOW many in one tank?
Best kept in male/female pairs, but you should appreciate that this will double the potential problems caused by this species.

HOW does it behave?
A peaceful fish. Territorial disputes with members of its own species are assumed to be between rival males.

WILL it breed in an aquarium?
Possible but unlikely, given the problems associated with keeping this fish in the long term.

Fascinating variety

This section features an assortment of species that are not closely related to each other or those described elsewhere in this book. They include the large and predatory snappers, the raptorlike lionfishes, and the aptly named hawkfishes. These species must be housed with care, as they feed on small fish and crustaceans. Dragonets and jawfishes are similar in that they have a substrate-dwelling existence, but jawfishes actually dig holes and therefore require a good depth of substrate. Dragonets prefer sand or rock. Tilefishes and dartfishes are

Price guide

★	$20–$35
★★	$35–$60
★★★	$60–$90
★★★★	$90–$175
★★★★★	$175+

goby-like pelagic fish that swim actively in the water column, yet are not closely related. The species featured in this section are of direct interest to aquarists, since understanding their behavior and aquarium demands can help to foster better husbandry techniques for similar or closely related species not contained in this book.

Nemateleotris decora
Purple firefish

HOW do I sex it?
Females are often stockier than males, but this is not immediately apparent unless you have a male/female pair to compare.

WHAT kind of tank?
Fish only; live rock-based fish-only system; or a reef aquarium.

WHAT minimum size tank?
20 gal (75 l).

HOW do other fish react?
Do not house with aggressive tankmates, as it will spend prolonged periods hiding in the rockwork. It is not uncommon for specimens that feel threatened to hide away for several weeks and then suddenly appear, albeit in an emaciated condition. Avoid keeping fairy wrasses and other active planktonivores with the purple firefish.

▶ *The rounded head of the dartfishes is reminiscent of the gobies, but dartfishes belong to the Family Microdesmidae.*

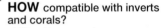

▼ *The stunning colors of this species have made it a firm favorite with marine aquarists.*

WHAT to watch out for?
This species is prone to leaping from an uncovered tank and is notorious for finding the tiniest hole through which to escape. Take care when undertaking work in the aquarium itself, as this can be stressful enough for the fish to begin leaping.

HOW compatible with inverts and corals?
Will not harm corals or ornamental shrimp.

WHAT area of the tank?
Settled, non-threatened individuals are open water swimmers.

HOW many in one tank?
Best kept in male/female pairs, as this is often how they are encountered in their natural environment. Male specimens can be extremely territorial towards conspecifics. Mixing individuals can be problematic and is not recommended.

HOW does it behave?
This shy species often remains close to a suitable bolthole into which it will retreat if threatened.

WILL it breed in an aquarium?
Potentially yes.

Nemateleotris helfrichi

Helfrich's (lavender) firefish

FISH PROFILE

An exquisite rarity, highly desirable among aquarists, yet only a select few have the budget or confidence to invest in a specimen or two. Despite this, it is as hardy as the other members of the small genus *Nemateleotris* and thrives in an aquarium situation.

WHAT size?
Males and females 2.3 in (6 cm).

WHAT does it eat?
Zooplankton in the wild. Offer regular feeds of brineshrimp, chopped shellfish, mysis shrimp, etc. If newly imported specimens need to regain lost weight, provide frequent feeds before adopting a more sensible regime.

WHERE is it from?
A fish with a scattered distribution throughout the Western Pacific, including the Ryukyu Islands to the south of Japan and Tuamotu Islands and Palau. Many aquarium specimens are sourced from the Marshall Islands and exported through Hawaii.

WHAT does it cost?
★★★★☆ ★★★★★
Expensive. The fact that it is most commonly encountered in water at least 120 ft (40 m) deep and in the more remote tropical reefs of the world partly explains the premium it commands.

HOW do I sex it?
This species is available fairly regularly as mated pairs. However, determining male and female specimens is not easy unless you can observe a pair. In general, females appear to be stockier.

WHAT kind of tank?
Fish-only with excellent water quality; live rock-based fish-only; or a peaceful reef aquarium.

WHAT minimum size tank?
20 gal (75 l).

HOW do other fish react?
Do not house with any other territorial species or active mid-water swimming species that feed on zooplankton in the wild.

WHAT to watch out for?
Ensure that specimens are feeding before you buy them and try to avoid newly-imported specimens that appear slightly emaciated. With a sensible choice of tankmates, *N. helfrichi* will prove as hardy as other firefish species.

HOW compatible with inverts and corals?
Will not harm shrimp, corals, or other invertebrates.

WHAT area of the tank?
Often inhabits more shaded areas of the aquarium, especially following introduction. Although its confidence grows in time, it rarely strays from a suitable bolthole.

HOW many in one tank?
Keep singly or in a mated pair.

HOW does it behave?
As with many members of the Family Microdesmidae, this firefish is capable of prodigious jumps, so cover the aquarium to prevent the loss of a prized specimen.

WILL it breed in an aquarium?
Potentially, yes.

▼ *A beautiful rarity that rewards the aquarist with hardiness and longevity.*

Nemateleotris magnifica

Flame firefish

FISH PROFILE

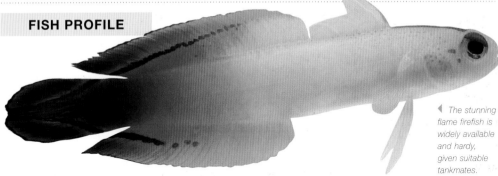

◀ *The stunning flame firefish is widely available and hardy, given suitable tankmates.*

The flame firefish is one of the most instantly recognizable marine fish and often referred to as a goby, but is in fact included in the family Microdesmidae, the dartfish. Only three species exist in the genus *Nemateleotris* and all are very popular aquarium fish.

WHAT size?
Males and females 3.5 in (9 cm).

WHAT does it eat?
Wild specimens feed on zooplankton. Aquarium specimens will accept most suitable substitutes, including finely chopped shellfish, brineshrimp, and mysis.

WHERE is it from?
Tropical Indo-Pacific, from East Africa to Hawaii.

WHAT does it cost?
★☆☆☆☆
Relatively inexpensive.

HOW do I sex it?
Females are often stockier. Closely observing individuals in the dealer's tanks should enable you to identify pairs.

WHAT kind of tank?
Fish only; live rock-based fish-only system; or reef aquarium.

WHAT minimum size tank?
20 gal (75 l).

HOW do other fish react?
Do not house *N. magnifica* with aggressive tankmates, such as fairy wrasses and other active planktonivores, as it will spend prolonged periods hiding in the rockwork. It is not uncommon for specimens that feel threatened to hide away for several weeks and then suddenly appear, albeit in an emaciated condition.

WHAT to watch out for?
This species is prone to leaping from uncovered aquariums and can escape through the tiniest hole. Take care when undertaking work in the aquarium, as this can be stressful enough for the fish to begin leaping.

HOW compatible with inverts and corals?
Will not harm corals or ornamental shrimp.

WHAT area of the tank?
Settled, non-threatened individuals are open water swimmers.

HOW many in one tank?
Best kept in male/female pairs. Single individuals can be maintained, but may not have the confidence of a pair.

HOW does it behave?
Hovers in the water, often making short darting movements forward. These coincide with a flick of the sickle-shaped dorsal fin.

WILL it breed in an aquarium?
Potentially yes.

Cirrhitichthys oxycephalus

Coral (spotted) hawkfish

FISH PROFILE

One of the commonest species of hawkfish available to marine hobbyists, due to its abundance and huge collection region. Both its hardiness and reasonable price make the coral hawkfish an ideal choice for the aquarist on a tight budget. However, it is an insatiable carnivore and failure to appreciate its cosmopolitan tastes can only result in disaster.

WHAT size?
Males 4 in (10 cm); females 3.3 in (8.5 cm).

WHAT does it eat?
In the wild, small benthic animals such as crustaceans and fish. In the aquarium, it will accept almost anything meaty, including chopped shellfish, plus most other foods, including granules and flake. Feed frequently to suppress the huge appetite of this fish.

WHERE is it from?
Indo-Pacific, from the Red Sea to the Gulf of California and Central America.

WHAT does it cost?
★☆☆☆☆
Inexpensive.

▶ *This inexpensive species makes a hardy addition to an aquarium containing robust tankmates.*

HOW do I sex it?
Males are larger than females.

WHAT kind of tank?
Fish-only or live rock-based fish-only system.

WHAT minimum size tank?
26 gal (100 l).

HOW do other fish react?
May be targeted by other hawkfishes acting aggressively towards it. Otherwise largely ignored by its tankmates.

WHAT to watch out for?
This fish can jump from an uncovered aquarium.

HOW compatible with inverts and corals?
Will eat many small fish and invertebrates often associated with reef aquariums. Will also harm corals it perches upon.

WHAT area of the tank?
On rocks or similar perching points. Swims in a slightly labored fashion when food is offered.

HOW many in one tank?
Keep singly unless the aquarium is large enough to hold a pair (120 gal/450 l or more). Males are highly territorial and will occupy an area housing more than one female.

HOW does it behave?
Can be aggressive towards open-water-swimming species, such as dartfishes or smaller wrasse species. Best stocked after any sensitive species. Do not house with small fish, which are likely to be eaten.

WILL it breed in an aquarium?
Has not been recorded but is possible in a very large aquarium.

Cyprinocirrhites polyactis
Lyretailed hawkfish

FISH PROFILE

A fairly uncommon fish in the aquarium trade, yet one that should be much better known and more popular than it is. It combines the intriguing characteristics of the hawkfish family with some of the behavior of pelagic planktonivorous fish.

WHAT size?
Males and females 6 in (15 cm).

WHAT does it eat?
A planktonivore that swims in open water to feed in much the same way as anthias and similar fish species. It will accept a variety of substitutes in the aquarium, such as mysis, brineshrimp, chopped shellfish, and, with time, possibly flaked and pellet foods.

WHERE is it from?
East Africa to Western Pacific, plus East Coast of South Africa.

WHAT does it cost?
★★☆☆☆ ★★★☆☆
Varies according to the collection area. Ranges between inexpensive and moderately expensive.

▲ *The lyretailed hawkfish is one of the most peaceful representatives of the Family Cirrhitidae and rewarding to keep.*

HOW do I sex it?
No external visual differences.

WHAT kind of tank?
Fish-only; live rock-based fish-only; reef aquarium, with care.

WHAT minimum size tank?
120 gal (450 l).

HOW do other fish react?
Other fish that feed on plankton in the wild and are therefore active, open water-swimmers may behave aggressively towards the hawkfish and vice versa.

WHAT to watch out for?
The lyretailed hawkfish may not appeal to aquarists when it is first encountered in a dealer's tank, but if given a chance to settle in a home aquarium, it soon comes into its own.

HOW compatible with inverts and corals?
May eat small crustaceans. Should not harm corals unless it chooses one or two to act as perching points.

WHAT area of the tank?
Alternates between swimming in open water and perching on a suitable promontory.

HOW many in one tank?
Keep singly.

HOW does it behave?
Hovers in a "head-up" position when feeding. Otherwise it acts like a typical hawkfish, perching on rocks that offer a suitable vantage point from which to observe the arrival of food items.

WILL it breed in an aquarium?
No.

Neocirrhites armatus

Scarlet hawkfish

The smallest and most popular hawkfish commonly imported for the aquarium trade. It perches on small-polyp stony corals such as *Stylophora* and *Pocillopora* species, descending into the branches when threatened. With the ongoing advances in maintaining first-class water quality within the marine aquarium, it is easy to provide the excellent conditions this species demands.

▲ *The deep red pigments can be temporarily lost in the dealer's aquarium.*

WHAT size?
Males 3.5 in (9 cm); females smaller.

WHAT does it eat?
Feeds largely on small crustaceans on tropical reefs and will accept most meaty foods in an aquarium. Feed mysis, brineshrimp, and chopped shellfish. Be sure to vary the diet and enrich the food frequently with vitamin supplements.

WHERE is it from?
Most specimens are imported through Hawaii, but this species can be found from as far north as Southern Japan to the Great Barrier Reef and Micronesia.

WHAT does it cost?
★★☆☆☆   ★★★☆☆
Fairly expensive, especially when compared to other species of hawkfish.

HOW do I sex it?
These fish are protogynous hermaphrodites, meaning that individuals are female first and then become males. Thus, males are likely to be larger than females.

WHAT kind of tank?
A live rock-based, fish-only system or, better still, a reef aquarium.

WHAT minimum size tank?
53 gal (200 l).

HOW do other fish react?
Ignored by most fish species.

WHAT to watch out for?
Specimens can be prone to fading in fish-only aquariums, particularly in dealers' tanks if held long-term. The same effect is evident in fish housed in a sparsely decorated fish-only aquarium or one with white rockwork and sand. A varied diet helps the fish retain better coloration, but introducing it into a more natural environment, such as a coral-rich aquarium, can reverse the color loss without any other intervention from the aquarist.

HOW compatible with inverts and corals?
Will not harm corals unless it chooses to perch on a sensitive specimen. Take care when introducing it into an aquarium containing small ornamental shrimp. It has even been known to consume dwarf hermit crabs.

WHAT area of the tank?
Usually only swims into open water when feeding.

HOW many in one tank?
Best kept singly in the smaller aquarium, but it is possible to house more than one individual in aquariums greater than 132 gal (500 l).

HOW does it behave?
Can be aggressive towards other hawkfishes or similar rock-perching species. May even target other active zooplankton-feeders.

WILL it breed in an aquarium?
Potentially, yes.

Oxycirrhites typus

Longnose hawkfish

FISH PROFILE

An unmistakable species that has achieved huge popularity with aquarists on account of its entertaining behavior and apparent hardiness. Its natural habitat consists of dense growths of gorgonians and black corals, but it is highly adaptable, readily settling into most marine aquariums.

WHAT size?
Males 5.1 in (13 cm); females may be smaller.

WHAT does it eat?
In the wild, largely benthic and planktonic crustaceans. Accepts most aquarium substitutes, especially mysis and brineshrimp. Offer particulate shellfish-based feeds two to three times a day.

WHERE is it from?
Throughout the Tropical Indo-Pacific, from the Red Sea to Hawaiian Islands. Despite its wide range, it is not an abundant species anywhere in this region.

HOW do I sex it?
Males can be larger than females and some authorities report that they have an additional black margin on the anal and tail fins. This may not be immediately obvious in aquarium specimens.

WHAT kind of tank?
Fish-only; live rock-based fish-only system; or reef aquarium.

WHAT minimum size tank?
53 gal (200 l).

HOW do other fish react?
With the possible exception of other territorial hawkfishes, most other marine fish ignore *O. typus*.

WHAT to watch out for?
The longnose hawkfish has a reputation for jumping from uncovered aquariums. The lack of a swimbladder in this group can result in an ungainly swimming motion, but this is no cause for concern.

▼ *As with most hawkfishes, avoid stocking this species with very small fish as tankmates.*

HOW compatible with inverts and corals?
May chase and eat smaller species of ornamental shrimp. Should not harm any sessile invertebrates.

WHAT area of the tank?
Swims into open water only when food is offered, often hovering beneath the aquarist's fingers as its meal is distributed. More usually, it perches motionlessly on the decor, where it can watch everything that is going on.

HOW many in one tank?
Keep singly or in male/female pairs.

HOW does it behave?
May chase and consume small fish or harass medium-sized zooplankton-feeders, such as smaller microdesmids, *Anthias*, and similar species.

WILL it breed in an aquarium?
Yes, likely to breed where pairs are housed in larger aquariums.

WHAT does it cost?
★★☆☆☆ ★★★☆☆
A medium-priced marine fish.

Dendrochirus biocellatus

Fu Manchu lionfish

FISH PROFILE

The rarer of the two *Dendrochirus* species encountered with any degree of regularity in the hobby. Unfortunately, this species is also the most sensitive to the rigors of shipping; a specimen that is well settled in a dealer's aquarium should be highly prized. The common name is derived from the two tentacles on either side of the upper jaw that resemble the mustache of writer Sax Rohmer's cartoon and film villain.

▶ It is vital that you observe this species feeding before buying it.

WHAT size?
5.1 in (13 cm) is the maximum for wild and aquarium specimens.

WHAT does it eat?
In the wild, small fish and shrimp. In the aquarium, only the occasional individual will accept dead foods raght away; choose such fish where possible. However, if a specimen readily accepts feeder shrimp, then weaning to more easily-obtained foods should be relatively easy.

WHERE is it from?
Tropical Indo-Pacific.

WHAT does it cost?
★★☆☆☆   ★★★☆☆
One of the most expensive lionfishes available.

HOW do I sex it?
No external visual differences.

WHAT kind of tank?
Fish-only or fish-only with live rock. Could be housed in a large reef aquarium in the absence of ornamental shrimp, but may prove difficult to feed in such a system.

WHAT minimum size tank?
30 gal (300 l).

HOW do other fish react?
Most fish avoid this lionfish, not least because it has venomous dorsal spines. Nevertheless, the Fu Manchu is a shy species that will not thrive in an aquarium housing overly aggressive fish.

WHAT to watch out for?
Avoid individuals with elevated breathing rates (i.e., that appear to be panting), at least until they have settled down following importation. Good specimens move their dorsal fin spines in a rhythmic motion, presumably as a warning to potential aggressors.

HOW compatible with inverts and corals?
Will not harm corals unless it chooses one to perch on. Likely to consume ornamental shrimp.

WHAT area of the tank?
Likely to hide in cracks and crevices during the daylight hours of the aquarium. At night, individuals venture forth to hunt.

HOW many in one tank?
Keep singly or in pairs.

HOW does it behave?
Do not house with fish that are small enough to be consumed.

WILL it breed in an aquarium?
Yes, but the larvae are difficult to raise.

Dendrochirus brachypterus

Fuzzy dwarf lionfish

FISH PROFILE

This is one of the commonest species of venomous fish known as turkey- or lionfish. It is also one of the easiest to maintain in captivity, but appears to be surprisingly short-lived; two to three years is a decent average. This is somewhat surprising given its adult size and the apparent superior longevity of other, smaller species. It is a good candidate for a themed specialist aquarium dedicated to maintaining venomous species.

WHAT size?
Males 6.7 in (17 cm); females slightly smaller.

WHAT does it eat?
Although generally considered to be a crustacean specialist, the fuzzy dwarf will also consume small fish where possible. Small individuals (3-4cm) readily accept frozen brineshrimp and mysis and are generally much easier to feed than larger specimens. To tempt these, you may need to "animate" small whole fish by wriggling them in the water.

WHERE is it from?
Tropical western Indo-Pacific, including the Red Sea.

WHAT does it cost?
★☆☆☆☆   ★★☆☆☆
Inexpensive, particularly small specimens.

HOW do I sex it?
Males are likely to be larger, with more robust-looking heads. They are also reported to have more stripes on the pectoral fins (6 or more) than females (4–6).

WHAT kind of tank?
Fish-only or live rock-based fish-only aquarium. .

WHAT minimum size tank?
66 gal (250 l).

HOW do other fish react?
Seems to integrate well with larger fish, which mostly ignore it. Exceptions may include adult angels, triggers, and puffers that may nip at the lionfish's fins.

WHAT to watch out for?
Take care when moving rockwork or cleaning the aquarium, as this fish has the habit of perching upside-down under ledges

▼ *Despite its common name, this fish will grow large enough to present a threat to smaller tankmates!*

during the day. Lionfishes and scorpionfishes are venomous and can inflict painful injuries.

HOW compatible with inverts and corals?
May consume small ornamental or "useful" shrimp, such as *Lysmata wurdemanni*. Should not harm sessile invertebrates.

WHAT area of the tank?
In and among rockwork unless hunting at dusk or when food is in the water column.

HOW many in one tank?
Keep singly or in pairs. It is known to aggregate in small groups in its natural environment.

HOW does it behave?
Not aggressive, but may eat very small aquarium fish.

WILL it breed in an aquarium?
Yes, but the larvae are difficult to raise.

Pterois radiata

Clearfin lionfish

The clearfin or "radiata," lionfish is one of the smallest _Pterois_ species available to hobbyists. The maximum recorded wild size for this species is around 25cm, but it is unlikely to achieve this even in a very large home aquarium. This means that it is perhaps more suitable for hobbyists than some of the more commonly-available lionfish species.

WHAT size?
Captive individuals 6.3 in (16 cm) or so.

WHAT does it eat?
Wild specimens include a variety of small shrimp and crustaceans in their preferred fare of small fish. Offer aquarium specimens a variety of similar frozen foods, occasionally soaking these in vitamin supplements to ensure correct nutrition.

WHERE is it from?
Red Sea and East African coastline and throughout large parts of the tropical Indo-Pacific.

WHAT does it cost?
★★☆☆☆   ★★★☆☆
More expensive than many other lionfish species, but still not too costly compared with most other marine fish.

▶ _One of the smaller lionfish species. Good specimens should accept frozen foods, such as mysis, krill, or small fish._

HOW do I sex it?
No external visual differences.

WHAT kind of tank?
Fish-only or live rock-based fish-only aquarium.

WHAT minimum size tank?
120 gal (450 l).

HOW do other fish react?
Do not keep with aggressive species such as triggers, pufferfishes, or adult angelfishes, all of which are likely to nip at the elaborate fins of the lionfish. Do not keep it with moray eels, which are likely to consume the lionfish given the opportunity.

WHAT to watch out for?
Observe specimens feeding on dead food before buying them. Although it is possible to settle newly imported specimens and acclimatize them over a period of time to frozen foods using "river shrimp," it is best to acquire an individual that will take any food offered in the first place.

HOW compatible with inverts and corals?
Will not harm corals, but consumes ornamental shrimp.

WHAT area of the tank?
Hides in rockwork during daylight hours of the aquarium, becoming more active at feeding time or under blue actinic light. The latter simulates the lionfish's favorite hunting time—at dawn and dusk.

HOW many in one tank?
Keep singly, in pairs, or in small groups where space allows.

HOW does it behave?
Do not house with any fish small enough to fit in its capacious mouth. Otherwise, this peaceful species tolerates other lionfishes or similar species with no real problems.

WILL it breed in an aquarium?
Yes, but the larvae are difficult to rear in captivity.

Pterois volitans

Turkeyfish (volitans) lionfish

FISH PROFILE

This lionfish is probably the most commonly encountered in the marine aquarium hobby and often at very small (tempting) sizes. It is also one of the largest species, quickly outgrowing a small aquarium; tankmates that were once much too large to be consumed soon become "bite-size." Aquarists have a duty to the care of their fish and should not acquire species that cannot be housed long-term, no matter how beautiful or interesting.

WHAT size?
Males 15 in (38 cm); females 14 in (36 cm).

WHAT does it eat?
In the wild, crabs, shrimp, fish, and cephalopods. In the aquarium, most specimens feed readily on a variety of foods, including frozen fish and shellfish. With perseverance, very tame specimens can sometimes be acclimatized to accept large pellet food.

WHERE is it from?
Eastern Indian Ocean and the Pacific Ocean. *Pterois miles* is the equivalent species in the Western Indian Ocean and Red Sea.

WHAT does it cost?
★☆☆☆☆   ★★☆☆☆
Inexpensive.

▲ *Few marine fish are more spectacular or hardy than this species.*

HOW do I sex it?
Males are larger and more massively built.

WHAT kind of tank?
Fish-only or live rock-based fish-only aquarium.

WHAT minimum size tank?
120 gal (450 l).

HOW do other fish react?
Small specimens may be bullied by more aggressive species, such as triggerfishes or pufferfishes. Even large individuals may be bothered by mature and dominant angels.

WHAT to watch out for?
Small, inviting juveniles become monsters in no time at all.

HOW compatible with inverts and corals?
Consumes ornamental shrimp and crabs but should not harm corals. However, its large maximum size and appetite are likely to compromise the water quality demands of most sessile invertebrates.

WHAT area of the tank?
More likely than other similar species to swim in open water, particularly when hungry. Hides in caves and beneath ledges.

HOW many in one tank?
Can be kept singly, in pairs, or even small groups if the aquarium is large enough.

HOW does it behave?
Anything that will fit inside its huge mouth is threatened. Otherwise it tolerates other fish and will not react aggressively. Although it often becomes extremely tame, beware of "head-standing," where the fish assumes a vertical head-down position, with the venomous spines pointing forward.

WILL it breed in an aquarium?
Yes, but this is rare, given that few aquarists have an aquarium large enough to house pairs.

Opistognathus rosenblatti
Bluespotted jawfish

FISH PROFILE

An exquisite species, full of character and very rewarding to keep. Despite its high price it is fairly hardy and will thrive in most aquariums, providing it has deep sand in which to burrow and its tankmates are chosen with care.

WHAT size?
Males and females 4 in (10 cm).

WHAT does it eat?
Zooplankton in the wild, but accepts most aquarium frozen foods. Offer a varied diet with occasional vitamin supplements.

WHERE is it from?
Endemic to the Gulf of California.

WHAT does it cost?
★★★★★
Unfortunately, this species is very, very expensive.

Yellowhead jawfish
Given plenty of substrate in which to burrow, the yellowhead jawfish (*O. aurifrons*) will thrive in colonies in a home aquarium. Ensure fish feed well before purchase. Males brood clutches of eggs in their mouths and aquarists have raised the larvae successfully.

▲ *This beautiful rarity is highly rewarding to keep in the home aquarium.*

HOW do I sex it?
No external visual differences.

WHAT kind of tank?
A live rock-based system is ideal, but with a deep sandy substrate in which the fish will dig a burrow.

WHAT minimum size tank?
Actual size is not as important as the depth. Because this species prefers a deep substrate in which to burrow and is prone to leaping from an uncovered aquarium, the deeper the aquarium the better.

HOW do other fish react?
Do not keep this species with any other sand-dwelling fish.

WHAT to watch out for?
This jawfish is likely to jump when disturbed. Take particular care when carrying out essential aquarium maintenance, such as cleaning the glass.

HOW compatible with inverts and corals?
Completely safe with all sessile invertebrates. May attack smaller ornamental shrimp.

WHAT area of the tank?
Sandy substrates.

HOW many in one tank?
Best kept singly to avoid potential aggression.

HOW does it behave?
Once it has excavated a burrow, it will find a suitable stone with which to cover the entrance at night. Due to its slightly nervous nature, it is a good idea to introduce this species first and select its tankmates according to their compatibility.

WILL it breed in an aquarium?
Other jawfishes have bred in aquariums, but this is usually achieved by maintaining groups or definite pairs. This can be difficult to achieve in this rare species.

Synchiropus ocellatus

Pink scooter dragonet ("blenny")

FISH PROFILE

A firm favorite among aquarists. Several similar species are commonly referred to as "scooters," or "scooter blennies," despite the fact that they are not blennies (Family Blennidae), but rather species of dragonet (Family Callionymidae).

WHAT size?
Maximum 3.1 in (8 cm). Males are slightly larger with a more robust appearance.

WHAT does it eat?
More likely than its close relative the mandarin dragonet to pick frozen foods such as brineshrimp from sandy substrates, but make sure it is getting enough to eat. Aquarists are often tempted to introduce this species into an aquarium housing mandarins, but unless you are very careful, this can lead to a situation in which all similar species starve. *S. ocellatus* will thrive where there is plenty of live rock harboring natural populations of the copepods and amphipods that scooters love to eat.

WHERE is it from?
Southern Marquesas to Japan.

WHAT does it cost?
★☆☆☆☆
Inexpensive.

HOW do I sex it?
Males have a large first dorsal fin used in display. When not extended, it is still obvious as it flops over the back of the fish.

WHAT kind of tank?
A live rock-based fish-only system or reef aquarium.

WHAT minimum size tank?
18.5 gal (70 l) for a single specimen.

HOW do other fish react?
Scooters can often be introduced to aquariums with territorial fish already in residence and will be completely left alone. Fish that feed on similar food items may not do well when scooters are introduced.

WHAT to watch out for?
Avoid overly skinny specimens. If you are willing to invest time and energy in the care of such emaciated individuals they can recover well, but this is really the responsibility of the dealer not the hobbyist.

HOW compatible with inverts and corals?
Will not harm any ornamental invertebrate species.

WHAT area of the tank?
Over rockwork and sand.

HOW many in one tank?
Keep singly or in male/female pairs where possible. It is possible to house two females without any problems, but then you will not be able to observe the fascinating courtship behaviour of this fish.

HOW does it behave?
Does not behave aggressively towards any other fish species.

WILL it breed in an aquarium?
Yes. Courtship and spawning are fairly common.

▼ *Scooter blennies are beautiful fish with highly variable pigmentation, ranging from almost brown to bright pink and red.*

Synchiropus picturatus

Spotted mandarin dragonet

Although not as popular among aquarists as its very close relative *Synchiropus splendidus* (the psychedelic mandarin dragonet), it is still a very attractive species.

◀ *The rounded appearance of the body suggests that this specimen is feeding readily.*

WHAT size?
Males 2.5 in (6–7 cm); females 2 in (5 cm).

WHAT does it eat?
Feeds on small benthic invertebrates, but sometimes accepts frozen foods such as brineshrimp in the aquarium. Will not swim into open water to compete with more boisterous species, so often goes without at feeding time. It is essential to provide live rock or live rock rubble that will encourage the existence of small, self-sustaining populations of its natural food.

WHERE is it from?
Most aquarium specimens come from Indonesia and the Philippines, but it is also found in northern Australian waters.

WHAT does it cost?
★☆☆☆☆   ★★☆☆☆
Slightly more expensive than the psychedelic mandarin, but still one of the less costly species available to the marine aquarist.

HOW do I sex it?
Males have a spikier first dorsal fin. The very largest specimens are almost certainly males.

WHAT kind of tank?
Live rock-based, either as a fish-only or reef system.

WHAT minimum size tank?
A specimen that readily accepts frozen foods can be maintained in a 26-gallon (100-liter) aquarium. The larger the system, the more dependent on natural food sources the fish becomes.

HOW do other fish react?
Take care when introducing this fish to systems housing other *Synchiropus* species, as they may not react favorably. Some tangs and surgeons have been known to show aggression towards this species, but this may depend on the individual concerned.

WHAT to watch out for?
Avoid emaciated specimens as they are unlikely to have fed since capture. Try to establish whether an individual is accepting frozen brineshrimp before buying it.

HOW compatible with inverts and corals?
Perfectly compatible with corals and ornamental invertebrates.

WHAT area of the tank?
On sand and rocks.

HOW many in one tank?
Keep singly or in male/female pairs. Females can be maintained together.

HOW does it behave?
Male spotted mandarins are fiercely aggressive towards other males, often grappling by biting the spiny gill cover of their rivals. Otherwise, this fish will endear itself to the aquarist by its methodical scrutiny of every square inch of the aquarium in its search for food.

WILL it breed in an aquarium?
Yes. As with many dragonets, its courtship displays and spawning rituals are a wonder to behold and can take place regularly in most aquariums.

Synchiropus splendidus
Psychedelic mandarin dragonet

FISH PROFILE

The psychedelic mandarin dragonet is not only one of the most desirable tropical marine species, it is also one of the least understood. While many aquarists appreciate that it must have plenty of natural live foods in the aquarium, they do not realize that other fish may compete for these resources. Occasionally, you may encounter the red morph of this species in which the base color is crimson, not green.

WHAT size?
Males 3.1 in (8 cm); females 2 in (5 cm).

WHAT does it eat?
Should accept live brineshrimp, and the best examples will readily take frozen offerings of same. However, the presence in the aquarium of self-sustaining natural populations of crustaceans is essential. These will include tanaidaceans, copepods, and amphipods, all of which form the major part of this species' natural diet.

WHERE is it from?
Tropical Western Pacific. Large numbers are imported through Indonesia and the Philippines.

WHAT does it cost?
★☆☆☆☆ ★★☆☆☆
Relatively inexpensive.

▶ *The myriad different colors present in the skin of this fish explain its popularity with marine aquarists.*

HOW do I sex it?
Males have a long and extravagant first dorsal fin ray.

WHAT kind of tank?
An aquarium with plenty of live rock is essential. Fish-only is acceptable, but a peaceful reef aquarium is ideal.

WHAT minimum size tank?
26 gal (100 l) should be sufficient to hold the live rock essential for this species.

HOW do other fish react?
The occasional fish will take exception to this species for no tangible reason, but because it secretes toxic mucus from its skin, it will be ignored or even avoided by its tankmates.

WHAT to watch out for?
Avoid skinny specimens unless you are certain they are strong enough to gain sufficient weight. Starved individuals appear to have angular bodies, rather than a smooth, cylindrical appearance.

HOW compatible with inverts and corals?
Will not harm ornamental shrimp or sessile invertebrates.

WHAT area of the tank?
The base of the aquarium or close to rockwork. Rarely swims in open water.

HOW many in one tank?
Keep singly or in a male/female pair. Females can be housed together, but will obviously not demonstrate any of the fascinating breeding behavior.

HOW does it behave?
May react belligerently towards similar species such as other members of the same genus, but males save their real aggression for other males.

WILL it breed in an aquarium?
Yes. This species has been successfully raised in captivity.

Doryrhamphus excisus

Blue-and-orange cleaner pipefish

FISH PROFILE

Perhaps the only species of commonly-encountered tropical pipefish that is fairly easy to maintain in captivity without going to the effort of supplying live foods. A peaceful species when kept in pairs. They will reward the aquarist with behavior as close to natural as is possible, including courtship and parasite inspection and removal from larger fish, to name but two.

WHAT size?
Males and females 2.75 in (7 cm).

WHAT does it eat?
Wild specimens feed on zooplankton, benthic invertebrates, such as amphipod crustaceans, and also on parasites removed from larger fish species. In the aquarium they readily accept frozen foods such as brineshrimp and mysis, provided these are small enough to be ingested through their tiny mouths. Ensure that specimens for sale are feeding on frozen, not live, food.

WHERE is it from?
A very wide range, from the Arabian Gulf to the tropical coasts of Central and South America.

WHAT does it cost?
★☆☆☆☆
Relatively inexpensive.

HOW do I sex it?
Males have a series of bumps, hooks, and protruberences on the upper surface of their snouts. These may not be immediately obvious, but close scrutiny should reveal their presence.

WHAT kind of tank?
Best in a reef aquarium or a live rock-based fish-only system stocked with peaceful fish species.

WHAT minimum size tank?
12–13 gal (45–50 l) for a pair.

HOW do other fish react?
Do not house with predatory fish species.

WHAT to watch out for?
Pipefishes are not strong swimmers and may not enjoy the high flow rates in aquariums containing many small-polyp stony corals.

▼ *Check the snout of this species for bumps or notches, as these signify a male specimen. Smooth-snouted individuals are female. Pairs will spawn in the home aquarium and are fascinating to observe.*

HOW compatible with inverts and corals?
Compatible with all corals and invertebrates.

WHAT area of the tank?
Often found in shady areas of the aquarium during the day, but becoming more adventurous under blue actinic or moonlight.

HOW many in one tank?
A pair is best, as you can observe natural behavior without the potential conflicts that may occur among a group in the same tank.

HOW does it behave?
Two male specimens will fight, and if they cannot get away from each other, the dominant individual often harasses the weaker fish to death.

WILL it breed in an aquarium?
Yes. Females deposit eggs in a brooding pouch located at the base of the tail on the underside of the male fish. The eggs are supplied with oxygen by the rich blood supply of the pouch lining. The larvae are difficult to rear.

Hippocampus kuda

Yellow seahorse

FISH PROFILE

Seahorses are enigmatic creatures that evoke strong emotions in aquarists and non-aquarists alike. They are currently the subject of CITES restrictions, so the vast majority of specimens likely to be encountered by hobbyists will be tank-raised.

WHAT size?
Males and females 10 in (25 cm), including the curved tail.

WHAT does it eat?
Captive-bred specimens should be feeding on frozen food when acquired. It is much easier to keep such specimens. Live foods can be difficult to obtain in sufficient quantities year-round, so avoid seahorses that are unwilling to accept frozen food.

WHERE is it from?
Although the current classification of the seahorse genera needs revising, the range of this species, or group of species, is from the Indian Ocean to Central Pacific.

WHAT does it cost?
★★★☆☆
Captive-bred specimens are relatively inexpensive.

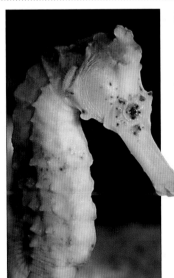

▲ *Tank-raised seahorses should prove hardy in a home aquarium, provided it is designed to meet their requirements.*

HOW do I sex it?
Mature males have a brooding pouch into which the female deposits her eggs.

WHAT kind of tank?
A species aquarium is best, with plenty of holdfasts and a lack of strong flow.

WHAT minimum size tank?
Seahorses generally require high water quality but plenty of food, so small aquariums with large sump reservoirs can be perfect. However, any size system is acceptable, provided it is set up to meet this species' demands.

HOW do other fish react?
Seahorses are slow, methodical feeders, so do not keep them with any fish species that can collect food more quickly.

WHAT to watch out for?
Pairs of seahorses kept for any length of time will almost inevitably breed successfully. While raising this species is not difficult, it does requires a certain amount of dedication and can be time-consuming.

HOW compatible with inverts and corals?
Although seahorses can be maintained with sessile invertebrates it is not recommended, as the fish can be stung by corals or do damage to them with their prehensile tails.

WHAT area of the tank?
Usually found holding onto branching structures. Include artificial corals, algae or gorgonians for this purpose.

HOW many in one tank?
Several individuals.

HOW does it behave?
A peaceful fish with fascinating courtship and breeding behavior.

WILL it breed in an aquarium?
Yes.

Lutjanus sebae

Emperor snapper

FISH PROFILE

The widespread availability of this species in the aquarium hobby sadly does not reflect the number of aquariums capable of sustaining the fish long-term. Juveniles are attractive and hardy, but their growth rate is phenomenal and they soon outgrow all but the very largest home aquarium. Be aware of the demands that such a large carnivore will place on the aquarium filtration system.

▲ *This sizeable species is one to avoid unless your aquarium is sufficiently large to cope with its long-term needs.*

WHAT size?
Males and females 39 in (100 cm).

WHAT does it eat?
A carnivorous species, specializing in crustaceans and fish. It has a large mouth and the types of food accepted vary as it grows, but it should readily accept most meaty foods. Mysis, chopped shellfish, whole fish, and marine pellets are all useful.

WHERE is it from?
Indo-Pacific, from the Red Sea to Australia.

WHAT does it cost?
★☆☆☆☆ ★★☆☆☆
Inexpensive.

HOW do I sex it?
No external visual differences.

WHAT kind of tank?
Fish-only or very large live rock-based fish-only system.

WHAT minimum size tank?
264 gal (1,000 l).

HOW do other fish react?
Most fish will ignore the emperor snapper when it is first introduced to the aquarium. However, it is unwise to add a small juvenile to a system containing big fish in case it is bullied or eaten. Instead, stock all fish at a similar size.

WHAT to watch out for?
Many individuals are imported directly and should therefore be well settled and feeding before you buy them.

HOW compatible with inverts and corals?
Not recommended with corals or any ornamental invertebrates.

WHAT area of the tank?
A juvenile sometimes stay close to rockwork, but becomes increasingly pelagic as it grows.

HOW many in one tank?
Keep singly. Juveniles can be housed together, but few aquariums are likely to be large enough to house them as they grow.

HOW does it behave?
Small juveniles will dominate and harass other fish, but this behavior gives way to general laziness as the fish grows and it becomes quite mellow except when feeding

WILL it breed in an aquarium?
No.

Symphorichthys spilurus

Blueline snapper

FISH PROFILE

A very large species of snapper that changes from an attractive juvenile into an exquisitely colored adult. However, you should only contemplate buying it if you have a system capable of providing plenty of swimming space and sufficient filtration to deal with the copious amounts of waste produced by such a large fish.

WHAT size?
Males and females 23.6 in (60 cm).

WHAT does it eat?
In the wild, molluscs, including cephalopods, fish, crustaceans. In the aquarium, chopped and whole shellfish, fish, and large shrimp, such as mysis and krill.

WHERE is it from?
Western Pacific, including the Philippines, Australia, and Tonga.

WHAT does it cost?
★★☆☆☆ ★★★☆☆
Moderately expensive.

HOW do I sex it?
No known external differences.

WHAT kind of tank?
Fish-only or very large live rock-based fish-only system.

WHAT minimum size tank?
264 gal (1,000 l).

HOW do other fish react?
Juveniles may be bullied by aggressive or territorial species, but adults are plenty large enough to look after themselves.

WHAT to watch out for?
A hardy species, but make sure that specimens in the dealer's aquarium are feeding and have a steady breathing rate.

HOW compatible with inverts and corals?
Do not keep with corals, other sessile invertebrates or ornamental shrimp.

WHAT area of the tank?
An active, open-water-swimmer that requires suitably-sized retreats when alarmed or for a short time after its initial introduction.

HOW many in one tank?
Keep singly.

HOW does it behave?
The behavior of this species is exactly what might be expected from such a large and robust species. Don't worry whether it will bully other fish; be more concerned about whether it will eat them.

WILL it breed in an aquarium?
No.

▼ *Long fins can prove tempting to nippy fish such as puffers or triggers.*

Caracanthus maculatus

Spotted coral croucher

A small species more closely related to scorpionfish than the *Gobiodon* spp. gobies that it

▶ *This beautiful fish has evolved to live among the branches of hard corals in much the same way as gobies from the genus* Gobiodon.

resembles. Its laterally-flattened body is an adaptation to its life among the branches of small-polyp stony corals, where it hunts for small crustaceans. Witnessing how superbly coral crouchers are adapted to their environment is a privilege, but bear in mind that in systems with large colonies of branching hard corals, the chances of observing these small fish are diminished.

WHAT size?
Males and females 2 in (5 cm).

WHAT does it eat?
Captive specimens accept any meaty food particles small enough to ingest.

WHERE is it from?
Tropical Indo-Pacific.

WHAT does it cost?
★☆☆☆☆ ★★☆☆☆
Once very expensive due to its scarcity, it is now more affordable for the budget-conscious aquarist.

HOW do I sex it?
There is no easy way to determine the sexes. The best method is to observe a group in an aquarium and look for individuals that tolerate each other and form pairs.

WHAT kind of tank?
To encourage its natural behaviour, house this species in an aquarium with branching forms of small-polyp stony corals. Otherwise, provide a live rock-based system with plenty of hiding places and non-aggressive fish.

WHAT minimum size tank?
13 gal (50 l) upwards, with plenty of hiding places.

HOW do other fish react?
Gobiodon spp. gobies may bicker with coral crouchers as they not only share similar physical characteristics, but also compete for the same type of environment.

WHAT to watch out for?
This species may appear emaciated in dealers' tanks,

because some individuals can prove reluctant to feed, or are unable to compete with more boisterous species in a mixed species aquarium. Target feeding with a syringe is often useful.

HOW compatible with inverts and corals?
Coral crouchers can damage small colonies of *Acropora* stony corals; do not consider the fish for any system where these are present.

WHAT area of the tank?
Among rockwork and corals.

HOW many in one tank?
Groups can be safely housed in a system with sufficient retreats.

HOW does it behave?
Peaceful.

WILL it breed in an aquarium?
Yes. Vigilant aquarists could be treated to fascinating courtship and, potentially, spawning displays.

Hoplolatilus marcosi
Skunk tilefish

FISH PROFILE

The Family Malacanthidae contains many species. Of these, the tilefishes are the most popular with marine aquarists, and this species is the most commonly encountered.
As it naturally lives in relatively deep, dimly lit waters, it is an ideal candidate for a themed "low-light" aquarium, housing sponges and non-photosynthetic organisms.

WHAT size?
Males and females 4.7 in (12 cm).

WHAT does it eat?
A natural zooplankton-feeder in the wild, but accepts most frozen meaty foods as substitutes in the aquarium. This busy fish needs feeding several times each day.

WHERE is it from?
Large island chains in the Western Central Pacific, such as Indonesia, the Philippines, Papua New Guinea and the Solomon Islands.

WHAT does it cost?
★★☆☆☆
For their size, these fish are not expensive.

▶ *Take care that this sometimes nervous fish does not jump from an uncovered aquarium.*

HOW do I sex it?
No known visual differences.

WHAT kind of tank?
Fish-only; live rock-based fish-only system; or reef aquarium.

WHAT minimum size tank?
Single specimen: 66 gal (250 l). Pairs: 120 gal (450 l) or more.

HOW do other fish react?
Conflicts can occur if this fish is stocked after other active midwater-swimming species, such as fairy wrasses, or territorially aggressive species such as surgeonfishes.

WHAT to watch out for?
Unusual swimming action may be a sign of a fish being poorly captured or decompressed. Make sure that specimens are feeding before buying them.

HOW compatible with inverts and corals?
Should not harm corals or other invertebrates.

WHAT area of the tank?
Swims in open water off steep edge-of-reef drop-offs or over sandy or rubble zones in deep water. It should therefore be active in open water, but this may only occur under subdued light, for example when blue actinic lights are on.

HOW many in one tank?
Best kept singly or in pairs.

HOW does it behave?
Relatively peaceful; should not present a problem to any other fish. May take some time to settle down and is likely to jump from an uncovered aquarium throughout this period. The risk of discovering it on the floor never disappears completely.

WILL it breed in an aquarium?
Not recorded in captivity, but possible where pairs are housed in a system that is sympathetic to their natural environment.

Credits

Unless otherwise stated, photographs have been taken by Geoff Rogers © Interpet Publishing.

The publishers would like to thank the following photographers for providing images, credited here by page number:

Aqua Press (M-P. & C. Piednoir): 69, 83, 96, 109, 183, 190

Bioquatic Photo – A.J. Nilsen, NO-4432 Hidrasund, Norway (email: bioquatic@biophoto.net. Web site: www.biophoto.net): 11, 16, 24, 40, 42, 47, 94, 108, 123, 135, 138, 151, 152, 163, 169, 173, 198, 199, 202, 203, 206

Tristan Lougher: 67, 74, 139, 140, 167, 177

Scott Michael: 144, 179

Lisa Page: 90

R. Patzner: 175

Photomax (Max Gibbs): 45, 92, 113 (Top), 115, 128, 155, 160, 188

J.E. Randall: 101

Erling Svensen, UWPhoto ANS: 12, 191

Iggy Tavares: 33, 70, 89, 121, 124, 130, 137, 141, 143, 146, 150, 161, 162, 164, 168, 170, 171

Kevin Webb: 43, 145, 174

Author's acknowledgments

The author would like to thank Steve, Faye, and Lisa Birchall for their continued support and assistance throughout the writing of this book. Dr. Rick Winterbottom and Dr. J.E. Randall provided invaluable assistance in the identification of species new to the hobby. Chris Higinbotham and Paul Culcheth of the Tropical Marine Centre in Manchester assisted in obtaining specimens for aquarium study.

Publisher's acknowledgments

The publishers would like to thank the following for their help in providing facilities for photography:

Amwell Aquatics, Soham, Cambridgeshire
Cheshire Water Life, Northwich, Cheshire
Maidenhead Aquatics, Crowland, Lincolnshire
Shirley Aquatics, Solihull, Warwickshire
Swallow Aquatics, East Harling, Norfolk
Swallow Aquatics, Aldham, Colchester, Essex
Swallow Aquatics, Southfleet, Kent
Tropical Marine Centre, Chorleywood, Hertfordshire
Tropical Marine Centre, Wythenshawe, Manchester
Wharf Aquatics, Pinxton, Nottinghamshire

Publisher's note